Birds *of* Prey

Birds *of* Prey

Hawks, Eagles, Falcons, and Vultures of North America

Pete Dunne

with Kevin T. Karlson

PHOTO RESEARCH AND PRODUCTION BY
KEVIN T. KARLSON

HOUGHTON MIFFLIN HARCOURT
BOSTON • NEW YORK • 2017

Address requests for permission to make copies of Houghton Mifflin Harcourt material
to trade.permissions@hmhco.com or Permissions, Houghton Mifflin Harcourt Publishing Company,
3 Park Avenue, 19th Floor, New York, NY 10016.

www.hmhco.com

Library of Congress Cataloging-in-Publication Data is available.

ISBN 978-0-544-01844-0

Book design by Eugenie S. Delaney

Printed in China

SCP 10 9 8 7 6 5 4 3 2 1

*To the many hundreds of raptor biologists, with thanks for your insights and
in partial compensation for the squadrons of sweat bees sharing your airspace in the
rainforest canopy, the clouds of black flies, and mosquitoes that gather precisely when
eyes fuse to the eyepiece of a spotting scope and a prey transfer is imminent.*

*Beyond recompense are the hours of downtime spent in crummy motels and on
the floors of friends' homes while you waited for lost luggage and promised permits
to arrive or the weather to clear so you could finally get "out there" and
engage the birds that give elevated meaning to our lives.*

With thanks and admiration, this book is dedicated to you.

PETE DUNNE, Mauricetown, New Jersey, March 2016

Contents

Acknowledgments

THIS BOOK STRIVES TO OFFER A CONTEMPORARY PROFILE OF NORTH AMERICA'S diurnal raptors. It was written to appeal to anyone who has ever been inspired by these magnificent birds and designed to compile in comprehensive fashion the biological particulars that both distinguish and unite this bird group.

Invaluable in this regard are the following resources, whose combined wealth of knowledge allowed me to cherry-pick facts and weave them into a biographical narrative, a profile for each species.

First and foremost I acknowledge the significance of the *Birds of North America* series, which for so many species served as a primary resource. The significance of this monumental effort cannot be gainsaid and were it not for this resource, it is likely that I would not have attempted this book. The *Handbook of the Birds of the World* proved another useful resource, as did several informative and inspirational works whose information and insight-packed pages made this project both fruitful and fun. These include Helen and Noel Snyder's *Birds of Prey;* Leslie Brown and Dean Amadon's incomparable *Eagles, Hawks, and Falcons of the World;* Tom Cade's *The Falcons of the World;* and Richard R. Olendorff's masterpiece, *Golden Eagle Country.* Bill Clark and Brian Wheeler's concise and precise *Hawks of North America* was a perennial source of information, as was

Paul Johnsgard's *Hawks, Eagles & Falcons of North America.* This prolific and indefatigable writer seemed ever able to provide missing facts when other resources failed. Also invaluable was Colin Harrison's *Field Guide to the Nests, Eggs, and Nestlings of North American Birds,* as well as Keith L. Bildstein, Jeff P. Smith, Ernesto Ruelas Inzunza, and Richard R. Veit's *State of North America's Birds of Prey.* But at the heart of all these works and these pages are the many hundreds of raptor biologists who have indentured their lives to the study of the birds profiled in these pages, beginning with Alexander Wilson and extending now to such notable contemporaries as Helen and Noel Snyder, Tom Cade, Ted Swem, Brian Millsap, Laurie Goodrich, Carol McIntyre, and Keith Bildstein.

All credit for the visual appeal of this book goes directly to my good friend Kevin Karlson, with a due measure of thanks apportioned to the many fine nature photographers whose talent and dedication to their craft is underscored by the many superlative images found herein. Accordingly and with gratitude,

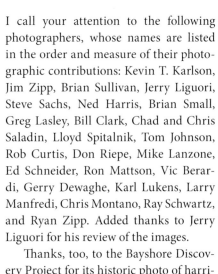

I call your attention to the following photographers, whose names are listed in the order and measure of their photographic contributions: Kevin T. Karlson, Jim Zipp, Brian Sullivan, Jerry Liguori, Steve Sachs, Ned Harris, Brian Small, Greg Lasley, Bill Clark, Chad and Chris Saladin, Lloyd Spitalnik, Tom Johnson, Rob Curtis, Don Riepe, Mike Lanzone, Ed Schneider, Ron Mattson, Vic Berardi, Gerry Dewaghe, Karl Lukens, Larry Manfredi, Chris Montano, Ray Schwartz, and Ryan Zipp. Added thanks to Jerry Liguori for his review of the images.

Thanks, too, to the Bayshore Discovery Project for its historic photo of harriers murdered on New Jersey's Delaware Bayshore.

My very special thanks is extended to René Buccinna and Dr. Laurie Goodrich, who found time to review this manuscript, and to Trish Miller and Michael Lanzone for their insights on Golden Eagles. All residual errors are, of course, the responsibility of the author. Additional thanks to Bill Clark and Brian Wheeler for reviewing the manuscript and providing important comments and corrections.

Final thanks and recognition are accorded to my splendid editor of many years, Lisa White at Houghton Mifflin Harcourt, and my sage and supportive agent, Russell Galen, who is, like you, like me, a raptor fan.

Previous page: *Adult Bald Eagle,* Haliaeetus e pluribus unum, *chosen by Congress to be the national bird of the United States in 1782.* Jim Zipp

Left: *Red-tailed Hawk, like this juvenile, is the most widespread raptor in North America. Namesake red tails are assumed during the birds first molt and complete by the second autumn of the bird's life.* Jim Zipp

---

The Allure of Raptors

"Peregrine," I announced, directing people's attention, with raised binoculars, to the stiletto-winged bird soaring over the hawkwatch platform at Cape May Point, New Jersey.

Around me I felt others imitate the gesture, including the gentleman beside me, Dr. Harold Axtell, retired curator of biology at the Buffalo Museum of Science.

The bird stopped circling and lined out southeast over the Atlantic Ocean. Next stop? South America, perhaps.

Lowering my binoculars, I took in the sea of faces still studying the bird. Most were creased by smiles. A few had mouths contorted by appraising O's.

Into the early 1970s, even in such celebrated hawk-watching junctions as Cape May, New Jersey, Peregrines remained an uncommon species, their North American population still suppressed by DDT poisoning.

"Harold?" I invited, after my friend had concluded his appraisal, "why do you think people are so captivated by birds of prey?"

"I think," he replied, "that people are drawn to their fierceness and freedom. These qualities are suppressed in human society so we project them upon the birds."

The quickness of Harold's response did not surprise me. The senior ornithologist was blessed with a keen and incisive mind, and this was certainly a subject the lifelong student of birds had turned over in that mind before.

But the substance of his response did surprise me, coming as it did from a trained biologist and mild-mannered individual who was even known to share bits of sandwich with foraging skunks.

Fierceness is a human attribute, inapplicable in nature. Formidable, yes; evolutionarily refined, yes; but fierce? I say no. But then Harold did say his pronouncement was a projection. And the expression of many raptors does indeed appear fierce to the human eye.

As for *freedom*, as a biologist Harold knew that birds of prey live lives as hemmed in by necessity as our own. To our earthbound eyes, the Peregrine cleaving

Opposite: While most raptors appear fierce to our eyes, the pugnacious Merlin, a small bird-catching falcon, looks particularly nefarious. This male taiga Merlin was photographed in Cape May, New Jersey. Kevin T. Karlson

The Peregrine Falcon's swiftness of flight and mastery of the air make it a favorite among ornithologists and bird watchers alike. Steve Sachs

a path through open sky might ignite a sense of freedom in us, but the bird was simply responding to biological necessity, fleeing her Arctic breeding grounds for the shorebird-rich mudflats of eastern Brazil, where she would remain until her biological clock announced it was time to return to her Arctic nest ledge to pair, breed, and begin the Peregrine life cycle anew.

The species accounts that are much the substance of this book summarize the biological elements that distinguish and define the 33 species collectively called "the diurnal birds of prey" that breed in North America, north of Mexico. It is a diverse assemblage with an array of refinements, an array that only adds to the broad appeal of these noble birds and has inspired many books treating this evocative bird group, including, now, this one.

But as so often happens with writing projects, this book started out one way and ended up another. My initial objec-

tive was to craft a companion to *Hawks in Flight,* a book whose focus is identification. What I set out to do with this book was put some biological flesh and feather upon the bare outline of an identification. I found myself instead assembling a species-by-species compilation of personal observations and ornithological insights that are the fruits of thousands of hours of field time amassed by hundreds of raptor biologists whose fascination with and dedication to birds of prey are the substance of scores of publications. This book is a testimony to their efforts and, as underscored by the book's dedication, a tribute to them.

There is nothing self-congratulatory in this tribute. However many thousands of hours I have spent observing birds of prey, I am, I freely admit, not a raptor biologist. I am a writer, a scribe, one who recounts more than gathers insights. It is my hope that the information assembled

Pomarine Jaegers are large powerful fliers, but this adult jaeger is clearly outclassed by this harassing adult Peregrine. The jaeger survived the contest when the Peregrine lost interest in the chase. Chris and Chad Saladin

here will serve as a contemporary profile of North America's hawks, eagles, falcons, and vultures, and inspire readers to become ardent advocates of this exciting bird group. Supporting this ambition are the scores of superior images that both enliven these pages and bear testimony to the level of dedication nature photographers, too, have lavished upon this fascinating group of birds.

This book does not include the owls that, while similar in many ways to the birds that are my focus here, are taxonomically disjunct, found as they are in the order Strigiformes. They are only distantly related to the Accipitriformes, which comprise the bulk of the species covered in this book.

Some may, then, be perplexed to find that I have chosen to include the New World Vultures, the Cathartidae, in these pages. After a period of taxonomic estrangement, vultures are once again considered to have close genetic kinship to the diurnal birds of prey, the order Accipitriformes, although some authorities place vultures in a separate order, the Cathartiformes.

It is the falcons that are currently considered genetic outliers. It has been determined that they are not closely linked to the Accipitridae and are in fact more genetically allied to the parrots, even to their passerine prey, than to kites, hawks, and eagles. Falcons are currently placed in the order Falconiformes.

These taxonomic determinations, while not universally accepted—and perhaps subject to future change—do have a biological foundation.

Why, then, include the falcons in a book whose focus is North America's diurnal birds of prey?

Three compelling reasons: convention, convergence, and convenience.

Convention because, since the beginning of American ornithology, the manifest similarities among hawks, eagles, vultures, and falcons have cast a binding spell upon observers even though biological dissimilarities have long been recognized.

Convergence because it is precisely the convergent evolutionary traits that unite these birds and have long argued in favor of inclusivity.

Circle of Raptors: *Try to identify these raptors by species, age, and/or color morph/plumage. Answers are provided at the end of the chapter. Moving clockwise, start at 12 o'clock on the outer and first inner circle, and then at 1 o'clock for the third circle, starting with Osprey. Finish with the two large birds in the center.* Photos by Jim Zipp

Convenience because to tease either the vultures or falcons out of the ranks of the diurnal birds of prey poses the awkward question: what to do with them? Vultures, for all their storklike affinities, do not stand comfortably or well among their mostly long-legged kin. And while falcons may indeed be akin to meat-eating, turbocharged parrots, it is precisely this refinement that has carried them away from their mostly fruit-munching cousins and squarely into the raptorial ranks, which in a strictly literal sense they are. Unlike vultures, whose feet are too weak to grasp prey (the defining characteristic of a *raptor*), falcons are very adept at wrapping their talons around prey, thus earning them a pragmatic as well as a semantic talon hold among the raptors.

Honesty compels me to admit that it is mostly convention that prompted me to take a broad and inclusive view when selecting the species to be covered in this book.

When I started this project, the vultures were purged from the raptorial ranks, but to my mind, excluding California Condor, a vulture and our greatest soaring bird, from the ranks of birds of prey is heretical. Its relationship to the birds of prey is now supported by biological fact. While sometimes classified among the Accipitriformes, New World vultures are now relegated to a separate but closely related order, the Cathartiformes.

And while the Arctic Gyrfalcon would seem manifestly out of place seated among the ranks of its tropical fruit-eating cousins, it does sit comfortably among the diurnal raptors—birds whose diet, like the Gyrfalcon's, is flesh.

Furthermore, it is likely that only card-carrying systematists might lose sleep over the question of taxonomic versus convergent kinship. For my part, I believe all the birds housed in this book deserve to be collectively known as "birds of prey," their disparate routes into this celebrated assemblage notwithstanding.

Since prehistoric times, humans have

Falcons typically kill their prey with a swift decapitation. Protests notwithstanding, this adult Peregrine is about to administer the coup de grâce to the Killdeer. Chris and Chad Saladin

embraced the obvious commonality shared by the birds covered in this book. We have imbued them with a binding reverence, integrated them into our legends and religions. Literally etched their emblematic likeness into the fabric of our lives—on uniforms, flags, football jerseys, tepee walls—and even invoked them as elements in our written language.

Unlike most other bird groups, to my mind, the diurnal birds of prey are less an assemblage of offshoots from a common biological tree than a grove of trees representing bird families whose trunks are tangent and whose branches (representing different genera and species) converge and overlap in the canopy. Such a commonality is, in fact, precisely one of the unifying characteristics of the birds of prey—a group of birds specialized to locate their prey from lofty places, and in the case of some species, capture that prey in the air. For others, acquisition requires a descent to the earth below. All the species included here, however, are citizens of the sky and of lofty places, including, and perhaps most importantly, our esteem.

In thematic accord, I likewise submit that prowess in flight is then another trait binding hawks, eagles, falcons, and New World vultures, a trait that has long inspired awe, even envy, in our species. All

---

This American Goldfinch is about to move on to the next trophic level, the fate of most living things. While Peregrine Falcons typically target larger bird species, with hungry young in the nest, adult male Peregrines cannot be too choosy. It is precisely the smaller size of males that permits them to target smaller and more agile prey while the larger female tends to young. Steve Sachs

Top: *This juvenile Red-shouldered Hawk is displaying not just its namesake trait, but also the broad wings that rank this forest species among the buteos.* Jim Zipp

Bottom: *The bulging crop on this large adult female Cooper's Hawk attests to a successful hunt, which is by no means the assured outcome when hungry hawks bring their skills to bear.* Brian Small

Top: *Birds of prey, such as this Red-tailed Hawk, are creatures of elevated places, including, and perhaps most significantly, human esteem.* Jim Zipp

Bottom: *The bills of birds of prey are hooked, specialized for tearing and rending flesh. The head of the Turkey Vulture, like other members of the carrion-feeding Cathartidae, is unfeathered, a refinement that permits these birds to delve deep into carcasses without sullying head and neck feathers with gore. While some consider vultures loathsome, I personally find the Turkey Vulture striking.* Brian Sullivan

birds of prey are capable of dramatic flight, and many species spend much of their lives in the air. Zone-tailed Hawk and Swallow-tailed Kite spend much of their time aloft in search of prey. Swainson's Hawk spends as much as one-third of its life migrating to and from breeding and wintering areas. Condors may cover over one hundred miles in a single day in search of food. In winter, some Gyrfalcons live a life that is essentially nomadic, circumnavigating the edge of the Arctic ice in search of prey.

And prey is precisely the binding element that lies at the heart of predation and serves to define and unify the birds of prey. True, many bird species feed upon other living organisms, including American Robin. But the diurnal birds of prey are celebrated for their specialized capacity to capture and consume other animals, often in dramatic fashion. Prey species vary, as does the manner of capture, but among the birds covered in this book only one species is known to stray from a strictly meat diet. This is the Swallow-tailed Kite, a ferocious predator of large flying insects and treetop vertebrates, but one that in winter in South America has been known to eat fruit.

As befits a meat-eating group, the bills of the birds of prey are hooked, specialized for tearing and cutting flesh. Many of these bills are very highly specialized, customized to meet the challenges presented by very specific prey.

Of course, before food can be consumed, it must be located. Visual acuity is, then, yet another defining hallmark of this assemblage. In fact, so celebrated are the eyes of diurnal birds of prey that we have integrated their elevated visual acuity into our language: we say that those of

Taloned feet are a defining attribute of birds of prey. At top, a Harris's Hawk shows off its offensive array—one capable of dispatching full-grown jackrabbits. At bottom, a curiously warm-toned juvenile light morph shows the small rodent–calibrated feet and fully feathered legs of Rough-legged Hawk. Top: Kevin T. Karlson; bottom: Ed Schneider

Among most birds of prey, females are considerably larger than males. This "reverse sexual dimorphism" gives pairs the latitude of targeting different-sized prey and may benefit females, who must vie with other females for prime mates and territories. Here a male Gray Hawk is offering a lizard to its mate. Ned Harris

our species who are visually gifted have "hawk eyes" or "the eyes of an eagle." Even the Turkey Vulture, which is able to locate its carrion prey by smell, uses its keen eyesight to mark the movement of other vultures to lead it to food and to locate carrion on the ground.

Vultures excepted, the birds of this group also have highly specialized feet, equipped with sharp, curved talons, designed to grasp and lacerate or penetrate prey. Prey that can, in the case of some species—most notably Golden Eagle—be as large as the bird itself. However sized, the feet of raptors—like their bills—are customized to specific prey and tailored to complement the hunting style of the species, whether this means hawking dragonflies high over the forest canopy, plunging into water to grasp fish, snatching songbirds out of the air, securing a hare plunging through brush, or knocking a Dall Sheep off mountain ledges to die on the rocks below, a testimony not only to Golden Eagle's cunning but also to its size and strength. And while the vulture's feet are ill-suited for grasping, they do serve to anchor the bird as it rends flesh from the bones of moribund animals with its flesh-tearing bill. Philadelphia ornithologist John Krider speaks to the vulture's flesh-rending capacity: "I have seen more than two hundred of these birds at once on the body of a dead horse and in less than thirty minutes there was nothing left but the bones."

Large size is also a general hallmark of this bird group. While birds of prey come in an array of sizes, ranging from the Mourning Dove–sized American Kestrel to the turkey-sized Bald Eagle, most are physically large, thus capable of subduing large prey. In addition, most birds of prey show a marked size difference between sexes of the same species, with females averaging larger than males—a morphological differentiation called *reverse sexual dimorphism*.

Impressive size, taloned feet, hooked bills, elevated visual acuity, vaulted powers of flight, and air supremacy. All of these traits help define and bind the diurnal birds of prey and, taken in sum, are the foundation of our species' elevated regard, envy—even emulation—and my grounds for including them all in this book. But of all these unifying attributes, it is certainly their mastery of the sky that inspires us most and enjoys the greatest range of expression among them, a feature that relates directly to wing shape.

It is precisely here, with the flick of a wing, that the search for commonality ends and divergence within the families ascends. Each of the groups that comprise the diurnal birds of prey can be broken out and defined by the adaptive shapes of their wings and how these contribute to the lifestyle of each family.

These families are the Pandionidae (Osprey), Accipitridae (hawks, harriers, eagles, kites, and Old World vultures), Falconidae (falcons and caracaras), and Cathartidae (New World vultures).

Answers to Circle of Raptors: 1. Outer circle, clockwise from 12 o'clock: Swainson's Hawk, light morph adult; Rough-legged Hawk, light morph; Ferruginous Hawk, dark morph; Red-tailed Hawk, light morph adult Western; Harris's Hawk, adult; White-tailed Hawk, adult; Sharp-shinned Hawk, juvenile; Cooper's Hawk, juvenile male; Northern Goshawk, juvenile; Short-tailed Hawk, adult light morph. 2. First inner circle, clockwise from 12 o'clock: Zone-tailed Hawk, juvenile; Gyrfalcon, gray morph; Prairie Falcon, adult female; Peregrine Falcon, adult; Common Black Hawk, adult; Red-shouldered Hawk, adult; Broad-winged Hawk, adult; Gray Hawk, juvenile. 3. Second inner circle, clockwise from 1 o'clock: Osprey; Merlin (at 6 o'clock); American Kestrel, male; Northern Harrier, juvenile. 4. Inner two raptors at center: Golden Eagle, top, Bald Eagle adult, bottom.

Osprey, like this adult, are specialized to capture fish at depths that may result in the birds' being completely submerged. This successful hunter is ferrying dinner to hungry nestlings. Kevin T. Karlson

The Birds *of* Prey

FAMILY: Pandionidae

This family is represented by a single, highly specialized, cosmopolitan species, Osprey. This bird is specialized to capture fish swimming beneath the surface, a feat it accomplishes by diving into the water from above, often fully immersing itself in the process. Osprey's long, crooked wings may in fact be an adaptation to withstand the jolting impact of a large bird striking water. Other plunge-diving, fish-eating birds, most notably pelicans and boobies, show a similar wing configuration. The feathers of Osprey are uncommonly greasy so water sheds quickly when the birds muscle themselves aloft. The crook-shaped wing may also help Osprey reach up and forward as it lifts off the water, often with prey in tow.

FAMILY: Accipitridae

A large and diverse family encompassing most of North America's diurnal birds of prey, it includes the buteos, accipiters, fish and aquila eagles, harriers, and kites. While all the members of this family are capable of soaring flight, specialization is the element that defines the various groups.

The twelve species of large soaring hawks in North America (the buteos and their allies) are characterized by long broad wings. Some are forest dwelling, while others are specialized for more open habitats, but all have wings suited to exploit thermal lift, and many hunt from aloft and/or engage in long migrations that may carry them hundreds or thousands of miles. Spirited, aerial courtship displays are also a hallmark of this group. Closely related to the *Buteo* genus are two closely related genera, *Parabuteo* and *Buteogallus*. Another hallmark of the buteos is their adaptive array of specializations. For every predatory opportunity, there seems a buteo specialized to meet the challenge.

Also closely related to buteos are the *Aquila* eagles, represented in North America by Golden Eagle. This is essentially a very large buteo, but one whose size and power have elevated it into a separate category sustained largely by our esteem.

The accipiters are typically shorter-winged birds of forest or forest edge. Their wings are suited for flying in tight vegetative confines and for rapid acceleration. These low-level bird-catching specialists also typically have long, rudderlike tails that make accipiters highly maneuverable, an adaptation that serves them as they pursue nimble birds in flight—the group's forte.

While gray squirrels are not accounted among the planet's great strategists, it is equally certain that this adult Red-shouldered Hawk has lost the element of surprise raptors depend upon to give them the winning edge in the age-old competition between predators and prey. Steve Sachs

Top: *Sharp-shinned Hawks are small bird–catching machines. Note the long, extended middle toe that is common to bird-catching raptors.* Kevin T. Karlson

Bottom: *White-tailed Kites, like this adult, were once persecuted to near extinction because of the mistaken belief that they preyed upon game birds. White-tailed is actually a mouser and its population is now much recovered thanks to the blanket protection afforded it and all birds of prey.* Brian Small

The kites are a group of nimble, buoyant hunters that may be divided into two subgroups: the "paddle-winged prey specialists," represented by Hook-billed Kite and Snail Kite, and the "pointy-winged aerialists," including Swallow-tailed, Mississippi, and White-tailed Kites.

Haliaeetus or "sea" eagles are ancestrally aligned more to kites than to aquila eagles. Our Bald Eagle is very representative of the genus, showing long, broad, planklike wings that make it a masterful soaring bird, able to stay aloft for hours or travel, at need, great distances.

The light, buoyant, slender-winged clan of active hunters in the genus *Circus* is represented in North America only by the Northern Harrier. Distinguished by a very light wing-loading, this ground-hugging hunter spends hours coursing low over open terrain that lies beyond the exploitable reach of perch-hunting raptors. While other hawks sit and wait, harriers hunt.

FAMILY: Falconidae

In North America, we find six of these speedy, blade-winged sentinels of open spaces and open sky, plus Caracara. Most falcons are bird-catching specialists, but several use their agility and speed to also target mammalian and insect prey. The

Open, fish-bearing water is requisite where Bald Eagles winter and breed. Jim Zipp

Top: *Northern Harrier, the only harrier species found in North America, is a buoyant, nimble, low-altitude specialist whose low coursing flight lacks the flash and dash of other raptors in the eyes of some.* Steve Sachs

Bottom: *Crested Caracara is a versatile, opportunistic hunter, and while it feeds heavily upon carrion, it is fast and nimble enough to overtake live prey.* Brian Small

The numbered wing tag identifies this adult California Condor as one of the birds playing a role in the successful reintroduction program that spared North America's grandest soaring bird from certain extinction. Ned Harris

Crested Caracara, ranked among the falcons, is a raptorial polyglot, a bird genetically related to falcons but in its foraging behavior more akin to the next somewhat disparate family.

FAMILY: Cathartidae

The New World vultures, which include California Condor, our largest bird of prey, have long broad wings, ideally suited to exploit updrafts and thermal lift.

Opposite: *Feathers are not only the defining characteristic of birds, they are the mechanism that gives birds their vaulted powers of flight. Daily feather care is therefore essential for birds that strive to maintain their predatory edge; bathing is an important part of this routine, as demonstrated by this adult Peregrine Falcon.* Steve Sachs

Feeding almost exclusively upon carrion, much of a vulture's day is spent aloft, commonly at very high altitudes where it can search vast areas for carcasses or note the bellwether behavior of other vultures and carrion-feeding birds that then guide vultures to food.

Note to readers: Having already broken with taxonomic tradition in the assembling of birds in this book, it is but a venial transgression to also alter slightly the taxonomic order. I have elected to conclude rather than begin the species accounts with the New World vultures, as a strict adherence to the AOU order would dictate, thereby allowing these carrion feeders to bat clean-up just as they do in real life. In true taxonomic order, the vultures, the Cathartidae, precede all the other families just outlined.

Species
Accounts

OSPREY

Pandion haliaetus

FAMILY: Pandionidae
One species, one genus

ETYMOLOGY: Originally ranked among the *Falco* by Linnaeus, the Osprey was later reclassified by Savigny and relegated to its own new genus, *Pandion,* after the mythical King of Athens, an innocent third party in one of those tragic Greek dramas involving daughters and a love triangle—complete with fratricide, the inevitable intervention of gods, and humans being turned into birds, including a hawk whose task it was to pursue the murderous daughters of the king through eternity. Apparently Savigny confused the name of the king with that of his son-in-law Tereus, the instigator of the tragedy, thus ascribing the wrong name to the hawk. Were Savigny following the script correctly, the Osprey genus would have been named after Tereus.

It hardly matters; while Savigny had a flawed grasp of Greek mythology, he did make amends by assigning the species name *haliaetus* to the bird—literally "sea eagle" from the Greek *halos* for "sea" and *aetos* for "eagle."

As for the etymological foundation of "Osprey," that name hails from a misinterpretation of a different sort, this one biological, insofar as it derives from the Latin *ossifragus,* "bone breaker," a name more aptly applied to the Old World Lammergeier, a vulture that does indeed shatter bones by dropping them upon the substrate below. That said, Osprey do carry all manner of odds and ends into their nests—including bones. It is not inconceivable that an Osprey ferrying a bone to the nest fumbled its prize, which then fell to earth in the bone-breaking manner of Lammergeier, thus giving rise to its reputation as an *ossifragus* "bone-breaking" species.

PROFILE: This large, handsome, altogether remarkable bird of prey is distinguished by its sheer volume of specialized characteristics, including the distinction of being placed in its own monospecific family within the Accipitriformes, the family Pandionidae, thus serving taxonomic accuracy by affirming Osprey's close ties to eagles, hawks, and Old World vultures.

The species has a worldwide distribution (found on every continent except Antarctica) and breeds on all but South America, which hosts wintering North American birds. Some second-year birds elect not to return to North America to breed until their third year. Among birds of prey, only the Peregrine has a greater worldwide distribution.

While the Osprey is not in taxonomic fact accounted among the sea eagles (the genus *Haliaeetus,* an eight-member genus also ranked among the Accipitridae), it does—perhaps even more than those birds classed as sea eagles—deserve this label. As a bird whose diet is all but exclusively fish, Osprey is wholly wedded to the aquatic environment and is specialized to extract fish from water like no other raptor. While Osprey plunge to a depth of one meter, sea eagles merely dabble—snatching dead and dying fish from the surface or pirating them from successful Osprey.

The only semantic problem with calling this large, handsome fish-catching specialist a "sea" eagle is its extensive use of nonmarine aquatic environments (such as lakes and rivers). It is true, however, that the largest concentrations of breeding Osprey are typically found near sea coasts, whose open, clear shallows are fish-rich much of the year—especially and most significantly during the breeding season.

Almost eagle-sized, Osprey is endowed with many biological refinements well suited to a bird specialized to capture live fish by diving from the air into an aquatic environment. These include a dense oily plumage; relatively long legs; large, long-taloned feet; and a reversible outer toe that presents slippery prey with a four-cornered net of talons. Feet are also arrayed with sharp spicules on the pads of each foot, creating a nonslip surface tailored to grasp slimy prey.

Upon examination of the Osprey's uropygial glands (the "two glands which supply birds with the oil used for lubricating feathers"), nineteenth-century ornithologist Alexander Wilson found those of the Osprey to be "remarkably large, capable, when opened, of admitting the end of the finger, and contained a large quantity of white greasy matter, and some pure yellow oil." As one who has run my hands over the back of an Osprey, I can attest to the oiliness of the feathers, although my physical examination of the bird's waterproofing adaptations stopped there. While the plumage of other birds of prey feels dry, Osprey's feels distinctly greasy.

Also linked to the bird's diet, the small intestine of Osprey is "long and narrow for a hawk, probably an adaptation to help digest tough scales and bones." The digestive tracts of other fish-eating specialists all show similar characteristics.

Authors Helen and Noel Snyder suggest that the "curiously crooked" wing may be an adaptation that helps Osprey absorb the "jolting" impact when the bird plunges into water. It may also facilitate liftoff from an aquatic substrate. It is probably no coincidence that the wings of gulls, which also launch themselves from the water, are similarly configured.

DESCRIPTION: A large, handsome, fairly narrow-winged, boldly patterned bird of prey, between the size of a large Buteo and a Bald Eagle. It is all dark above (blackish brown) except for a white crown, and mostly bright white below except for a dark bib or necklace (on the

upper breast), which is usually heavier on females. Eyes are bright yellow. On perched birds, long wings extend beyond the tail. The posture of perched birds is mostly upright.

Juveniles are similar to adults but lack the dark necklace and, for a few weeks after fledging, show a buffy band across the breast. Juveniles' upper parts are also browner and feathers have pale edges, making the backs of young birds appear overall scaly. In flight, both adults and young fly with wings angled back, and crooked down, in a gull-like configuration. In flight, the leading edge of the underwing (the underwing coverts) is white, the trailing edge of the wing blackish. Outer primaries are splayed (finger-like), unlike gulls, whose primaries fuse to a point.

MEASUREMENTS
Length: 21–26 inches
Wingspan: 59–67 inches
Weight: 2.2–3.9 pounds

Females average 15 to 20 percent larger than males.

SYSTEMATICS/SUBSPECIES: Four Osprey subspecies are currently recognized, two in North America: *P. h. carolinensis*, which occurs widely across much of North America, and *P. h. ridgwayi*, heralding from the Caribbean. The other subspecies include *cristatus* from coastal Australia and the nominate *haliaetus*,

which breeds from Scandinavia to Japan. As a cosmopolitan species with fossil records going back to the Miocene (10 to 15 million years ago), the question naturally arises as to why this bird has not demonstrated a greater degree of specialization—as has, by comparison, the genus *Haliaeetus* (sea eagles), which comprises eight species.

VOCALIZATIONS: The classic call is a high, piping whistle repeated in a series. It is sometimes measured and mellow sounding, at other times (most notably when birds are excited) strident and hurried.

DISTRIBUTION: Extensive but by no means uniform. In North America the breeding range extends from western Alaska and the Aleutians east to Nova Scotia and Newfoundland. Along the Atlantic Coast it breeds the length of the coast from the Maritimes to Florida; on the West Coast, from Alaska to northern California. In interior North America, breeding distribution is patchy. The Snyders isolate five main population centers for this species in North America: Atlantic Coast, Florida and the Gulf Coast, Great Lakes, Northern Rocky Mountains, and Pacific Northwest. But no matter where this species is located, be assured it lies in close to fish-bearing water—lakes, rivers, or coastal areas.

In winter, northern birds retreat primarily to South and Central America, but some Osprey winter along the southern Oregon, California, and Mexico coasts and very locally inland (including the lower Colorado River in Arizona). Coastally Osprey are year-round residents from North Carolina to Louisiana. Birds also winter in south Texas, eastern Mexico, and the West Indies and Cuba and from the Carolinas to Florida.

MIGRATION: Alexander Wilson, writing in the early 1800s, noted that Ospreys arrive on the coasts of New York and New Jersey about the 21st of March and retire south about the 22nd of September. As for our local breeders, this timetable is fundamentally unchanged; however, increasingly, a few migrant Ospreys continue to be recorded at Cape May into November, which is late by historical standards. Most fall migration is conducted between mid-August and mid-October. Birds typically migrate alone but may join Broad-winged Hawks in thermals, where they quickly rise through the swirling ranks.

Notes Wilson about the bird's spring arrival: "The first appearance of the Fish Hawk in Spring is welcomed by the fishermen, as a happy signal of the approach of those vast shoals of herring, shad that regularly arrive on our coasts . . ." While most birds of prey have been regarded with a degree of hostility by coastal residents, the Osprey is a notable exception. Continues Wilson: "A sort of superstition is entertained in regard to the Fish Hawk. It has been considered a fortunate incident to have a nest of these birds on one's farm."

While the number of farmers has diminished in our corner of the Garden State since Wilson's last visit to the Bayshore, where he worked on the field sketches that culminated in the Wilson Osprey print that graces the walls of our den, the popular acclaim for Ospreys has not diminished. In our village of Mauricetown, the strident piping of circling adult Osprey is as much a part of summer as the hum of lawnmowers in suburbia.

At top, an adult male and a very young Osprey at the nest; two older juveniles are below. Two or three young are typical. Kevin T. Karlson

In fact, as I type these words, the piping whistle of multiple birds is cascading through my office windows. Now in August, the measured calls of adults have been joined by the strident food-begging calls of newly fledged young. Once again it has been a banner year for breeding Ospreys along the Maurice River, with most of the nearly 70 nests along the 40-mile watercourse fledging three young each.

HABITAT: While the bird's requirements are not numerous, they are—as befits a prey specialist—exacting. Proximity to open, clear, fish-bearing (some authorities also suggest "shallow") water is mandatory. Breeding territories must offer an ice-free period long enough to support the bird's three-month breeding period plus easily accessed trees or structures strong enough to support the weight of the bird's bulky nest, although in some places the bird locates its nest on cliffs and even on the ground. Breeding pairs may be solitary or—where food is plentiful and suitable nest sites are few but clustered—birds may form loose breeding colonies, which provides a greater degree of nest defense and perhaps offers adults greater freedom to forage. Where I live in southern New Jersey, both strategies are used.

Ospreys spend a great deal of time aloft, searching for prey or interacting with other Osprey. Wilson called the bird "vigorous-winged." Most large birds of prey are more lethargic or energy-conscious. But Osprey adopts somewhat the casual, sky-embracing behavior of Swallow-tailed Kite, a bird that it also somewhat resembles in size, plumage, and wing configuration. Soaring when it can, Osprey's flight is also energetic; it flies directly with steady wingbeats that are regular, shallow, and punctuated by brief, energy-saving but momentum-sapping glides. That the bird is a master of flight is evidenced at hawkwatches where Osprey are known to fly late, even as darkness settles—and hours after more thermal-dependent species have quit the sky. This species is also capable of making extensive open-water crossings.

BREEDING: Observed Wilson of the productivity of the birds: "About the first of May, the female Fish Hawk begins to lay her eggs, which are commonly three in number, sometimes only two, and rarely four."

The nests themselves are large bulky affairs, in most places constructed primarily of large dead branches that the adults snap off in flight from standing trees. In some places the nests are made mostly from clumps of seaweed or grass. The species is famous for carting all manner of artifacts into nests, including muskrat skulls, flip-flops, deflated beach balls, beach chair webbing, and, sometimes with tragic consequences, tangles of fishing line that can ensnare and injure nestlings.

Ospreys are quick to adopt manmade structures for nest sites, including (increasingly) Osprey platforms designed specifically to support nests. Other commonly used structures include utility poles, communication towers, channel markers, and duck blinds. In my town, one pair built their nest on the superstructure of a moored yacht.

Wherever the nest is placed, the birds are strident in their defense of it, calling loudly when human intruders approach. I once saw a circling adult stoop upon and strike an adult Black-crowned Night-

The two advanced juveniles on the top are apparently eager to test their wings while the juvenile on the bottom is about to test the water. Top: Don Riepe/American Littoral Society; bottom: Kevin T. Karlson

Heron that had the ill fortune to fly by the nest while a biologist was banding the young. This act of redirected anger resulted in the death of the heron, which was struck on the back with such force that both wings snapped upon impact.

Wilson describes the eggs this way:

"They are somewhat larger than those of the common hen, and nearly of the same shape. The ground color varies in different eggs, from reddish cream to nearly a white, splashed and daubed all over with Spanish brown, as if done by art."

Worth including in full is a footnote

The Osprey's overall fishing success rate must allow for shrinkage by pirating Bald Eagles.
Ryan Zipp

inserted by Wilson that supports my belief that Wilson's studies of Osprey were done locally. "Of the palatableness of these eggs I cannot speak from personal experience; but the following incident will show that the experiment has actually been made. A country fellow near Cape May, on his way to a neighboring tavern, passing a tree on which was a Fish Hawk nest, immediately mounted and robbed it of the only egg it contained, which he carried with him to the tavern and desired the landlord to make it into egg-nog. The tavern-keeper, after a few wry faces, complied with this request, and the fellow swallowed the cordial; but, whether from its effects on the olfactory nerves (for he said it smelled abominably), the imagination, or on the stomach alone, is uncertain, it operated as a most outrageous emetic, and cured the man, for that time at least, of his thirst for egg-nog. What is rather extraordinary, the landlord (Mr. Beasley) assured, that to all appearance the egg was perfectly fresh."

BEHAVIOR/HUNTING: When hunting, birds typically circle or fly a transect over fish-bearing water at altitudes between 16 and 130 feet (5–40 meters) above the surface, sometimes hovering and doubling back if they sight prey. They generally forage within half a mile of shore, and often just beyond the breakers. The stoop is all gravity, with wings mostly folded, the dive micromanaged with subtle manipulations of the wings and tail. They enter the water feet first and may be completely submerged.

With or without prey, Ospreys do not linger in the water. After a brief, usually less than 20-second pause (perhaps to better secure prey), the birds launch themselves with a powerful, rowing wingbeat—followed then by a hurried series of wingbeats to gain altitude and momentum and, often, to outpace the pirating Bald Eagle that is almost certain to be closing should the Osprey's effort prove successful (which, depending upon conditions and targeted prey, is 30 to 90 percent of the time). Young Ospreys, however, are only about half as successful as adults. The angle of the dive is generally steep but calibrated to depth and prey: long, shallow dives are directed at fast-moving fish near the surface, steeper dives for sluggish fish in deeper water.

Ospreys also perch-hunt, particularly, it seems, in winter when adults unencumbered by the food demands of young are able to resort to this less energetic but time-consuming feeding strategy.

PREY: Ospreys are opportunistic hunters that target whatever fish species is most common and accessible, and these

Only in years of prey abundance do adult Ospreys (like the bird on the right) succeed in fledging three young. Kevin T. Karlson

tend not to vary much. For example, here on the Delaware Bayshore, menhaden, weakfish, and bluefish are the most commonly captured species. Audubon reports seeing an Osprey carrying "with difficulty" a weakfish that he judged to weigh more than five pounds. At the report of Audubon's gun, the bird dropped the fish, which Audubon presumably retrieved. Audubon's estimates notwithstanding, the preferred prey range of this species is 0.3 to 0.7 pounds.

Most treatments of Osprey mention occasions when they latch onto prey that is too heavy for them to lift. Audubon mentions such incidents in his species treatment but admits he is unable to corroborate these reports. Ornithologist Alan Poole suggests that 400 grams is about the upper limit for a male Osprey. He also notes that the birds can release fish underwater as well as in the air.

I can add two accounts to the larder of Osprey-drowning lore. Cape May resident Clay Sutton advises that his father, an avid fisherman, once secured a large bluefish that had two detached Osprey feet embedded in its back. It should be pointed out that feeding bluefish have a piranha-like quality and that, upon hitting the water, the bird was likely set upon by fish in the "blitzing school."

And once, at Cape May Point, New Jersey, I watched an Osprey make what I surmise was a successful dive, except then it could not launch itself from the water. The bird was about 40 yards offshore and in about 20 feet of water. After watching for half a minute as the bird struggled, half-submerged on the surface, I looked away, then back, but was unable to relocate the bird, nor was there any Osprey to be seen within the range of my vision. After waiting several minutes, I departed, concluding that the bird had indeed been pulled under by a fish too large to handle—very possibly a striped bass or perhaps a large bluefish, both of which are common in Delaware Bay.

STATUS: More recently, specifically the last half of the twentieth century, Osprey eggs were central to a biological tragedy when it became evident that the eggs of predatory birds and a chemical agent called DDT did not mix, with the result that the shells of Osprey eggs became too thin to bear the weight of incubating adults, and—perfectly fresh or not—fractured. The result was near-blanket nest failure, leading to a widespread and dramatic decline in Osprey populations. The decline was so catastrophic that many, myself included, presumed that the bird was headed for extinction. While other raptor species were similarly affected, owing to their manifest presence and popularity, the decline of this golden-eyed raptor was particularly apparent and lamented. I submit that this bird's decline did as much to move public opinion in favor of banning DDT in America as the decline of the Peregrine, which has come to be the raptorial poster child of the DDT debacle.

But as I conclude this account, and as the chorus of Osprey calls cascading into my open window attests, Osprey populations here and elsewhere have recovered from their brush with extinction. The bird is once again a common breeder and migrant across much of North America, and I would not be surprised if the local breeding population was now as large as it was when Alexander Wilson visited these fecund shores two centuries ago.

KITES
Five species, five genera

Hook-billed Kite
Chondrohierax uncinatus

ETYMOLOGY: The genus name comes from the Greek *chondros*, meaning "composed of cartilage," and *hierakos*, for "a falcon." The bird's limber and somewhat rough-and-tumble feeding behavior lends itself to the supposition that the bird is made of something more flexible than muscle and bone. The species name *uncinatus* is Latin for "hooked," a presumed reference to the bird's prominent bill.

PROFILE: A goofy-looking, bulbous-billed tree snail specialist that comports itself below the forest canopy in the manner

An adult female Hook-billed Kite shows the bird's distinctive paddle-shaped wing profile. Note the tree snail in the bird's bill. Bill Clark

of a feathered sloth. It does, at times—particularly at midmorning—soar high above woodlands, showing a long-tailed paddle-winged profile that is all field mark.

DESCRIPTION: A medium-sized tropical and subtropical forest raptor that when perched is shaped somewhat like a robust but inverted bowling pin. Observers are immediately struck by the bird's large, heavy bill, which seems disproportionately large for the head, and pale eyes that give the bird a crazed look. Bill size in this species is variable, divided between large-billed and smaller-billed types whose bill is nevertheless substantial. These large- and small-billed types are not believed to represent separate subspecies. But this species is sexually dimorphic, with adult males and females having markedly different plumages. There is also a rare dark morph that has occurred in the United States.

Most adult males are slate gray above with an all-gray head and throat, and a heavily barred long gray tail bisected by several broad dark bands. Most adult females show a brown back and wings, a gray face, and a dark cap; the breast and belly show orange barring that coalesces into an orange breast and neck, extending to form a collar. The female's tail, like the gray morph male's, shows broad dark bands. Very short yellow legs give perched birds a sawed-off appearance. Note that males are sometimes found in brown morph like the female.

Juveniles are like brown morph/female but show a whitish cheek and whitish underparts, lightly barred or vermiculated.

It has also been advanced that rather than being strictly sexually dimorphic, Hook-billed Kite is simply polymorphic, showing a gray, brown, and dark morph and that more males are gray morphs and more females brown. On dark morphs, with sexes similar, the entire body is leaden black. The black tail is bisected by one to two broad pale bands and shows a whitish tip.

MEASUREMENTS

Length: 16–20 inches
Wingspan: 34–38 inches
Weight: 8–12 ounces

SUBSPECIES: Three subspecies are generally recognized. *C. u. uncinatus* is our resident group, ranging from the Rio Grande Valley south through Central and South America to Paraguay and northern Argentina. *C. u. mirus* is resi-

An adult female Hook-billed Kite perched (left); a mostly adult male (right). Only a trace of a first-year's tail pattern at the base of the tail allows for the aging of this bird. Left: Brian Small; right: Kevin T. Karlson

A dark-morph Hook-billed Kite. This black color morph is a very rare occurrence in the United States. Bill Clark

dent in Grenada and the Lesser Antilles. *C. u. wilsonii* is resident in eastern Cuba.

VOCALIZATIONS: "A very musical whistle with notes resembling an American oriole." The Snyders liken the call to the mellow vocalizations of Field Sparrow and call it very "unhawk-like." Also makes "a clucking or rattling chatter . . ."

DISTRIBUTION: In the United States, Hook-billed Kite is an uncommon to rare resident in the flood plain of the lower Rio Grande Valley of Texas in Hidalgo and Starr Counties. The Texas population appears to be small, with two or three pairs nesting regularly. It was considered "accidental" by Oberholser in 1974, with only a single unsuccessful nesting effort in Santa Ana National Wildlife Refuge in 1964. This initial failure was then fol-

lowed by a successful nesting effort there in 1976. Today the birds are seen regularly in the riparian forests bordering the Rio Grande from Santa Ana NWR north and west to Falcon Dam.

MIGRATION: Mostly sedentary, but in some parts of its large range, small soaring flocks of 20 to 30 individuals "apparently on migration" have been noted. At the Veracruz, Mexico, hawkwatch, a seasonal average of 145 Hook-billed Kites are counted during fall migration, 3 in spring.

HABITAT: This is a tropical and subtropical forest species occupying the lower forest canopy and (dense) undergrowth. It is particularly partial to dry tropical forest but also found in humid tropical forest as well as forest edge, clearings,

An adult female Hook-billed Kite at left, a juvenile at right; classic Rio Grande Valley thorn scrub habitat in between. Unless a freeze reaches the Rio Grande Valley, there are plenty of snails to go around. Left and center: Brian Sullivan; right: Bill Clark

and disturbed forest and coffee plantations. In Mexico, Hook-billed Kite occupies acacia thorn scrub woodlands. In the United States and elsewhere, Hook-billed Kite inhabits areas where tree snails are abundant.

BREEDING: In Texas, Hook-billed Kite breeding occurs mostly in May and June. In some places it nests in "loose colonies." The cup-shaped stick nest is built by both sexes and is situated at mid- to upper levels of the tree. The clutch contains one or two eggs, buffy white and marked with dark reddish brown. Snyder describes the nests as "frail, tiny, very much like that of a dove." Incubation lasts 35 days and the male reportedly brings most of the food to the nest. There is no information about fledging, but young apparently remain with the parents for several months.

BEHAVIOR/HUNTING: Hook-billed Kite has been described as "unobtrusive and sluggish, usually skulking within the canopy," and " . . . found singly or in groups of two or three." It's not a well-studied species, but spends much of its time, particularly mornings, foraging be-neath the canopy for tree and land snails. Perch-hunting is typical, but it is also reported to reconnoiter by circling low over open ground. When a bird sights prey from a strategic perch (which we humans can often identify by the accumulation of discarded snail shells below), it flies directly and unhurriedly to the snail-bearing tree (which is commonly not far away) and thrusts its legs forward, appearing to fuse to the tree trunk in an upright position. Then, stretching its neck up and to the side, it grasps the snail with its bill, prying it free, before pushing (or falling) back, whereupon it flaps to gain stability and direction, before returning to a favored perch. The capture process is accomplished in seconds and repeated until the bird is satiated. Once perched, the bird transfers the prey to its left foot. Then, using its bill, it attacks the membrane covering the shell's aperture and chips away the whorls, exposing and extracting the snail before dropping the characteristically holed shell to the pile below. It is also reported to hang upside down to reach prey and to hop about among branches, as well as forage on foot on the forest floor.

Compared to the surgical process of snail extraction practiced by Snail Kite, the Snyders liken Hook-billed Kite's technique to the application of "brute force," and suggest the bird's heavy bill is designed to withstand the abrasive wear and tear of fracturing snail shells. Bill size differs markedly within populations, a distinction that is not related to age, sex, or race but is presumed to enable birds to target a wider spectrum of snails. In point of fact the greatest variation in bill size between individuals correlates with places where snails of different sizes are available. However, it is not known whether large-billed and smaller-billed individuals interbreed freely.

When conditions are good, birds may be seen soaring over the canopy, sometimes very high but not commonly for long.

PREY: Hook-billed Kite preys primarily upon arboreal and terrestrial snails but is also reported to eat frogs, salamanders, insects, and caterpillars, although the manner of capture is not described and, given the bird's very short legs, the capture of non-snail prey might prove challenging, indeed.

An adult female Hook-billed Kite (left) and a dark morph of indeterminant sex (right). Note the robust size of the shell-crunching bill. Bill Clark

STATUS: Where they're found, they're generally considered uncommon to rare and often "declining." The two races in the West Indies are endangered.

Swallow-tailed Kite
Elanoides forficatus

ETYMOLOGY: The genus name comes from the Greek *elanos,* for "kite," and *oides,* meaning "resembling." The species name, *forficatus,* is Latin for "deeply forked."

PROFILE: A large, elegant, gregarious, splay-tailed aerialist whose beauty and fluid flight would incite envy in heaven.

DESCRIPTION: Large, nearly Osprey-sized, with crooked but slender wings; our only bird of prey with a deeply forked tail. This kite is conspicuously and contrastingly black and white, with head, underparts, and wing lining brilliant white. Upperparts, tail, and flight feathers are blue-black in good light. Sexes are similar and, except for a buffy wash on the head, neck, and breast, the juvenile is much like adults. Unlike most raptors, males and females of this species are similar in size.

MEASUREMENTS
Length: 20–25 inches
Wingspan: 47–54 inches
Weight: 11–18 ounces

SUBSPECIES: Two subspecies are recognized: *E. f. forficatus,* which breeds in the southeastern United States and winters in South America; and *E.f. yetapa,* which breeds from southern Mexico south through the northern two-thirds of South America.

VOCALIZATIONS: Generally silent, but in flight Swallow-tailed Kite utters shrill piping and ringing whistles.

DISTRIBUTION: Occurs in the southeastern United States, Mexico, Central America, and most of South America, south to northern Argentina. In the United States, breeding is mostly limited to Florida, also southeastern Georgia, the coastal lowlands of South Carolina, coastal Alabama, southern Mississippi, central Louisiana, and eastern Texas. It was formerly much more widespread, with a breeding range extending north to North Carolina, central Minnesota, southwestern Wisconsin, and southwestern Ohio and west to the prairies. John Krider noted, "I have found it very abundant in Iowa, Minnesota and Kansas where they breed . . . " It has been estimated that this species currently occupies only 5 percent of its historic range.

In late summer, the entire population withdraws into South America. Band recoveries of U.S. birds in southern and southeastern Brazil and telemetry studies support the determination that Brazil is where North American breeders spend much of their winters—soaring over the rainforest canopy.

MIGRATION: This species spends only half of its year in North America, arriving in Florida in late February and departing by September. Preparations for departure begin before September in Florida, with roost counts of birds staging for migration in late July and early August exceeding 1,200.

The Swallow-tailed Kite is a bird beautiful and graceful enough to turn biologists into poets.
Kevin T. Karlson

More than a dozen highly social Swallow-tailed Kites forage in the skies over the tropical forest canopy where North America's breeders spend the northern winter. This shot was taken at the Canopy Tower in Panama. Brian Sullivan

This kite is among North America's earliest fall and spring migrants. The entire U.S. population withdraws by mid-September to begin the 10,000-mile odyssey. Radio telemetry has confirmed what biologists have long suspected: the birds use two routes to reach wintering areas in Brazil. One circumnavigates the Gulf of Mexico, while the other crosses the Gulf of Mexico using south Florida as the point of departure and western Cuba as a steppingstone to the Yucatán Peninsula. The birds then pass through Costa Rica and Panama to western Colombia, where they are obliged to cross the Andes before continuing south to southern Brazil. There they remain until late January, at which time birds begin their return, crossing the Andes once again for an interim stop on the Yucatán Peninsula from where at least some birds launch themselves directly north across the Gulf of Mexico, as many passerines do, making landfall somewhere along the Gulf Coast of the United States. To vault the Gulf, birds must necessarily fly day and night. Some birds evidently take a land route that circumnavigates the Gulf.

In spring, Swallow-tailed Kites arrive in south Florida in the third or fourth week in February; birds that breed farther north arrive later. On the Dry Tortugas, one morning in late April, I observed a pair of Swallow-tailed Kites fly in off the Gulf of Mexico and continue north toward the mainland. The birds were about 100 to 200 feet above the Gulf and did not land or tarry, despite what was apparently an all-night flight across open water. Cross-Gulf migrants evidently suffer high mortality.

HABITAT: Primarily a denizen of open sky, over tropical and subtropical forest as well as marshes and swamps along river systems, it uses its four-foot wingspan to soar and glide for hours over the canopy and along riverine forest edge. The kite typically forages where it finds concentrations of large insect prey that it catches on the wing, and also snatches arboreal prey from forest canopy. It generally avoids dry areas.

Formerly, in the upper Mississippi drainage, it nested in riparian forest, small woodlands, and groves in proximity to prairie and marsh. Now, in the southeastern United States, its breeding habitat is typically a combination of pine forest, swamp, wet prairies, freshwater and brackish marshes, hardwood hammocks, tall trees edging sloughs and bayous, mixed hardwood-cypress swamp forest, and mangrove. It typically forages in open country, often in the same air space occupied by Mississippi Kite.

BREEDING: Swallow-tailed Kite breeds in March through July, with birds arriving in south Florida the third week in February; pairs may be formed upon or shortly after arrival. Courtship and territorial behavior is immediate. Says Audubon: "The Swallow-tailed Hawk pairs immediately after its arrival in the Southern States, and as its courtship takes place on the wing, its motions are then more beautiful than ever." The nest, he says, "is usually placed on the top branches of the tallest oak or pine tree, situated on the margin of a stream or pond." The Snyders concur, observing that the species nests at the "very tops of the tallest trees available . . . with many nests over 100 feet from the

Pine forest is a common component of Swallow-tailed Kite's North American nesting habitat profile. This bird was nesting next to the University of Miami in suburban habitat. Kevin T. Karlson

Swallow-tailed Kites are adept at feeding on the wing, as evidenced by this photo of a bird relishing a frog. Steve Sachs.

ground . . . " Sprunt says nests are typically placed in pines or cypresses at heights of 75 to 130 feet but specifically references a Texas nest "recorded at a height of over 200 feet in a cottonwood."

Both sexes aid in construction of the nest. Audubon likens the structure to that of "Common" (now American) Crow, " . . . being formed of dry sticks with Spanish moss and is lined with coarse grass and a few feathers." Nests are not usually used for more than one season. It is common for new nests to be located near the previous year's nest. Typically two creamy white eggs are laid and they are embellished with dark brown to reddish brown markings. These hatch in about 28 days. Fledging occurs 35 to 42 days later. Juveniles may be tended by adults for two to eight weeks, then may remain in natal ranges for two or three months, a timetable that coincides with the onset of migration. Both parents share in all aspects of rearing young. Pairs produce a single clutch per season, and while several pairs may nest in close proximity, pairs are monogamous.

BEHAVIOR/HUNTING: In migration and in winter, Swallow-tailed Kites are gregarious, roosting together and hunting in loose assemblages where food is concentrated.

While birds are in flight, they capture all prey with the feet, snatching it in the air or gleaning it from the surface of vegetation. They hunt by gliding or soaring in search of flying insects or gliding low over the tree canopy in search of arboreal prey. The capture of insects is usually straightforward and direct, with birds overtaking insect prey from behind, but at times birds are obliged to maneuver deftly, diving or rolling to capture insects located behind and below. Adults consume prey on the wing.

PREY: Insects are the primary prey throughout the year. But when the birds are nesting, adults deliver vertebrate prey to young, sometimes including nestlings of smaller birds still wrapped in the nest. At all times of year, adults and larvae of stinging insects (such as wasps) are an important component of the diet, and adults frequently return to nests bearing whole wasp nests. Other prey includes dragonflies, tree frogs, anole lizards, snakes, birds (including nestlings), and small mammals. Fruit eating in winter is reportedly common in the tropics. Swallow-tailed Kites are opportunistic foragers, and any large concentrations of dragonflies can be counted upon to draw numbers of hunting kites. They do not pursue prey, relying mostly upon surprise. In mid-April, in south Florida, I have seen multiple foraging flocks in excess of 80 individuals foraging in dragonfly-rich skies over marshes.

Holy Elanoides! This unique shot shows 34 of 66 birds migrating as a group through Limón, Costa Rica, in late February 2016, en route to breeding grounds in North America. Kevin T. Karlson

STATUS: In the early twentieth century, this species entered into a dramatic range reduction, which is believed to have been caused by persecution and habitat alteration to favor agriculture. Egg collecting has also been implicated as a cause of decline, with clutches going for $80 to $120. In Florida, development (and the ensuing loss of habitat) has been implicated as a cause of population decline.

This is a popular and intensely studied species. Presently listed as endangered in South Carolina, it nevertheless remains relatively common in proper habitat within its now greatly reduced range but has been recommended for listing as a federally endangered species. Notes Alexander Sprunt, speaking for everyone who has observed this bird: "If any bird in the country deserves protection from an aesthetic standpoint, this kite stands at the top of the list"—or, perhaps more appropriately, "soars" at the top of the list. Summarizing point count data from Gulf Coast hawkwatches (1995–2005), Bildstein et al. note a "positive rate of change" at those hawkwatch sites.

White-tailed Kite
Elanus leucurus

An adult White-tailed Kite, an angelic bird with demonic eyes. Brian Small

ETYMOLOGY: *Elanus* is Latin for "kite"; *leucurus* is Greek for "white-tailed."

PROFILE: Dapper, elegant, and almost angelic, this geographically restricted raptor of open, usually grassy habitat combines the coursing flight of a harrier with the hovering finesse of an American Kestrel, thus making it ideally suited to hunt open, perch-impoverished habitat. As much as the Condor or Peregrine, this species is a totem to the conservation realignment that transformed raptors from vermin and villains into valued symbols of a healthy environment. But before this philosophical realignment

and as a result of human persecution, by the early twentieth century this species had become exceedingly rare—even extirpated—in the eastern portion of its North American range. In the early twentieth century Arthur Cleveland Bent failed to locate the species in former breeding strongholds in Florida or Texas and was unaware of any recent records from those states. "Only in California" Bent notes, did the species seem to be "holding its own . . ."

As far back as 1886, the consensus among ornithologists was that the White-tailed Kite was a doomed species. Shooting appears to have been the principal cause of the bird's decline. Its low, slow flight over open marshes occupied by men with guns, coupled with the mistaken belief that the bird fed upon quail, ducks, and other game birds, was a lethal combination. Notes Milton S. Ray of birds in California, "this kite is peculiarly friendly and unsuspicious and therefore exceptionally easy to shoot."

The bird's fortunes were not improved by the fact that its eggs were coveted for their beauty precisely during a time when egg collecting was at the height of fashion among Victorian gentlemen. William Leon Dawson estimates that the eggs of White-tailed Kite were "quite the handsomest of the raptors." Very happily, the kite beat the odds, survived persecution, and now appears to be expanding its range in Texas, California, and even Oregon and Washington, as well as Mexico and Central America.

DESCRIPTION: This is a medium-sized, somewhat gull-like raptor. Adults have pearl gray wings and back; a whitish head, tail, and underparts; and boast a large, elongated, black shoulder patch and bright white underparts. A black eyepatch sets off the demonically red eye of adults—a trait at odds with its otherwise angelic appearance. Sexes are similar. The bill is petite, the feet are yellow, and the legs are short. When the bird is perched, the namesake white tail is mostly concealed beneath folded wings.

Elliott Coues describes juveniles as "marked with dusky and reddish brown; wing feathers white tipped; tail feathers marked with a substantial ashy bar." Very young birds show a buffy wash on the breast that fades within weeks.

A White-tailed Kite can only be confused with an adult male Northern Harrier, which typically hunts lower and does not hover extensively or at a kite-high altitude of 25 feet.

MEASUREMENTS
Length: 20–25 inches
Wingspan: 47–54 inches
Weight: 11–18 ounces

Hunting White-tailed Kites typically course over rodent-rich grasslands. When they sight prey, they may hover briefly or parachute to earth with wings raised and legs extended. Brian Sullivan

SYSTEMATICS/SUBSPECIES: This species has occasionally been considered conspecific with the Black-shouldered Kite, *Elanus caeruleus,* which is found in the Old World and Australia. White-tailed does share some plumage and habitat similarities with Black-shouldered, but overall White-tailed is more delicately proportioned, and in 1993 the AOU determined that evidence warranted the return to a previous determination that *E. leucurus* is, in fact, a distinct species represented in the Americas by two subspecies: *E. l. majusculus* in North America and the smaller *E. l. leucurus* in South America.

VOCALIZATIONS: When startled, White-tailed Kite emits a low, dry, raspy yelp. Juveniles make an Osprey-like whistle.

DISTRIBUTION: In North America the bird's principal stronghold is California, west of the Sierras, south to Baja, where it is resident. This West Coast population is gradually expanding northward and now occurs sparingly to southwestern Washington and the far western counties of Oregon. It is also reestablishing itself in historic strongholds, becoming once again a common breeder in south Texas and reestablishing itself in south Florida (beginning in the 1960s). At present, the species distribution, while disjunct, is the most extensive since Audubon was introduced to it as a live specimen in 1835, the gift of Dr. Ravenel of Charleston. This species also occurs in Mexico and locally in South America to Chile and central Argentina. It is reported "common" in northern Argentina.

MIGRATION: Populations are believed to be mostly resident but somewhat nomadic, relocating in response to prey availability, at which time range expansion may result.

The juvenile White-tailed Kite on the left has made a successful catch, while the bird on the right parachutes upon prey. Left: Chris Montano; right: Brian Sullivan

Luckily for some rodent, this time those rodent-calibrated talons are reaching for a perch.
Brian Small

HABITAT: Typically a bird of low-elevation grasslands, the White-tailed Kite also hunts wetlands, agricultural lands, and open areas adjacent to riparian woodlands. Grassy highway borders and median strips constitute prime foraging areas. The most important consideration is an abundance of prey. For breeding it uses isolated trees or groves. It generally avoids regions subject to prolonged winter freezes and also selects in favor of ungrazed grasslands.

BREEDING: Pairs are found together year-round but most particularly December through August. According to J. R. Dunk, nest building occurs "slowly over the course of weeks and pairs spend more time near nesting areas after courtship begins." Nests are placed in trees (willows in particular), frequently near water and twelve to sixteen feet high. Both sexes contribute to nest construction. Colin Harrison describes the nests as "loose but well built twig structures with the small nests of other species used as the foundation." California ornithologist William Dawson describes the eggs as "basically creamy white, the surfaces are half buried or altogether covered with chocolate in several intensities and each of ravishing richness." Dawson regarded them as "quite the handsomest of the raptors and that is high tribute of praise." He goes on to appeal to zoologists to restrain their "cupidity."

A typical clutch has four or five eggs, with incubation by the female lasting 30 to 32 days. Fledging occurs four or five weeks after hatching, and young have been known to capture prey a month later.

In seasons marked by high prey density, pairs may start a second brood after a successful first nesting, but one nesting effort per season is typical.

BEHAVIOR/HUNTING: Dawson considered the bird "unsuspicious" and "confiding." Outside the breeding season, it is a social, even gregarious species with more than 100 individuals counted at key communal roosts. Dawson calls the bird "more or less gregarious." While nests may be only 600 feet apart, this species is reported to be "antagonistic toward most large raptors." Winter roosts are situated in groves of trees.

Birds typically hunt by hovering 20 to 75 feet high, facing into the wind, searching the ground below. Once it sights prey, the bird parachutes downward on wings raised in an acute V. (See photo on page 46.) It often checks its descent and engages in another bout of hovering before making a final vertical drop with its legs extended. Prey secured, the bird flies to a favorite perch.

When not hunting, birds are commonly seen perched atop trees or shrubs, often in pairs. However, this species does not commonly practice perch-hunting.

PREY: Small mammals, particularly mice, are the kite's principal prey, although Fisher reported a varied diet that also included birds, lizards, and insects. But this species is first and foremost a

A hovering adult White-tailed Kite, very obviously intent upon prey. Brian Small

The adult male Snail Kite never appears to be in a hurry. Low and slow is its forte. Kevin T. Karlson

mouser, one that targets mice and voles. Its early reputation as a destroyer of game birds is wholly undeserved.

STATUS: Persecution in the early twentieth century gave way to legislated protection that covered both wanton shooting and scientific collecting. This species' survival and current expansion may be attributed in part to the widespread respect for raptors that is now the prevailing attitude among sportsmen, as well as the alarm sounded by ornithologists beginning in the nineteenth century.

The element of human persecution now greatly diminished, this species seems to be doing well in agricultural California, Texas, and Florida. But the bird's future may be tied to agricultural practices that accommodate the prey-bearing grassy edges of managed croplands—and, of course, to rainfall.

Snail Kite
Rostrhamus sociabilis

ETYMOLOGY: The genus name comes from the Latin *rostrum,* for "beak," and *hamus,* for "a hook," and the species name from the Latin *sociabilis,* for "gregarious," for its nesting in loose colonies.

PROFILE: The Snail Kite is one of the planet's most specialized raptors. Despite decades of active management and study, it is arguably North America's most endangered raptor. For over a century, this iconic resident of central and southern

Florida has been the poster child for those striving to restore the free-flowing integrity of Florida's River of Grass. It is distinguished in the United States by its persistently low population, limited range, and near total dependence upon its aquatic prey, freshwater apple snails (*Pomacea* sp.).

DESCRIPTION: A medium-large (Red-shouldered Hawk–sized) raptor of marshy tropical and subtropical regions, brandishing a deeply curved, surgically slender bill, specialized to extract the body of the apple snail from its shell. Males appear uniformly dark slate gray except for a white undertail and base to the tail. The legs and the base of the bill are bright red-orange. The dark-backed adult female has an overall browner plumage, a bold face pattern, and heavily streaked underparts. The juvenile is similar to the female but is browner, lacking any grayish tones, with a less distinctly patterned face and bright yellow legs and base to the bill. The long and extremely slender bill is evident in all cases. Despite pronounced differences in plumage, the sexes differ little in proportions, the female being only slightly larger than the male.

MEASUREMENTS
Length: 16–19 inches
Wingspan: 41–44 inches
Weight: 12–21 ounces

SYSTEMATICS/SUBSPECIES: The genus *Rostrhamus* has one other member, the Slender-billed Kite, *Rostrhamus hamatus,* of South America. Like Snail Kite, it is a *Pomacea* snail specialist, but one specialized to forage in the flooded forest margins of rain forests.

Three or four subspecies of Snail Kite are described. *R. s. plumbeus* is a year-round resident in peninsular Florida. It is also resident in Cuba. *R. s. major* is found as a local resident in the lowlands of eastern and southern Mexico, as well as Belize. *R. s. sociabilis* is found from Nicaragua to Argentina. This race is smaller than other races. Brown and Amadon also recognize *R. s. levis* of Cuba and Isle of Pines, separating it from the Florida-based "Everglades Kite," *R. s. plumbeus.*

VOCALIZATIONS: They are usually silent, but both sexes make a "harsh cackling" *ka-ka-ka-ka-ka.*

DISTRIBUTION: This is a New World species found across tropical and subtropical America from Florida to Argentina and Peru. Outside Florida's Everglades, this raptor species is local but common in proper habitat in Central and South America. In the United States, the subspecies *R. s. plumbeus* is a permanent resident in the southern half of the Florida Peninsula, where its range is restricted to watersheds of the Everglades, Lakes Okeechobee and Kissimmee, and the upper St. Johns River. Florida birds are considered to be a single population showing considerable distributional shifts that relate to seasonality and water conditions. Where this species does occur, it commonly outnumbers all other birds of prey.

MIGRATION: *The Birds of North America* says the Snail Kite is "Non-migratory but semi-nomadic in response to water depths, food availability and aquatic vegetation growth." As go apple snails, so go Snail Kites. Dispersal to other breeding areas may be "annual, seasonal, or short-

The mating strategy of the Snail Kite is fickle and dynamic with both sexes practicing desertion and new mate selection near the conclusion of a successful breeding cycle. This mated adult pair (female on left, male on right) had just copulated. Note the larger size of the female. Kevin T. Karlson

term." There is no evidence of passage from Florida to Cuba, but in colder winters birds tend to range farther south on the peninsula.

HABITAT: In Florida, Snail Kites breed, roost, and forage in large, inland freshwater marshes or edges of shallow lakes where apple snails abound. The marsh profile is typically sawgrass, but openwater areas for foraging are an essential habitat component, plus a scattering of "low trees and shrubs to support nests and accommodate roosting birds. Almost continuous flooding of wetlands for one year is needed to support a healthy snail population." Roosting sites are "almost always over water."

BREEDING: This is a somewhat dynamic, multifaceted affair that typically involves multiple nestings and mates over the course of a breeding season that—under favorable conditions—may span 10 to 11 months. Mate desertion during the later part of the breeding cycle may be part of this strategy and a practical application of the old adage "Don't put all your eggs in one basket." The strategy may have developed to offset losses caused by the frequent problem of nest collapse. The "River of Grass" constitutes a supportive environment against human encroachment, but grass is, for the most part, a poor substrate for supporting bulky raptor nests.

In Florida, most birds pair late November to early June, but nesting activity is noted every month of the year, and the breeding season varies widely year to year, depending upon rainfall, water levels, and apple snail abundance. Kites situate their nests from 3 to 15 feet above the water.

Nesting material consists of sticks and grass. Substrate is typically woody growth, often in a stand of willows, or it may be a low bush or stand of reeds ("sawgrass clumps"), but the standing water component is important as a predator deterrent. Nevertheless, predation is the primary cause of death for nestlings. The nest, which is described as "small, flat in form, composed of sticks somewhat carelessly arranged," may stand alone or be situated in a loose colony. Whatever the substrate, nests are accessible from above. Those supported by cattail and willow are prone to collapse, particularly during severe drought. Most such nests fail when wind, rain, and rapid water-level changes weaken cattails, spilling eggs and young overboard. Kites readily adopt special artificial nest baskets, which are a more stable platform than natural vegetation, resulting in reduced nest failure due to toppling.

While juveniles come fully equipped with bills and talons calibrated to a life of hunting snails, the extraction process takes time to master, resulting in a protracted period of dependence upon one or both adults after fledging. This plumage of a fresh juvenile (left) is rarely depicted in field guides, and the bold buff fringing and head shading changes to resemble the plumage shown in the photo on the right, which is probably a first winter bird due to the pale yellowish leg color and amount of whitish feathering on the head (adult females can sometimes resemble first winter birds). Kevin T. Karlson

Modern clutch size ranges from one to six brown to reddish brown speckled white eggs, but larger clutches of four to six eggs were typical before 1940. The incubation period is 24 to 30 days. Fledging takes 23 to 28 days. The adults continue to attend to their young after fledging. Notes Menge: "They feed and care for their young longer than any other birds I know of, until you can scarcely distinguish them from adults."

This parental devotion is possibly related to the difficulty inherent in mastering the snail extraction technique. As noted by Snyder, "The young birds had special difficulties learning how to hold a snail against a perch with the feet . . . Obviously unsure how to proceed, they eyed the captured victims curiously, then positioned them in orientations in which further progress was unlikely if not impossible." How then to reconcile this protracted parental care with the species' "fickle nesting strategy," one in which one member of the pair deserts the nest when young are three to five weeks old, leaving one adult to complete the nesting cycle while the deserter initiates another nesting cycle with a new mate? Mate desertion is practiced by both sexes and is most common in years when apple snails are abundant and foraging conditions are good.

The abandonment strategy makes sense when, as noted by Snyder, it is realized that when snail numbers are high, young kites have little difficulty securing prey: "Once the young kites fledged from the nests . . . they very quickly became as adept as adults in grabbing snails from the water surface." For this species, the challenge parents face during the fledging stage and in times of apple snail abundance is not one of finding or providing prey. The challenge lies in young birds mastering a difficult feeding technique for which they have the adaptive mechanisms but not the skill, which can be gained only through trial and error, nothing adults can instill whether singly or in pairs.

Very possibly, then, the "fickle" or dynamic mating strategy may have evolved precisely because of the protracted learning period young kites require to gain independence. Given a five- to ten-month breeding season, Snyder calculates that this mating strategy may offer one adult bird the opportunity to produce three or four broods per year if it continues the strategy sequentially through the nesting season, but only two broods if both adults tended young to full independence.

BEHAVIOR/HUNTING: Birds are social throughout the year, roosting communally, often in association with anhingas, assorted herons, ibis, and vultures. They spend 85 percent of daylight hours perched, and the balance of the time foraging and capturing snails. They hunt by flying low and slow (somewhat harrier-like) over open marsh, seeking out some favored open freshwater pool free of tall or surface-covering vegetation. Spotting an apple snail at or close to the surface, the birds initiate a hovering descent from which they pluck prey.

The birds do not plunge or dive, as some accounts allow. The descent is more of a "swoop." Palmer describes the maneuver as a stall and drop, in a manner that does not even dampen the birds' feathers. Snail secure in one or both feet—or sometimes following a transfer to the bill—the kite flies to a favorite

perch and decants its prey. As described by Sprunt, "The Everglades Kite never seems in a hurry. It is a deliberate bird, never flustered or erratic. With deep strokes of its wings it slowly searches the water beneath, peering keenly downward, then swings around and covers another sector. When prey is sighted, the bird towers slightly, hovers, then drops downward, with dangling legs, seizes the prey in its talons . . . "

Hunting success varies with the weather. In moderate temperatures, snails come to the surface to breathe. When cold fronts pass and temperatures fall, snails stay deeper. Given cold conditions, what was typically a two- to three-minute hunting endeavor may stretch to 20 minutes or longer.

Much has been said about the kite's highly specialized bill, but its feet, the snail-catching end of the bird, are equally evolved to their highly specialized task. The exceptionally long, thin toes and talons are wonderfully designed for seizing and grasping their shelled prey.

One account describes the decanting process this way: "Snail secured and perch taken, the bird holds the snail with one or both feet, twists the operculum covering the snail's body away from the shell, tear-

This female Snail Kite is brandishing one of the smaller, native apple snails. Kevin T. Karlson

ing it off and usually discarding it. The bird then inserts its long, pointed bill into the shell's aperture and cuts the muscle attaching the snail's body to the inside of the shell. The snail is then extracted and eaten whole or torn to pieces . . . "

STATUS: One might presume, given the protracted nesting period and dynamic breeding strategy, that the North American Snail (or Everglades) Kite would be flourishing, but for several reasons this seems not to be the case. Nesting success varies greatly year to year and is directly linked to water levels.

The current Snail Kite population is doing better than it was during the 1950s when perhaps fewer than 40 birds remained. Since 1981, annual winter surveys conducted by the U.S. Fish and Wildlife Service have ranged from 109 birds to 996, with great variation year to year, with water levels constituting the principal influence on Snail Kite populations in Florida.

Future challenges to this species include habitat loss and alteration linked to planned or proposed water management strategies. Compounding challenges are the proliferation of invasive matting plant species, which hinder the kite's ability to locate snails, and, of course, the great and looming threat posed by global warming, which may result in the tidal inundation of this low-lying freshwater habitat, threatening not only Snail Kite but the entire Everglades ecosystem. Uncertain is the impact of the larger, invasive channeled apple snail (*Pomacea canaliculata*), which may compete with the native apple snail (*Pomacea paludosa*) but may also (as seems to be the case) constitute a new food resource for Snail Kite.

Mississippi Kite
Ictinia mississippiensis

ETYMOLOGY: *Ictinos* is Greek for "a kite," and *mississippiensis* for the location from which Alexander Wilson procured the type specimen. Says Wilson in his account, "This new species I first observed in the Mississippi territory, a few miles below Natchez . . . "

PROFILE: A neat, trim, dapper-looking, highly social aerialist that recalls a splay-tailed Peregrine Falcon in size and shape, and a cross between a swallow and thistledown in flight, moving as adroitly through air as a trout through a stream.

DESCRIPTION: What a privilege to quote here, intact, Alexander Wilson's description of this splendid raptor, an adult male:

The Mississippi Kite measures fourteen inches in length, and thirty-six inches or three feet in extent. The head, neck and exterior webs of the secondaries are of a hoary white; the lower parts a whitish ash; bill, cere, lores, and narrow line around the eye, black; back, rump, scapulars, and wing-coverts, dark blackish ash; wings very long and pointed, the third quill the longest; the primaries are black, marked down each side of the shaft with reddish sorrel; primary coverts also slightly touched with the same; all the upper parts at the roots is white; the scapulars are also spotted with white; but this cannot be perceived unless the feathers be blown aside; tail slightly forked, and, as well as the rump, jet black; legs, vermillion, tinged with orange and becoming blackish towards the toes; claws black; iris of the eye dark red, pupil black.

These two adult Mississippi Kites are in the early stages of moving their genetic heritage forward. The population is healthy and expanding both numerically and geographically. Ned Harris

An adult Mississippi Kite on the left, a subadult on the right, brandishing the retained juvenile flight feathers. The second-year bird bred in Sterling Forest, New York, in 2012. Left: Kevin T. Karlson; right: Lloyd Spitalnik

You just don't find descriptions like this anymore. Sexes are similar.

Wilson did not describe the juvenile plumage, but from Clark and Wheeler, also verbatim: "Head is dark brown, with fine whitish streaks and a short buffy superciliary line. Creamy throat is unstreaked. Iris color is dark brown. Back and upperwing coverts are dark brown with rufous feather edging. Underparts are creamy, with thick, dark reddish brown streaking. Flight feathers have white tips. Underwing has light brown coverts and somewhat darker flight feathers, often with white area at base of outer primaries. Dark brown tail has 3 incomplete light bands."

Subadults have mostly adultlike gray bodies but retain the banded tail of the immature.

MEASUREMENTS

Length: 16–19 inches
Wingspan: 41–44 inches
Weight: 12–21 ounces

Wilson's specimen, then, appears to be somewhat small.

SUBSPECIES: None recognized. This species is closely related to the Plumbeous Kite (*Ictinia plumbea*) of Central and South America, and the two are sometimes regarded as a superspecies.

VOCALIZATIONS: According to David Sibley, the call is a "high, thin whistle similar to Broad-winged but descending."

DISTRIBUTION: In Wilson's time it was found only in the southeastern United States. But this species has expanded both north and west, and now breeds as far west as Arizona and Colorado. Since the 1990s it has begun breeding in the New England states, most notably New Hampshire. It has also been breeding in Virginia since 1995. However, the core population remains southern and ranges from South Carolina throughout the upper and lower coastal plain, south

The aspired-to end game of a nesting cycle: a juvenile Mississippi Kite in these superb shots of juvenile plumage. Left: Vic Berardi; right: Greg Lasley

A not-so-smooth food exchange between adults. The male seems unwilling to part with his intended gift. In this species, both sexes deliver food and feed nestlings. Rob Curtis

through the southern half of Georgia and west into the Florida Panhandle, much of Alabama, southern and western Mississippi, and across much of Louisiana into southeastern Oklahoma and northeastern Texas. It also breeds in the southern coastal plain of Texas. A disjunct Great Plains population breeds in the Texas Panhandle, north-central Texas, central Oklahoma, central Kansas, and eastern Colorado, according to J. W. Parker.

Mississippi Kite also breeds in scattered locations in Arizona and New Mexico.

In Winter (October to March) the entire population vacates the United States to wintering areas presumed to be in South America.

MIGRATION: Beginning in early August, shortly after the breeding season, all Mississippi Kites, adults and juveniles, begin their migration to wintering areas in South America east of the Andes—possibly Manaus, Brazil. By the time the birds reach south Texas they are gathered in large flocks similar to those formed by Swainson's and Broad-winged Hawks. These flocks may number in the hundreds and thousands of kites and might pass key concentration points like Veracruz in a single day. On average, at Veracruz, Mexico, 210,279 Mississippi Kites are tallied over the course of a fall migration that spans late August to mid-September. Northbound migrants are noted in Central America beginning in mid-March, with large numbers again appearing over Veracruz in early to mid-April and birds reaching natal areas in the United States between late April and mid-May.

In years marked by the irruptive emergence of 17-year cicadas, some

Mississippi Kites use the opportunity to expand beyond their established range.

HABITAT: Mississippi Kites use a variety of habitats. Key components are tall trees for nesting close to open habitats, including the air above closed-canopy forest environments. Access to a reliable supply of large insect prey is likely a crucial requirement. This species' traditional—and perhaps preferred—habitat is mature bottomland forest, but in the 1960s it began nesting in urban and suburban areas, riparian woodlands, and golf courses. It also breeds in mesquite and oak shrub prairie with small dense groves of taller trees. In eastern woodlands, it prefers old-growth trees in large forest tracts, but in the Great Plains it uses a variety of planted tree groves, shelter belts, and even isolated trees. Communal nest trees are usually well foliated, and favored old sites are used repeatedly.

BREEDING: Birds appear to be paired when they reach breeding areas between early May and early June (which is, by raptor standards, late). Nest building begins soon after arrival. Kites nest communally, and colonies might include 20 pairs. The Snyders suggest that a reliance upon large insect prey may account for the relatively late nesting period.

Nest building may take up to two weeks, and both adults participate in construction. Situated in the upper canopy, the structure is described by J. W. Parker as "circular to oval, constructed of dead twigs and located in a limb fork or crotch in the upper canopy. The cup is shallow and where found lined with Spanish moss."

A typical clutch is one to three, usually two bluish white eggs. Incubation is conducted mostly by the female and lasts 29 to 32 days. Both parents deliver food and feed nestlings. Fledging occurs when birds are 25 to 30 days old, and adults may continue to feed for 15 to 20 days.

BEHAVIOR/HUNTING: Mississippi Kites are gregarious when breeding, roosting, even hunting. Foraging birds seek out and concentrate in prey-rich skies. Observes Alexander Sprunt of the bird's behavior and habits: "This kite takes prey on the wing and devours it in the air, seeming to be independent of the earth much of the time." However, incautiously approach a Mississippi Kite's nest and the sky is no barrier. This species has an earned reputation for intolerance when humans approach nest sites too closely, as not a few golfers pursuing balls hooked into the trees have learned. While few humans have actually been struck by territorial birds, the determined attention of territorial kites can throw your game off.

Most prey is snatched from the air somewhere above canopy height, even in excess of 200 yards. In early morning, hunting flights are typically lower; they get higher as thermal production increases by midmorning. Sometimes kites pluck prey from tree limbs, but for the most part Mississippi Kite is an aerialist, searching for prey while aloft either soaring or quartering across the sky. A kite will both ascend and descend to engage prey, which it captures with one or both feet. It consumes larger prey from a perch. When closing on prey, it may flap to accelerate or correct its course. Now soaring with prey secured, the bird uses its legs to extend the prey toward the bill for dismemberment. Birds may hunt solo

Mississippi Kites are infrequently seen perched. Note the cicada in this bird's bill. Range expansion by kites is sometimes spurred by cicada outbreaks. A celebrated aerialist, this species also hawks insects from exposed perches. Greg Lasley

or in flocks of up to 100 individuals. It frequently hunts close to the nest, but it may also forage several miles away. It also hawks insects from exposed perches.

PREY: Mississippi Kites eat mostly large flying or arboreal insects. Beetles, leafhoppers, grasshoppers, and cicadas are its most important insect prey. Dragonflies are important prey during migration and in South America. They also consume some vertebrate prey, including frogs, reptiles, birds, bats, and small mammals. No golfer's remains or attire have ever been collected in or near nests.

STATUS: Judging from recent range expansion and evident capacity to adapt to the human environment, Mississippi Kite's future might be regarded with some optimism. Of primary concern would be any reduction in mature bottomland, the bird's preferred habitat in its southeastern stronghold. Average counts of Mississippi Kites passing through Veracruz, Mexico, August through November are about 210,000, although recent counts have shown a marked increase in numbers. In 2013, 329,592 birds were counted; in 2014, 362,514 were counted. This probably constitutes the entire North American population. Evaluating point count trends at Gulf Coast hawkwatches between 1995 and 2005, Bildstein et al. note a "positive rate" of change at all sites during the period.

SEA EAGLES
One species

Bald Eagle
Haliaeetus leucocephalus

Outside the breeding season and where food is plentiful, Bald Eagles can be quite social. These birds are weathering a typical snowstorm in Homer, Alaska. Jim Zipp

ETYMOLOGY: From the Greek, the genus name *Haliaeetus* means "sea eagle." In the species name *leucocephalus, leucos* means "white" and *kephalos* is "head," for the white plumage of the head of adult birds.

PROFILE: The Bald Eagle is our national emblem, designated as such by Congress in 1782. In emblematic form it has been borne all over the globe by America's armed forces and diplomatic missions. Owing to the United States' prominence on the world stage, Bald Eagle must rank among the most recognized (if not nec-essarily acclaimed) bird species on the planet.

It is a long-lived species. Speculated Wilson: "It is said to live to a great age, sixty, eighty, and as some assert, one hundred years." (It's probably the fish diet.) In deference to the Father of American Ornithology, contemporary estimates are much more conservative. One wild Alaska bird is known to have lived 28 years. One celebrated eagle, known as Old Abe (see account on page 68) died in captivity in 1981 at the tender age of 20, killed by inhaling fumes from a solvent fire near its enclosure.

The United States' emblematic Bald Eagle is one of eight "sea eagles," a genus that enjoys worldwide distribution, South America excepted. This summary description of the genus taken from Brown and Amadon is so apt, I quote verbatim. While it treats sea eagles in general terms, it nevertheless applies well to the present species. Members of this genus, including Bald Eagle, are "large to very large, wings long, broad; tail medium to rather short; rounded to wedge shaped [not so Bald Eagle]. Bill large . . . legs rather short, tarsi unfeathered except at the base; toes and talons powerfully developed . . . Frequents chiefly coasts, lakes, rivers; scavenges on fish especially, but catching live fish, mammals and birds."

As North America's second-largest bird of prey, second only to California Condor, the adults with their all-white head and tail contrasting with blackish brown body are not just distinctive, but iconic. It is unlikely that a single American given a respectable view could fail to recognize the bird on sight.

At least the adult bird. Immature Bald Eagles, lacking the all-white head and tail, are more problematic. Birds do not assume a white head and tail until they are four to six years old. Juvenile birds are easily confused with Golden Eagle, and before the Bald Eagle's successional plumages were recognized, non-adult Bald Eagles were even presumed by some early authorities to constitute a different species.

In point of fact is Alexander Wilson's account of Sea or Gray Eagle, *Falco ossifragus,* in which he was mistakenly describing the immature Bald Eagle while at the same time admitting to personal reservations about this separation in his account of Sea Eagle: "I have strong suspicion, notwithstanding ancient and very respected authorities to the contrary, of its being the same species, only in a different stage of color." Wilson could not ignore the many similarities between the bird he and others called "Sea Eagle" and Bald Eagle, noting as he did that the brown birds (the bird he mistakenly

Adult Bald Eagle (left) and late first-year bird (right). Both show the classic plank-like wing configuration. Kevin T. Karlson

called "Sea Eagle") and the white-headed birds were "often seen in company."

His initial confusion notwithstanding, Wilson's praise for the emblematic bird of his adopted nation could hardly be more lavish: "This distinguished bird . . . is the most beautiful of his tribe in this part of the world . . . and is entitled to particular notice."

The poet in Wilson was brought to pen this verse describing the foraging finesse of Bald Eagle over Niagara Gorge. While other authors have labeled Bald Eagle a scavenger, even a thief, the Father of American Ornithology accords finesse and accomplishment:

> High o'er the watery uproar, silent seen,
> Sailing sedate, in majesty serene,
> Now midst the pillar'd spray sublimely lost,
> And now, emerging, down the rapids tost,
> Glides the Bald Eagle, gazing, calm and slow
> O'er all the horrors of the scene below:
> Intent alone to sate himself with blood,
> From the torn victims of the raging flood.

Thus waxed Alexander Wilson, poet and ornithologist, in 1814. Rival Audubon held a more jaundiced view: "I grieve that it should have been selected as the Emblem of my Country. The opinion of our great Franklin on this subject, as it perfectly coincides with my own, I shall here present to you . . . 'He is a bird of bad moral character; he does not get his living honestly; you may have seen him perched on some dead tree, where, too lazy to fish for himself, he watches the labor of the Fishing Hawk [now Osprey], and when that diligent bird has at length taken a fish, and is bearing it to his nest for the support of his mate and young ones, the Eagle pursues him, and takes it from him . . . '"

DESCRIPTION: An impressively sized, large-billed raptor. The body of the adult is overall blackish brown, except for the wholly white head and tail. The bill, eyes, and feet are bright yellow. Some individuals may have a dark-trimmed or yellowish tail.

The immature plumage is held for four years and is mostly brown with infusions of buff or dirty white, particularly on the back and belly. The plumage of subadult eagles is highly variable as compared to older immatures. The body of the juvenile bird is overall dark, showing little to no pale mottling, which is assumed as birds go through successional molts. Birds do not attain the white head and tail until they are four or five years old, but all birds are presumed to have an all-white head and tail by five and a half years. Following the juvenile year, the brown body becomes increasingly infused with pale feathers, to the point that some individuals appear piebald, even overall creamy to mocha-colored. Tails of young birds are mostly dirty white with a broad, dark terminal band that is typically not as crisply defined as that brandished by immature Golden Eagle and may, in fact, cover half the tail of an immature Bald Eagle.

Golden Eagles are similar in size to Bald Eagles, but *Aquila* eagles differ in shape, being smaller headed and smaller billed, structurally akin to buteos. Nevertheless, juvenile (first-year) Bald Eagles may be mistaken for the mostly dark-bodied adult Golden Eagle, and the golden hackles of Golden Eagles may gleam so brilliantly in bright light as to make their heads appear white. Golden Eagles tend to forage inland, while Bald Eagles tend not to stray far from seacoasts, riv-

An adult Bald Eagle and early third-year immature. It takes four or five years for immature birds to attain the iconic white head and tail of adults. Kevin T. Karlson

ers, or large bodies of water, except during migration.

MEASUREMENTS
Length: 27–35 inches
Wingspan: 71–89 inches
Weight: 4.4–13.6 pounds

SYSTEMATICS/SUBSPECIES: Bald Eagle is the only *Haliaeetus* eagle commonly found in North America; however, the White-tailed Sea Eagle (*Haliaeetus albacilla*) of Europe and Asia breeds on the southeast coast of Greenland, and birds of Asian origin are occasionally seen in the Aleutians where, in fact, this species bred in the 1980s (on Attu Island). There is also a sight record for this Old World species off the *Nantucket* lightship on November 14, 1914. It has been suggested by some authorities that White-tailed Sea Eagle and Bald Eagle may, in fact, constitute a superspecies.

As for Bald Eagle, two subspecies of *H. leucocephalus* are tentatively recognized: the larger northern Bald Eagle (*H. l. alascanus*), which breeds generally north of 40 degrees north, and the smaller southern Bald Eagle (*H. l. leucocephalus*), first described by Catesby.

VOCALIZATIONS: Bald Eagles have a weak, chirping twitter. In fact, so enfeebled is the sound that in movie sound tracks the whistled cry of the Red-tailed Hawk is often used.

DISTRIBUTION: A widespread but by no means uniformly distributed breeding, wintering, and resident species, in broad terms its range encompasses the North American continent south to Florida and Baja California. While absent as a breeder in the Arctic, it is found on Bering Sea and Aleutian Islands. In the continental United States it shows a patchy distribution with high breeding density in northern New England and also coastally from

New Jersey to Florida. High breeding numbers are also found around the western Great Lakes, major Midwestern water courses, the northern Rockies, and along the West Coast, coastally from the Cascades to Northern California.

In winter, deprived of open water, it withdraws from interior locations, but ranges coastally and along open-water courses across southern Canada and much of the United States south into northern Mexico. In winter, northern Bald Eagles resettle in the breeding zone occupied by resident southern Bald Eagles. Given open water, however, some wintering birds may be found as far north as coastal Maine, the Niagara Gorge, and coastal Alaska.

MIGRATION: Northern and southern breeders adhere to different migratory timetables, which makes the migratory pattern complex. But in the broadest sense, spring migration of northern birds is from late February to early June, fall migration mid-August to December. Southern and some northern birds breeding in more temperate coastal locations are resident. Immature eagles are essentially nomadic, moving among abundant food resources, so they may be found "migrating" any month of the year, including midwinter and midsummer.

HABITAT: Wherever it is found, this species is associated with ice-free aquatic habitat.

BREEDING: Bald Eagle courtship is energetic, involving much vocalizing and acrobatics, which may include clutching talons and cartwheeling display.

Breeding is very early, with nest building in Florida beginning September to early October. In Alaska, the onset of courtship begins as soon as migrating birds return to territories. In California, courtship and nest building occur from December to January. In New Jersey, resident females may be incubating as early as January so are frequently blanketed by snow.

The birds' large stick nests, which rank among the largest known among birds, are situated in the upper reaches of sturdy, mature trees, typically just below the crown. Sometimes they use a solitary tree, and other times a commandingly tall tree that projects above the forest canopy. Easy flight access and a commanding view are essential features of prime nest trees. Favored tree species vary by region, but the birds evidently prefer live trees. Both sexes contribute sticks to the structure, but the female does the arrangement. New nests require up to three months to construct, although nests continue to be added to throughout the year and in subsequent years.

The largest nest on record, in St. Petersburg, Florida, measured nearly 10 feet across and 20 feet deep. Another famous nest in Vermilion, Ohio, was occupied for 34 years and estimated to weigh two metric tons. In treeless regions, birds may place nests on the ground.

A typical clutch is one to three white eggs. Incubation by both sexes takes 35 to 46 days. Fledging occurs 63 to 70 days later. Especially in nests with three young, the smallest/youngest nest mate may not survive. After fledging, young may continue to use the nest as a feeding platform for several weeks as they gain flying and foraging skills. Nest departure can occur 8 to 14 weeks postfledging.

Bald Eagles may lock talons in midair and twirl around clockwise like tops during courtship or when involved with competing suitors. Sometimes young birds practice this maneuver. These two adults locked talons in front of the Cape May Hawkwatch in October 2015, and proceeded to spin three complete revolutions before breaking free. Often they release just short of crashing into the ground. This display resulted in a rousing chorus of cheers from lucky viewers. Kevin T. Karlson

BEHAVIOR/HUNTING: Outside of the breeding season, the Bald Eagle is a fairly social bird, roosting and sometimes foraging communally. Typical roost sites are secluded, often at higher elevations so that birds leaving roosts early can use gravity to propel them to foraging areas below. Stands of mature (often geographically elevated) trees offering a surfeit of sturdy limbs and a southern exposure are typical. Eagles frequently hunt from perches along water courses, but they also cruise and soar over food-bearing habitat. They generally attempt to secure most prey on the wing, snatching live or moribund fish from the surface of the water or forcing Osprey or other eagles to surrender their prey in the air. They also fly down water-

OLD ABE

The story behind the most famous Bald Eagle in history—an emblematic mascot of the 101st Airborne Division.

Captured by a Chippewa brave as a nestling in 1861, through a series of transactions the bird found itself under the protective custody of a Union Civil War regiment hailing from Wisconsin, the 8th Wisconsin Volunteer Infantry Regiment.

Named in honor of president Abraham Lincoln, Old Abe was appointed the regimental mascot and was involved in multiple campaigns in the Western Theater of the American Civil War, where he was carried into battle on a special perch held aloft by a company sergeant. During the battle of Corinth, Mississippi, Confederate General Sterling Price remarked: "that bird must be killed or captured at all hazards, I would rather get that eagle than capture a whole brigade . . . " The general failed to secure either objective, and after the war, Old Abe went on to tour the country as part of America's Centennial Celebration. He then lived out the rest of his life in an aviary in the Capitol building, before succumbing in 1881 to fumes resulting from a fire that broke out in a nearby cleaning closet.

But the bird's legacy endures. Since 1921, Old Abe's head, in profile, has served as the shoulder insignia of the United States Army's 101st Airborne Division (nicknamed the Screaming Eagles). Made famous by their epic defensive stand at Bastogne during the Second World War, the division headquarters of the 101st is at Fort Campbell, where Old Abe is exhibited in the atrium.

The nests of Bald Eagles are huge. Two young are a typical brood, although the survival of both young is far from assured. Left: Kevin T. Karlson; right: Steve Sachs

fowl in open flight. When foraging over water, they usually remain close to shore.

Bald Eagles frequently forage on carrion, including deer carcasses. Stealing fish from Osprey (as described by Audubon above) is a typical practice, with the eagle harassing the burdened Osprey until the Osprey releases its prize, which the eagle often secures before it hits the water. (See photo on page 30.) Eagles also take waterfowl as big as geese, usually after a brief tail chase. A typical maneuver is for an eagle to climb above and downwind of waterfowl flocks, then stoop and close

It looks serious, but these two immature Bald Eagles are just sparring, preparing for the day when jousts for mates and territory become serious. Appearances notwithstanding, neither bird was injured in the contest. Kevin T. Karlson

using level, powered flight when the flock lifts off and flees into the wind. Eagles sometimes hunt cooperatively, but larger and older birds often bully subordinate eagles (including mates) away from captured prey.

PREY: Eagles eat primarily larger fish, live or dead, the fish species varying with location, abundance, and season. They also feed upon large dead mammals, including marine mammals and winter-killed deer, as well as live mammalian prey, with raccoons reported to be the most common. My observations suggest they target muskrats during flood tides when the rodents are particularly vulnerable.

STATUS: This species has experienced dramatic population fluctuations since the founding of America. Early explorers reported it as "abundant." So abundant was the bird in Alaska that a 50-cent bounty was established in 1917, with 128,000 bounties paid out between 1917 and 1952. Now, in Alaska as elsewhere, this species is protected, as are all raptors. The bird became "rare" in the mid- to late twentieth century owing largely to the impacts of DDT. Populations have dramatically increased since 1980, and reproduction has returned to pre-DDT levels. This recovery is supported by point count data from eastern hawkwatch sites, which noted "uniform" increases from 1974 to 2000; at western count sites, numbers are assessed to be stable. The Alaska population alone is estimated to number 40,000 to 50,000 birds; British Columbia 20,000 to 30,000.

HARRIERS
One species

Northern Harrier
Circus cyaneus hudsonius

ETYMOLOGY: *Circus* is from Greek *kirkos,* a "kind of hawk"; *cyaneus* from Greek *kyaneous,* "dark blue," a reference to the adult male's blue back. *Harrier* comes from Old English *hergian,* meaning "to harass by hostile attacks."

PROFILE: A beautiful, buoyant, ground-hugging raptor of open country whose spirited courtship flight—dubbed "sky dancing" by the late Fran Hamerstrom—looks as though the bird was attempting to knit horizon and sky in a running stitch of U-shaped dives, UUUUUUUUU . . .

Northern Harrier is North America's sole representative of this worldwide genus, whose 17 or so species appear to have an Old World origin. North America's Northern Harrier is thought to have become part of North American avifauna during the early Pleistocene, crossing from Asia to North America via the Bering land bridge. However, as someone who has observed hundreds of harriers making open-water crossings, I am confident that a Bering Sea crossing would pose little challenge to this indefatigable migrant.

The bird's low cruising flight has led

some to mistakenly assume that this species lacks pluck and dash. Nothing could be further from the truth. Harriers are fearless defenders of their territory and will drive away birds as large as Red-tailed Hawk and Great Horned Owl when they test a harrier's tolerance.

This species exhibits a number of fascinating behavioral traits, not the least of which are its tendency to roost communally on the ground, its pronounced sexual dimorphism, and its use of audio detection to locate hidden prey.

DESCRIPTION: The harrier is a lanky medium-large, long-winged, long-tailed raptor whose signature characteristic is a well-defined, fist-sized white rump patch. Except for the rump, adult males are silvery gray above and bright white below, with a grayish bib and some sparse gray to reddish brown spotting on the belly and underwing. Folded wingtips appear blackish, and the long, banded tail extends beyond the wingtips on perched birds. The larger adult females are brown above, with heavily streaked buffy underparts. Juveniles in North America resemble females but are overall more rufous, showing cinnamon brown touches on the upperparts and a dark cinnamon wash on the underparts that makes the sparse darker breast streaking difficult to see. The owl-like facial disk and the white rump are evident in all plumages.

MEASUREMENTS
Length: male 16–18 inches; female 18–20 inches
Wingspan: male 38–43 inches; female 43–48 inches
Weight: male 10–14 ounces; female 14–21 ounces

SYSTEMATICS/SUBSPECIES: Some authorities consider the North American bird a race of the European Hen Harrier, *Circus cyaneus*, so *C. c. hudsonius*. It has also, at times, been suggested that *C. cyaneus hudsonius* may be conspecific with the smaller Cinereous Harrier (*C. cinereus*) of Central and South America.

A harrier sampler. From left (top and bottom): adult male, adult female, and cinnamon-tinged juvenile. The dead mallard was evidently not killed by the harrier, nor was it planted by the photographer. Bottom right: Jerry Liguori; top middle: Brian Sullivan; all others: Kevin T. Karlson

VOCALIZATIONS: Both males and females make a repetitive *kacking* sound when displaying. Females also make a very high, thin whistle, somewhat descending and two-parted, often in response to the appearance of another female in the bird's territory.

DISTRIBUTION: In North America, this species is widespread but has a spotty distribution, being limited to open habitats suitable for hunting and nesting. It breeds from western Alaska to the Maritimes and southwestern Newfoundland (mostly below the Arctic tundra) south to coastal Delaware, as well as states bordering the Great Lakes, and then widely across the prairies to northern Texas, northern New Mexico, most of Utah, and Nevada. In the West it also breeds in the Great Basin, Washington, Oregon, and California west of the Sierras, south to Baja.

In winter, birds from Alaska and most of Canada wholly vacate breeding areas and relocate across the United States from extreme southeastern and southwestern Canada south to Central America and to Panama. They also winter in the Caribbean. In coastal New Jersey (Delaware Bay), females may be resident. In winter, males and females typically occupy different habitats, with females hunting lusher, wetter marshlands supporting taller grasses, and smaller, more agile males hunting brushier but shorter grassed edge and upland fields.

MIGRATION: Fall migration is protracted, with some movement noted in mid-August (adults and juveniles) and some adult birds still seen passing in late December. Spring migration is more proscribed, with birds leaving southern wintering areas in late February and limited movement noted into late May. Spring peak is March and April; most fall migrants pass September to late November, with juveniles for the most part preceding adults.

Typical harrier habitat. While harriers do practice perch-hunting, they more typically course low over fields like winged bird-dogs. When they hear or spot prey, birds may stall and pounce or hover. Brian Sullivan

While harriers cannot fly backward, I wouldn't presume that they cannot fly inverted, as this juvenile seems eager to do. Note the owl-like facial disks that direct sound to the harrier's ears, aiding in the audio detection of prey. Kevin T. Karlson

Harriers are typically solitary migrants but at key concentration points they are occasionally seen in well-spaced groups (or strings) numbering up to ten birds. During migration they often fly at heights that challenge the limit of the unaided eye. This species frequently migrates during inclement weather, conditions that ground most other migrating raptors.

HABITAT: Northern Harrier lives in open, often grassy habitat, and both freshwater and tidal marshes.

BREEDING: Breeding is a subject open to interpretation by biologists as well as (apparently) adult harriers. Harriers are mostly monogamous, but they do practice polygamy and polyandry. Males sometimes bond with two or more females (perhaps in times of great prey abundance), and pairs in adjacent territories occasionally engage in overt, somewhat ritualized displays.

The aerial "sky dancing" display of Northern Harrier is energetic, acrobatic, and vocal, sometimes practiced by both sexes, but at other times and places, only the cock harrier displays. On windy days, displaying birds may go aloft before sunrise; otherwise they wait for thermals to bear them aloft. Typical display involves the male executing a series of U-shaped dives, with birds executing a loop or barrel roll at the apex of each climb. In New Jersey, males begin displaying in April and continue into May. Interestingly, where females are apparently resident, they begin sky dancing as early as March before males are present. Female displays, also involving the sky dancing acrobatics, are evidently triggered by the proximity or display of another female rather than the presence of male birds. This said, over most of the bird's breeding range, males arrive on territory earlier than females and sky dance to attract females and initiate mating.

I once observed two adult males from adjacent territories engage in what appeared to be a ritualized territorial display. Facing each other across open tidal marsh from a distance of about 15 feet, the presumed resident male stood between the "intruder" and the incubating female and stretched to his full height, displaying his bright white underparts. The other male responded by crouching, thus concealing his underparts. Point made and taken, both birds took wing, flying in opposite directions. Despite multiple visits, I never saw the display repeated.

In tidal marshes, if flooding tides severely deplete the rodent prey base and nests are washed out, pairs typically choose not to renest. Both birds contribute to nest construction, but the female incubates and tends to the young. The flat grass nests are situated on the ground, often at some vegetative break or transition, and are often placed within some taller, concealing stand of vegetation (phragmites). In forested regions, they nest in bogs.

The typical clutch is 4 to 6 eggs, but up to 12 have been reported. Eggs are white or very pale blue and generally unmarked, although some are spattered with pale brown or buff spots. Incubation is typically 28 to 36 days. In two weeks, young begin to move freely around the nest site, although birds usually wait until they are four or five weeks old for their first flight. Adults continue to bring food to nestlings after fledging.

The male is active in territorial defense and in the capture of prey—see the description of its "food pass" in the Behavior/Hunting section.

BEHAVIOR/HUNTING: Harriers spend a great portion of the daylight hours hunting, coursing low and slow over mostly open, usually grassy, flat, or rolling habitat. They locate prey by sight and sound, often doubling back to secure prey they've overflown. They capture prey with a short pounce or wingover to the ground, sometimes preceded by brief hovering. Males in particular may pursue birds in flight. They occasionally stoop on prey from a high altitude (most commonly during migration). Harriers hunt throughout the daylight hours but are most active at dawn and dusk. In tidal areas they frequently hunt high tides when flooded marshes displace and concentrate rodents.

Early in the nesting cycle, males do not bring food to the nest but transfer prey in midair via a "food pass" to the female, who rises and flies out to intercept the incoming male, adroitly catching the laterally tossed morsel in the air before descending to the earth, out of sight. Males depart immediately, and females returning to the nest may make one or more dummy landings before gaining the actual nest site, where young are fed in morsels.

Some days you're the harrier, some days you're the vole. Small mammals are the primary prey of harriers, although adult males in particular are adept at catching small birds too. Steve Sachs

Northern Harriers and Short-eared Owls frequent the same habitat and often engage in aerial "dogfights," in which the more buoyant and nimble owl typically dominates. Steve Sachs

In winter, females defend territories from other harriers, escorting intruders out of the area by flying lower and behind the subordinate intruder.

Harriers roost communally on the ground, with roosts forming before sunset. Roosts may exceed 100 birds (but typically fewer than 20) and may include other species, most notably Short-eared Owl, which also engages with harriers in spirited "dogfights," during which the more nimble and faster-climbing owl typically wins.

PREY: Frances Hamerstrom's observation that this is "a hawk ruled by a mouse" is apt. Small rodents (voles, mice, rice rats) are the primary prey. They also target birds, primarily (juvenile) passerines. Insects and reptiles have also been reported to figure in the diet. While some authorities have cited prey as large as hares and ducks, I have personally never seen Northern Harrier kill prey larger than a Clapper Rail, which, as evidenced by my securing the kill, proved too large for the hawk to carry.

Harriers also consume carrion. I have personally seen harriers eating putrefying muskrat and, during spring migration, on a beach in coastal Alaska, observed multiple harriers pausing to feed upon the carcass of a washed-up sea lion whose flesh had been partially consumed by wolves. They are also not above pirating prey; in Cape May I once observed a female harrier relieve a juvenile Peregrine of a just-captured Sharp-shinned Hawk. Approaching low and behind the burdened falcon, the harrier turned on her side and, reaching out with both legs, ripped the still-struggling Sharp-shinned out of the falcon's talons.

Kleptoparasitism is a road that runs two ways. One winter day I watched an adult male harrier robbed of what appeared to be a shrew by an adult Bald Eagle. Following a short pursuit, the harrier attempted to outclimb the pursuing eagle. The eagle responded by executing a classic ringing-up maneuver, driving the harrier higher and higher until the harrier evidently concluded that the morsel was hardly worth the effort and dropped the shrew, which the eagle deftly caught in midair, before descending to feed.

When not hunting, birds commonly take some low perch that offers a commanding view. Winter and summer, territorial birds often display their white rump patches when perched. In the sign language of harriers, the message reads: "This place is mine; yours is someplace else."

STATUS: In North America, this species has been experiencing a long-term population decline, a trend that is reflected globally. This decline may relate to the loss of wetlands and open, undisturbed grasslands. In Delaware Bay, the breeding population has experienced a dramatic decline, going from 43 nests in 1983 to fewer than 10 in 2009. Increased coastal flooding due to rising sea levels, resulting in the loss of their preferred nesting habitat (high marsh, which hosts *Spartina patens*), and the decline of rodent prey during the breeding season are the suspected causes.

Once, they were persecuted for killing waterfowl as well as other game species. This now illegal practice seems much diminished across most of North America, including the marshes of Delaware Bay, where waterfowl hunting has a longstanding tradition and wintering numbers of harriers remain high, with winter point counts sometimes exceeding 50 birds in years of prey abundance.

ACCIPITERS
Three species

Sharp-shinned Hawk
Accipiter striatus

ETYMOLOGY: From the Latin, *Accipiter* is for "a hawk"; *striatus* is for "streaked," referring to the streaks on the undersides of juveniles.

PROFILE: A nimble, bantam-sized, bird-catching forest raptor. While all raptors by definition capture, kill, and consume live prey, none have been so vilified (even demonized) for this specialization more than Sharp-shinned Hawks. Among early ornithologists, Alexander

Wilson offers the most flattering assessment, calling it an "active and daring little hunter." Audubon referred to it as a "marauder," going on to express his "pleasure in rescuing different species of birds from the grasp of this little tyrant." Eaton called it a "bloodthirsty little pirate," and this prejudicial assessment was widely advanced by ornithologists and conservationists of the day.

In their efforts to vindicate hawks, ornithologists seemed to select the present species as a scapegoat, a hawk to be held accountable for the bad reputation of the tribe—a hawk to embody the sins that most raptors were wrongfully accused of and held accountable for. Even into the 1950s, decades after protection was secured for most other birds of prey, it was still legal to kill Sharp-shinned Hawks in my home state of New Jersey. (Ironically, the Peregrine Falcon was likewise unprotected—ironic because within decades it would become the poster child for raptor protection.)

Me? I side with Wilson. But even Wilson's assessment falls short of Sharp-shinned's skill as a hunter, one that very nearly inverts the fine balance that exists between predator and prey. Across most of the natural world, it is the prey species that enjoys superior speed or quicker reflexes, so that to be successful, predators must capitalize upon some balance-tipping advantage—such as surprise, the inexperience of the prey, or perhaps a hampering injury suffered by the prey. But Sharp-shinned's superior reflexes, boardinghouse reach, and maneuverability are so formidable a combination that it is the prey that seems to need a counterbalancing measure of fortune to survive the contest. While the demonization of this bird may not be warranted, it is not without foundation. Release a Sharp-shinned in front of a seemingly impenetrable latticework of branches, and the bird will pass through leaves and branches as easily as smoke. In the open, the Sharp-shinned's ability to react to the evasive maneuvering of prey seems as fast as a mirror can mimic.

Several years ago, while searching for migrating warblers at a local mi-grant trap known as East Point Light—in fact, standing with my back against the foundation of the lighthouse—I pished a Yellow-rumped Warbler out of a nearby red cedar; it flew directly at my face with a Sharp-shinned soon in pursuit. The warbler's evasive strategy was to fly behind my head, a maneuver the tiny bird accomplished with ease but no gain. The Sharp-shinned followed, and while the gap between my head and the lighthouse could not have exceeded four inches, neither bird so much as grazed my hatless head. The pursuit ended less than a foot from my right eye, but too quick to apprehend. Only the sound of impact and the warbler limp in the hawk's talons confirmed the outcome.

DESCRIPTION: A small, long-tailed, robin-sized, bird-catching hawk with a fairly compact body; a small, near neckless head; and an upright stance when perched. Its bill is fairly petite, and its yellow legs are thin and twiglike. The adult's eyes are red, the immature's yellow. Adults are blue gray above, and the crown is slightly darker than the back. Orange-barred underparts give way to white undertail coverts. The long narrow tail is gray with several blackish bands and a narrow and diffuse whitish tip. Sexes are similar, but the female is conspicuously larger. Juveniles are cold brown above with a brown head and white underparts showing coarse brown streaking that sometimes appears blotchy. The juvenile's tail is similar to the adult's.

As befits a bird-catching specialist, the legs and toes are long, and each toe is tipped with a needle-sharp talon. The unusual length of the middle toe is a point not often raised in field guide species accounts, but this is a trait common to bird-catching specialists.

MEASUREMENTS
Length: male 9–11 inches;
female 11–13 inches
Wingspan: male 20–22 inches;
female 23–26 inches
Weight: male 3–4 ounces;
female 5–8 ounces

SYSTEMATICS/SUBSPECIES: Brown and Amadon recognized ten subspecies. These have been grouped into three subspecies groups by the *AOU Checklist*, Seventh Edition: the *Accipiter striatus velox* group breeds in North America; the White-breasted (*chionogaster*) group resides in southern Mexico and Central America;

and the Rufous-thighed (*erythronemius*) group consists of the Rufous-thighed Hawk (*A. erythronemius*) of central South America and the Plain-breasted Hawk (*A. ventralis*) of the northern Andes in South America. Note: some authorities regard Rufous-thighed Hawk and Plain-breasted Hawk as separate species.

The North American *striatus* group is broken down into four continental subspecies (only two of which occur in North America) and three resident subspecies restricted to the Greater Antilles. *A. s. velox* is the most widespread of subspecies found at some time of the year throughout all of North America. It breeds north into Alaska and southern Canada, and south to southern California, Arizona, New Mexico, and

---

A Sharp-shinned sampler. From left (top and bottom): adult female, adult male, and juvenile. The short, rounded wings are designed for rapid acceleration and allow the bird to maneuver in tight woodland confines. The rudderlike tail confers a degree of maneuverability that is unsurpassed by any other North American raptor. Kevin T. Karlson

The bulging crop on this juvenile Sharp-shinned Hawk attests to its recent hunting success. Note the long middle toe on the extended leg—a refinement common to many bird-catching raptors. Kevin T. Karlson

Alabama. In winter, it vacates most of the Canadian interior and occupies the North American landmass south to Panama. This migratory subspecies, whose breeding population has its greatest density in the boreal forests of Alaska and Canada, is the bird most commonly seen at hawkwatches. *A. s. perobscurus* breeds on the Queen Charlotte Islands of British Columbia and possibly on the coastal mainland.

VOCALIZATIONS: A series of sharp *kek* notes. It sounds like Cooper's Hawk but is uttered with less volume.

DISTRIBUTION: The widespread *A. s. velox* group are primarily northern breeders, found south of the tundra from central Alaska across forested Canada to the Maritimes and Newfoundland. Excepting the northern prairies, they breed across the northern United States and south in the Cascades to central California, in the Rockies south to central Mexico, and in the Appalachians south to northern Alabama. In winter, they withdraw from more northerly breeding areas except along the coast of Alaska, the Yukon, and southeastern British Columbia. In the East, they vacate interior

New England and the western Great Lakes states but are otherwise widespread across the Lower 48 and extreme southeastern Canada. However, the proliferation of bird-feeding stations has prompted increasing numbers of Sharp-shinned Hawks to winter farther north than historic records support.

Populations breeding south of the United States (Mexico, Cuba) are probably resident.

MIGRATION: Fall migration extends from late August to early December, with peaks in late September (juveniles) and early to mid-October (primarily adults). Spring migration is March to June but mostly April to May. These timetables coincide with the migratory periods of Sharp-shinned's prey and periods of low prey density in both breeding and wintering areas.

In general, migration is conducted along a broad front. Spring and fall birds make extensive use of thermals to gain elevation. Migrating birds are also attracted to the updrafts associated with mountain ridges, thus concentrating there. While able to make water crossings of many miles, birds occasionally winter on Bermuda, where they do not breed. This species is generally averse to extensive open-water crossings, so they follow the contours of lakeshores and coastlines. There is some evidence that birds may selectively avoid urban areas, but one observer reported Sharp-shinneds migrating down city streets utilizing updrafts off of high-rises. Birds may also follow bridges or other man-made structures across water barriers (such as Chesapeake Bay). In general, the greatest concentrations of migrating Sharp-shinneds occur in coastal locations where it has been noted prey species are also concentrated.

In migration, they roost and forage in any arboreal setting, including parks and cemeteries, preferring forest tracts exceeding 200 acres. During windy conditions they may fly very low—two to ten feet above the ground—often following some vegetative leading line. When thermal activity is favorable, they commonly migrate very high (to the limit of binocular-assisted vision). In migration, they average 50 miles per day, with stopovers of one to five days to rest and feed fairly typical.

Sharp-shinneds may migrate alone, in pairs, or in small, loose groups of up to a dozen individuals in locations of high concentration. In airspace frequented by migrating Cooper's Hawks, Sharpies typically fly above them. They migrate during daylight hours but most heavily in the morning, and birds may begin migration at first light. They feed opportunistically but daily during migration, with high-flying birds frequently seen to stoop, occasionally disappearing into foliage in pursuit of prey. They occasionally pursue passerine migrants in midair but generally without success. Juveniles in particular harass and pursue each other, as well as other, larger species that they have no intention of consuming (examples include Bald Eagles and Black-crowned Night-Herons).

HABITAT: Sharp-shinneds occupy a variety of forest types, "from sea level to near alpine," but they prefer forests that have conifers. In winter, they occupy an array of habitats, from deciduous woodlands and suburbia to coastal dune forest and

An adult male Sharp-shinned Hawk, beautiful but deadly. Judging by the intensity of the bird's gaze, if you were an inattentive junco foraging on the forest floor, you were likely only moments away from being double-wrapped in songbird-calibrated talons. Jim Zipp

city parks. A surfeit of small woodland passerine prey is an essential component of prime winter habitat; thus Sharp-shinneds haunt bird-feeding stations.

BREEDING: Birds particularly favor large forests with a coniferous component. Nests are frequently situated in dense, frequently younger stands with a closed canopy, but also frequently near one bordering a break or open area within the grove.

In New Jersey, nests are most commonly found in dense 70-year-old planted stands of spruce and white pine surrounded by extensive tracts of mixed native Canadian-zone forest. These stands are also used for nesting by Cooper's Hawks and Northern Goshawks (but not simultaneously).

Owing to its northern breeding range, Sharp-shinned Hawk is a late-nesting species, with courtship beginning in early April in many locations.

Nest building begins soon after arrival of the pair. Both adults gather nest material, but the female does most or all of the construction. The stick nest itself is about crow-sized but overall flatter and less bulky and typically situated 40 to 60 feet high, often near the trunk or supported by a spoke-like array of branches below the canopy. In northern forests, the primary component is spruce twigs. The nest interior may be lined with bark flakes. Favored groves are commonly used over and over again, although a new nest is typically built every year.

Typically, a clutch is four or five bluish white, variously marked eggs, which are incubated for 31 to 36 days. Fledging occurs 21 to 27 days later.

BEHAVIOR/HUNTING: Sharpies are generally solitary, although multiple individuals may hunt in the same prey-rich environs, such as suburban songbird feeding stations or coastal brush/hedges

---

"Hmmm. This looks like a good place to hunt." An assessment underscored by the female Red-winged Blackbird and Mourning Dove pinned to the earth. Sharp-shinned Hawks frequently haunt backyard feeding stations—to the consternation of some suburban homeowners—but, like all raptors, the hawk is just doing what the evolutionary dynamic called predation has designed it to do. Left and middle: Kevin T. Karlson; right: Jim Zipp

The superbly maneuverable juvenile female Sharp-shinned Hawk seems all but able to nullify the laws of physics. If you were a migrating Yellow-rumped Warbler, this is not what you'd want to see over your shoulder. Kevin T. Karlson

and places where wintering Yellow-rumped Warblers are abundant. They frequently forage in forest interiors, flying to strategic perches below the canopy and changing perches every few minutes. In more broken/open areas, they may hunt from perches (sometimes the ground). Hunting perches are often tucked within the outer branches, offering partial concealment. They also cruise-hunt, flying 5 to 20 feet high along open corridors, using flanking vegetation and structures for concealment, in an attempt to flush or surprise prey, which is then overtaken most commonly in flight after a brief acceleration and tail chase. If the hawk does not secure prey quickly, it typically breaks off the pursuit.

PREY: This is a bird-catching machine: a bushwhacker and close-quarters specialist. The literature is replete with references about the bird's quickness: "faster than the eye can . . ." is a common observation.

One veteran hawk counter at Hawk Mountain once observed to me: "If Sharp-shinneds were the size of eagles, there wouldn't be a cow in Pennsylvania"—a statement that is an accurate assessment of the bird's prowess but woefully awry with regards to prey selection. While small mammals are among their prey items, forest songbirds up to the size of American Robin and flicker are Sharp-shinned's typical prey. However, small, warbler-sized species are the hawk's primary prey.

STATUS: This species' population was sorely depleted in the 1950s when DDT was widely applied. By the 1960s, following the ban on DDT, Sharp-shinned Hawk entered into a population boom fueled by high nest productivity, followed by another decline in the 1990s. Eastern and western hawkwatch point counts have noted recent declines at most locations since 1980 and 1998, respectively. Despite population ups and downs, this species remains one of North America's most common raptors. So long as the boreal forests remain intact, songbird numbers remain stable, and our species refrains from folly, this doughty raptor should fare well.

Cooper's Hawk
Accipiter cooperii

ETYMOLOGY: Cooper's Hawk was named by French naturalist Charles Lucien Bonaparte in 1828 to honor New York ornithologist William C. Cooper.

PROFILE: A slate-backed torpedo-shaped cruise missile of a raptor. This common and widespread raptor is almost universally described as a "woodland raptor," a label I have been guilty of using myself. In the *Birds of North America* series, it is, in fact, called "a quintessential woodland hawk with short, powerful, rounded wings . . . ," a label and structural assessment I now very respectfully take exception to. Perhaps in summer when chipmunks are active and attractively sized bird prey species are nesting, this hawk forages more in woodlands, but having spent hundreds of hours hunting deer and observing from tree stands situated in deciduous woodlands between November and February, I cannot recall a single occasion when I have observed Cooper's Hawks hunting beneath the forest canopy, despite the presence of a resident pair that nests in a white pine grove not 50 yards from my tree stand. Sharp-shinneds, Red-shouldered Hawks, even Red-tailed Hawks hunt there. I typically find Cooper's sitting upon a commanding perch surrounded by open or broken habitat or cruise-hunting along the open woodland edge.

Another habitat where I frequently find Cooper's Hawks in winter and during migration is wetlands, where birds are typically seated atop some low perch (such as a fencepost) or perhaps on some strategic patch of elevated terrain (such

Juvenile female Cooper's Hawk showing tapered wings characteristic of this accipiter species and a look of focused intent, directed this time at a photographer rather than prey. Kevin T. Karlson

as a sand dune). In this regard, Cooper's Hawks behave much like the Northern Harriers that occupy much the same habitat. In fact, I have come to think of Cooper's Hawk as something of a harrieresque accipiter that specializes in broken or edge habitat more than a forest obligate, as it is commonly regarded. Upon reflection, the only woodland habitat where I note Cooper's Hawks hunting consistently is open riparian corridors bracketed by sparsely vegetated arid hillsides in the West. And riparian woodlands are essentially edge habitat in a linear configuration.

I note, too, that wherever I travel, Mourning Dove seems to be a prey favored by this hawk—and few would label Mourning Dove a forest species. Most observers would agree that Mourning Dove is a species that thrives in open habitats, including suburbia, where Cooper's Hawks are increasingly common. Even urban centers, with their abundance of pigeons and tree-lined manmade canyons, are fast becoming prime habitat for Cooper's Hawk. In May 2012, I studied a Cooper's Hawk cruise-hunting an unvegetated alley in New York's lower East Side.

As for Cooper's Hawk's wing structure, I have long labored to reconcile the party-line description "short and rounded" with the configuration I often note in the field. As compared to Sharp-shinned Hawk, whose short, blunt-tipped wings seem well suited for woodland confines, and do conform to the description "short and rounded," the wings of Cooper's Hawks, particularly females, are to my eyes tapered, a wing configuration better suited to open habitats than woodlands.

I consider Cooper's Hawk's success as a hunter more a matter of the hawk's speed and clever use of cover than any vaulted maneuverability in woodlands. It seems a hunter well suited for broken habitat and semiopen environments. Add to this the bird's size, which permits it to secure larger avian prey. As described by Audubon, "It passes along in a silent gliding manner, with a swiftness even superior to that of the Wild Pigeon (*Columba migratoria*) [Passenger Pigeon], seldom deviating from a straightforward course, unless to seize and secure its prey." Audubon goes on to explain that in the southern states where Cooper's Hawk winters in "considerable numbers," the bird was known by the name "Great Pigeon Hawk."

The Passenger Pigeon is gone, but this raptor so superbly suited to hunt this

While woodland nesters, Cooper's Hawks, like this juvenile male, hunt in an array of habitats in winter and during migration, including open marshes. Kevin T. Karlson

large, swift pigeon continues to target doves and domestic pigeons. Insofar as Passenger Pigeon was a forest pigeon, it is possible that two centuries ago Cooper's Hawk was a more dedicated woodland hunter, but since the pigeon's eradication, it appears to have adjusted to more open-country prey.

DESCRIPTION: Cooper's Hawk is a crow-sized accipiter showing a lanky and fairly large-headed profile and a decidedly long, narrow tail. The stance of perched birds is upright. Its legs are thicker than Sharp-shinned Hawk's, and the larger bill imparts to the birds a "Roman-nosed" appearance. Adults are slaty blue above, often showing faint touches of brown in the wings and back. The crown is darker than the back and, in combination with the paler nape, gives birds a distinctly capped appearance. The eyes of adults are red to orange-red. The underparts are barred orange from the throat to the legs. The undertail is white. The narrow, round-tipped tail is gray with dark bands and tipped with a crisply defined white terminal band.

Juveniles are shaped like adults but brown above, including the head, which often has a warm or orangy cast, especially on the face and collar. Whitish underparts are overlaid with crisp, narrow, dark streaking that is sparsest on the breast. This, in combination with the bird's dark head, imparts to immature birds a hooded appearance. Juveniles' eyes are yellow.

Except for size, sexes are similar. When birds are alert, they often raise their hackles, giving the head a squarish look never seen on Sharp-shinned Hawk.

MEASUREMENTS
Length: male 14–16 inches; female 16–19 inches
Wingspan: male 28–30 inches; female 31–34 inches
Weight: male 10–14 ounces; female 17–24 ounces

SYSTEMATICS/SUBSPECIES: At this time, there are no recognized subspecies, but some authorities consider North American birds conspecific with *A. gundlachi* of Cuba. Eastern and western birds have at times been considered different subspecies (*A. c. cooperii* and *A. c. mexicanus*). While no plumage variation exists, eastern and western birds do differ in size, with western birds being somewhat smaller, so closer to Sharp-shinned Hawk in size.

VOCALIZATIONS: The most typically heard call is a loud, harsh *kack,* given in a rapid series and most commonly heard when birds are disturbed near their nests. They also give a mewing whistle reminiscent of a sapsucker.

DISTRIBUTION: Cooper's Hawks breed widely across southern Canada and most of the United States, excluding only areas bordering the Gulf of Mexico, extreme southern Florida, extreme southern Texas, and southwestern Arizona, although the breeding range extends south into central Mexico. In winter, northern breeders withdraw from southern Canada and northern New England, apportioning themselves across the entire United States and Mexico south to Central America. South of Canada, birds are mostly resident.

A Cooper's Hawk sampler. From left (top and bottom): adult female; adult male; juvenile male perched and juvenile female in flight. Kevin T. Karlson

MIGRATION: Northern breeders retreat south before winter, flying mostly singly along a broad front, relying heavily upon thermal lift to save energy, so they soar frequently. Like many diurnal raptors, their course is directed and their numbers concentrated along migratory leading lines, such as mountain ridges and coastlines. Thermal use in spring migration is particularly common when sunlight and denuded landscapes cause widespread and strong thermal production. Spring migration occurs from early March to late May; fall from late August to early November, with juvenile birds preceding adults. Unlike Sharp-shinned, Cooper's is very much a solitary migrant, but they will opportunely join other raptors in thermals.

Probably as a result of their reliance upon thermals, Cooper's Hawks typically do not begin their day's migration until midmorning, when thermal production waxes. During migration, Cooper's often uses early morning hours to hunt.

HABITAT: Cooper's Hawk nests both in extensive forests and smaller woodlots and occasionally in isolated trees. In the East it may nest in mature broadleaf forest or mixed deciduous and conifer forest. It has acclimated itself well to small woodlots of less than five acres in suburbia and may even nest near high pedestrian traffic areas, such as park trails. It particularly favors planted pine plantations in forested areas and parts of the Midwest and the Northeast. In the West it often nests in the "thin fringe of trees along streams."

In winter, it frequents open or broken habitats, including cemeteries, parks, grasslands, and marshes dotted with trees and shelterbelts. It particularly favors older suburban neighborhoods rich in bird feeders, especially if near a sizable woodland for roosting. It also increasingly uses urban centers where pigeons abound and roost trees are available.

It haunts icterid roosts in the mornings and evenings. In migration, it prefers large woodland tracts for roosting.

BREEDING: Cooper's Hawks breed in late March to mid-July, with birds in northern regions on territory in late April to early May. The territorial display incorporates slow, exaggerated wingbeats and wings raised in a V and recalls the "sky dancing" display of Northern Harrier, including a series of U-shaped dives over the bird's nest site. During display flights, birds commonly fluff their white undertail coverts, giving themselves the semblance of a harrier's white rump patch. Resident birds display year-round, the action often precipitated by another Cooper's Hawk encroaching upon a resident bird's territory.

They nest in a variety of trees, with nest site selection very much influenced by prey availability. They are known to nest in solitary pines in suburban and urban environments.

Stick nests are typically situated below the canopy for concealment and perhaps shade. Nests are broad and flat (25 to 30 inches in diameter). It has been suggested that nests in conifers are broader and flatter than those situated in deciduous trees. Audubon likened the size and shape to a crow's nest. Cups are typically lined with bark flakes. The tail of the incubating adult commonly protrudes over the rim. Typically a new nest is built every year, frequently within sight of the previous year's nest, and old foundations, including old squirrel nests, are readily adopted and built upon.

Nests range 20 to 60 feet high, with many falling between 35 and 45 feet. Some authorities have noted a tendency for Cooper's to nest close to water. I suggest that the attraction may be linked to the bird's penchant for edge hunting and perhaps because of an abundance of attractively sized avian prey associated with marshy edge (such as Red-winged Blackbird and Least Bittern). An open understory is also sometimes suggested as a component of a prime nest site.

The typical clutch is three to five white to pale blue eggs. Incubation is 34 to 36 days. Fledging occurs 30 to 34 days later, but parents may continue to feed young for an additional seven weeks.

BEHAVIOR/HUNTING: Cooper's Hawks hunt early, typically at first light, using multiple techniques. For much of the year they appear to prefer perch-hunting from some point of concealment or from a perch, often high and deceptively distant from prey. They also—typically later in the day and during migration—may soar and stoop like a buteo. Occasionally they cruise-hunt like an accelerated harrier, hugging vegetation, hoping to surprise prey.

Cooper's Hawk is a fast and strong

A juvenile female Cooper's Hawk (lower bird) aggressively escorts a juvenile Northern Harrier out of its airspace (Cape May, New Jersey). Kevin T. Karlson

flier capable of rapid acceleration even in full flight. It closes upon unalarmed prey with rapid wingbeats punctuated by glides, particularly when crossing open areas and in the closing moments of an approach. The hawk's ground-hugging approach makes it difficult to detect, as does its clever utilization of concealing obstacles and vegetative backdrops along its course of attack. Sprunt describes the bird's attack as "secretive," with birds "appearing from nowhere and returning thereto as swiftly." Some authorities comment upon the tenacity of this species, which crashes through vegetation in pursuit of flushed prey or clambers amid vegetation in which prey has taken cover.

Young Cooper's Hawks, especially, will at times pursue prey on foot. Notes John Krider, "I have been shooting quail and seen this hawk chase a wounded bird until it reached some thicket."

With great amusement, I once watched a juvenile Cooper's Hawk stalking Semipalmated Sandpipers foraging in a shallow pool. In plain sight, the hawk walked back and forth along the edge of the open, muddy shore until evidently concluding the endeavor was futile.

When closing upon unsuspecting prey, they may set their wings and glide. They throw their feet forward to align with the body just prior to contact, thus putting just a little more oomph into the strike. They kill prey by force of impact, or by constriction or trauma caused by talon penetration. They sometimes drown their victims.

This species is evidently attentive to sound and may be attracted to squeal calls that imitate birds or mammals in distress. In point of fact, most of the Cooper's Hawks I tally on Christmas Bird Counts are attracted to the squeal call that is part of my pishing sequence. It is certainly no coincidence then that the face of Cooper's Hawk shows a semblance of the sound-directing, parabolic-reflecting feather pattern also found on harriers and many owls.

PREY: Most authorities agree that this is first and foremost a bird-hunting hawk, but small mammals (particularly chipmunks) and reptiles also figure in its diet. Many authorities also blame this species for the bad reputation hawks in general have among those who raise poultry, as noted by Leon Augustus Hausman: "No other hawk is so preeminently a 'chicken hawk.'"

Says Audubon about the bird's diet:

"This species frequently kills and eats the Gous [sic] commonly called the Pheasant . . . It also follows the Wild Pigeons in their migration and always causes fear and confusion in their ranks." Judging from the rings of plucked feathers beneath my feeders—a favorite foraging site for our local pair—I find few from small songbirds, and a disproportionate number of Rock Pigeon and Mourning Dove feathers. The Passenger Pigeon may indeed be gone, but the Cooper's partiality to the Columbiformes endures.

One bird species I no longer see at my feeders is Sharp-shinned Hawk, a bird that also falls within the prey range of Cooper's Hawk. Not many years ago, wintering Sharp-shinneds outnumbered Cooper's Hawks in our neighborhood. No longer.

Alexander Sprunt observes that Cooper's Hawk lives primarily upon birds the size of robins, quail, meadowlarks, and jays. But, as mentioned, I personally have come to regard Cooper's Hawk as something of a Mourning Dove specialist. This

---

Left: *An adult male Cooper's Hawk brings home the bacon (temporarily wrapped in chipmunk fur).* Right: *Two juvenile Cooper's Hawks vie for what's left of dinner.* Steve Sachs

A successful juvenile Cooper's Hawk mantles its prey. In the universal sign language of raptors, the message reads: "This is mine, your repast is somewhere else." Brian Small

widespread and attractively sized ground-foraging dove seems ever late to respond to the resident jay's alarm call and, while a fast flier, doves take time to get airborne and up to speed. These shortfalls make Mourning Doves particularly ill suited to defend themselves against Cooper's Hawks, whose attack incorporates stealth, great acceleration, maneuverability, and a boardinghouse reach.

STATUS: At the beginning of the twentieth century, Cooper's Hawk was considered a "common nesting raptor." John Krider, writing in 1879, pronounced the bird "quite a common bird all over the country . . . I have killed it at all seasons; it is very plenty [sic] in Virginia and Iowa and feeds on quail, young prairie chickens and meadow larks." Writing in 1923 in California, William Leon Dawson pronounced the bird a "Common resident at all levels . . . More in evidence in winter . . ." Given the species' historically common and widespread nature, it is perplexing that Alexander Wilson was evidently unfamiliar with it. No mention is made in the 1814 first edition of *American Ornithology*; inclusion awaited Charles Lucien Bonaparte's update in 1833.

While always persecuted for its taste for poultry and game birds, persecution seems not to have impacted the bird's numbers greatly. It wasn't until the widespread use of DDT in the 1950s and '60s that Cooper's Hawk's numbers plummeted. In my home state of New Jersey, Cooper's Hawk was declared an endangered species, a dubious status it maintained for two decades—although it should be noted that the population of breeding and wintering birds had recovered well before it was officially delisted in the 1990s. Given Cooper's Hawks' evident ability to adapt to habitats modified for human use, and barring some environmental catastrophe, it seems likely that Cooper's Hawk numbers will remain at least stable and may, in fact, increase as vegetation in suburban and urban neighborhoods matures and more suitably sized prey species (birds and mammals) integrate themselves into our urban and suburban environments.

At eastern hawkwatch sites, increased sightings were noted from 1974 to 2000, but increases may be slowing. At western sites, numbers increased from the 1980s to 1997, but since 1998 declines are noted.

Northern Goshawk
Accipiter gentilis

A Northern Goshawk shows the arresting blood red eye of an adult that has been many a snowshoe hare's last mortal sight. Jim Zipp

ETYMOLOGY: The Anglo Saxon *gos* means "goose," and *havoc* is for "hawk," for one of the birds on which the hawk might prey. *Gentilis* is Latin for "noble."

PROFILE: This large, handsome, smoke-colored forest raptor combines the size and strength of a buteo with the struc-tural refinements, reflexes, and hunting finesse of an accipiter. It is North America's largest and heaviest-bodied accipiter.

This large, powerful, tenacious street brawler of a raptor is celebrated in account after account for its defensiveness around the nest site, single-mindedness in pursuit of prey, and rapid acceleration. Many accounts relate the story of the goshawk that pursued a chicken into the kitchen of a farmhouse. The story, as well as others, is recounted in Forbush: "Dr. William Wood of East Windsor Hill, Connecticut, told of a Goshawk that followed a hen into a kitchen and seized her on the kitchen floor in the very presence of an old man and his daughter. The father beat off the hawk with a cane, while the daughter closed the door and finally killed the bird." Mr. J. A. Farley relates this tale from Lambert Lake, Maine, where a "Goshawk caught a half-grown hen. The hen, escaping, ran under a woman's skirts. The hawk followed right up to the skirt but was killed . . . "

The word *gentilis* was a term used by falconers who divided their birds into two classes. The members of the first class were the long- and pointy-winged falcons. These were called "noble" for their spectacular plunging after prey. In the lower, second class were the rounder- and shorter-winged hawks. As their catching of prey was less entertaining, they were called "ignoble." It says a great deal about this species, hailing as it does from the "ignoble" class, that its species name should elevate it to the ranks of the *gentilis*. Unlike our other two North American accipiters, Northern Goshawk's range straddles oceans, encompassing the northern forests of both the Old and New Worlds. If not for an intervening water barrier or two, Northern Goshawk's breeding range would be contiguous.

As for Goshawks subduing geese, I can only say that while not impossible, it seems to my mind quite improbable. While the ranks of Goshawk's prey are extensive, no modern resource lists any goose species of any size among them. Having said this, I submit that it would be very poor fortune to be a gosling Canada Goose in the vicinity of a Goshawk nest, especially during a year marked by low numbers of grouse, ptarmigan, and hare. While it is the smaller male that does most of the hunting, when birds are nesting it has been calculated that males are capable of killing prey 2.2 times their mass. While generally solitary, silent, and secretive, females are vocal and spirited in their defense of nest sites.

Reverend G. Eifrig of Ottawa tells of an Ontario farmer who went to inspect a pasture that adjoined extensive woods. He was attacked viciously again and again by a Goshawk that evidently had her nest in the woods nearby.

DESCRIPTION: A robust, heavy-bodied, long-tailed, near Red-tailed Hawk–sized raptor, the Goshawk is the largest of our accipiters. It is nearly twice the weight of Cooper's Hawk. Adults are mostly blue gray, overall paler gray above than Cooper's Hawk and Sharp-shinned. Finely barred underparts are likewise pale gray from the throat to the legs, contrasting with white undertail coverts. Barring on the larger females is generally coarser; otherwise, except for size, sexes are similar. The gray tail has three or four darker bands. The head pattern of the adults is distinctive, showing a blackish cap and a broad black eye stripe/patch, separated by a broad white supercilium. The blood-red eye is arresting.

The juvenile is similarly proportioned, with brown upperparts and a brown head creased by a prominent buffy white supercilium or eyebrow seated above the

An adult Northern Goshawk shows different flight profiles. Note the robust profile but small head relative to body mass and long accipiter-like tail. Top: Jerry Liguori; bottom: Jim Zipp

bird's bright yellow eye. Buffy underparts are heavily overlaid with coarse brown streaks from breast to legs, with streaking growing sparse on the white undertail coverts. (See photo, page 99.)

MEASUREMENTS

Length: male 18–20 inches; female 21–24 inches
Wingspan: male 38–41 inches; female 41–45 inches
Weight: male 24–36 ounces; female 26–43 ounces

SYSTEMATICS/SUBSPECIES: As many as ten subspecies are recognized. The AOU recognizes two subspecies for North America: the widespread *A. g. atricapillus,* which breeds throughout mostly northern forests of North America; and *A. g. laingi,* which breeds on the Queen Charlotte Islands and Vancouver Island north through British Columbia and coastal Alaska. Some authorities regard birds breeding from southern Arizona south into the mountains of Mexico a separate race, *A. g. apache,* which is overall larger and larger footed than *A. g. atricapillus.* The European or Eurasian Goshawk (*A. g. gentilis*) may, in fact, be a different species and has been considered such by some authorities. Audubon, for his part, was emphatic in his determination that the European and North American Goshawk were the "same" bird but at the same time apologetic to contemporaries who thought otherwise.

VOCALIZATIONS: Goshawks are mostly silent, but at the nest they make a loud, high-pitched, no-nonsense *kack* scream/call that is louder than a Cooper's Hawk's. It is intended to get your attention. If it doesn't, the bird that is threatening to decapitate you most certainly will.

DISTRIBUTION: Given the conspecific nature of North American and European Goshawk, this is a bird with an enormous breeding range. Its distribution is pan-boreal; it breeds in mostly boreal forest, generally south of the tree line, although some birds do breed in the tundra biome, finding suitable nesting habitat in large mature willow thickets even north of the Brooks Range in Alaska. In the United States, it breeds throughout northern forests from western Alaska to New Brunswick south into the Cascades of California, and in the Rockies south to southern Arizona and southern New Mexico (also in the mountains of Mexico). In the central and eastern United States it breeds in central Minnesota, northern Wisconsin, Michigan, northern Pennsylvania, and throughout New England south to northern New Jersey (also sparingly along the Appalachians to Tennessee). It is mostly resident throughout its breeding range, but some portion of the adult population and juveniles regularly winter south of the breeding areas, widely across northern states and the intermountain West east to the prairies.

This is an irruptive species that every few years stages a mass southern migration involving at least many hundreds of individuals (mostly smaller adult males and juveniles). These irruptive flights propel birds well south of the species' normal winter range.

MIGRATION: In most years the Goshawk is a "partial migrant," moving short distances to areas offering a greater abun-

Three juvenile Northern Goshawks show different flight profiles but heavily patterned under-parts that distinguish them from the lightly streaked and overall less robust juvenile Cooper's Hawk. Left to right: Jerry Liguori, Jim Zipp, Brian Sullivan

dance of prey. Fall migration is typically October through December, but the onset may be earlier in irruption years (beginning in August). Spring migration is very early—late February to early April—but poorly understood.

Irruptions occur every seven to ten years and are widely believed to be linked to the population cycles of Goshawk's two favored prey species, Ruffed Grouse and Snowshoe Hare. When grouse and hare numbers plummet, Goshawks head south in numbers.

In North America, large Goshawk irruptions were noted as far back as 1896–97 (this one apparently limited to the Northeast). In 1906–07 there was a famous invasion, widespread from New England to Minneapolis and Manitoba. Maurice Broun notes "invasions" in 1934, 1935, and 1936. Palmer lists "incursions" in 1859, 1870, 1905, 1926, 1935, 1954, 1962, and 1982–83. Totals from Hawk Mountain, Pennsylvania, attest to significant irruptions in 1982, 1983, and 1991–93.

HABITAT: At all seasons, this is mostly a bird of extensive mature forest, primarily boreal and temperate forest. When breeding, it is partial to clearings and edge.

In winter, the Goshawk is more eclectic in its habitat choices, but it still prefers large mature forest tracts and avoids young and middle-age-growth woodlands. Prey abundance more than habitat type and structure may be the primary determinant of winter habitat, although a preference for mature woodlands is evident.

BREEDING: Nests are typically situated in old-growth forests composed primarily of large trees. Some pairs remain near nests year-round. Those that migrate or relocate return between March and April, in places as early as February. They build their nests in coniferous or deciduous trees, typically the largest tree in the stand. The large stick nest is often snugged up against the trunk, where one or more main branches project, or at a major fork. Nests are typically 18 to 75 feet above the ground. Some authorities note a partiality to locations near the base of hills with sparse understory. Goshawks prefer forest with extensive, unbroken canopy, but nests are frequently located near or adjacent to some forest opening, such as a blowdown or logging road. They frequently use the same nest year after year, but they may construct and use up to eight nests. Construction of new nests takes approximately one week.

Nests are large, quite bulky, flatish, and often loosely constructed, with nest material draping over a support branch. One nest that Bent described was tightly constructed primarily of white pine and hemlock sticks; it measured between three and four feet across and was 35 inches in height. One ornithologist visiting a Goshawk nest proclaimed it to be "the most beautifully constructed large hawk nest that I have ever seen." Nests are sometimes garnished with fresh needle-bearing twigs.

A typical clutch is five unmarked bluish white eggs. The incubation period is 28 to 30 days. Pairs raise one brood per season. The male does most of the hunting but the female does the feeding. After delivering prey, the male does not linger. Branching of young occurs when nestlings are 34 or 35 days of age; the first flight away from the nest tree is at 35 or 36 days. Young birds remain together in the vicinity of the nest, where they continue to be fed by adults for several weeks or until they acquire hunting skills.

BEHAVIOR/HUNTING: The Goshawk is celebrated for its rapid acceleration. In the estimates of many, it is primarily a brief-

duration perch hunter, favoring multiple woodland perches below the canopy and targeting prey that occupies the forest floor or understory layer. Most prey ranges in size from sapsuckers to rabbits or hares and grouse—in fact, any accounting of Goshawk prey that fails to mention Snowshoe Hare and Ruffed Grouse by name is sadly remiss.

Palmer describes the attack as "sudden, at tremendous speed, over short distance." Few birds and perhaps no raptors are faster out of the blocks than Goshawk. They appear to attain full speed while the branch they just vacated still vibrates. Much has been said about the tenacity of this bird, including its willingness to plunge into thick vegetation in pursuit of prey.

There are multiple accounts of Goshawk pursuing prey on foot, even into vegetation. Once grasped, the prey is subdued by repeated contractions of the feet until it's dead—a so-called killing reflex. "A very persistent raptor, it will walk on the ground to flush or seize prey." W. E. W. Cram describes this interesting hunting technique used by Goshawk in snow-covered woodlands: "Walking much like a crow, but hopping for a few feet occasionally. At times it followed the tracks of rabbits for some distance. I have often known them to do this, and am inclined to think that they occasionally hunt rabbits in this manner where under-brush is too dense to allow them to fly through it easily. I have sometimes followed their

tracks through the brush until I came upon the remains of a freshly killed rabbit which they had eaten."

Audubon describes a more active hunting technique: "At times he [the Goshawk] passes like a meteor through the underwood where he secures squirrels and hares with ease. Should a flock of Wild Pigeon pass him, he immediately gives chase, soon overtakes them . . . " Imagine, if you can, the acceleration and speed of a bird that could overtake pigeons already in full flight. It is small wonder that this species has long been a favorite among falconers, nicknamed in days of yore the "cook's friend" because of its ability to capture pot-worthy-sized prey. I find this account from Alaska particularly illustrative:

> The tracts preferred by this Goshawk are the narrow valleys, borders of streams, and open tundras, which it constantly scans for ptarmigan and small animals; the lemming forming a considerable portion of its food. It will sit for hours in some secluded spot waiting for a Ptarmigan to rise on its wings. No sooner does its prey rise a few feet from the ground, than with a few rapid strokes of the wing and a short sail, the Goshawk is brought within seizing distance; it pounces upon the bird, grasping it with both feet under the wings, and after giving it a few blows on the head they both fall to the ground, often tumbling a few feet before they stop, the Hawk not relinquishing its hold during the time . . .

The observer goes on to note that displaying male Ptarmigan are a greatly favored target of Goshawk.

In winter and during migration, I have seen Goshawk use a different technique to good effect. Flying rapidly and at reed-top height toward a waterfowl-rich pond (evidently studied in advance), the Goshawk sets its wings and circumnavigates the edge of the pond or reeds in a gravity-defeating glide, not flapping until it targets a bird for pursuit.

PREY: Goshawks primarily target small and medium-sized birds and mammals up to the size of grouse, Cooper's Hawk, ducks, and hares. Red, gray, and flying squirrels are also frequent prey, as are jays and American Robin. At Donner Lake, California, American Robin and Steller's Jay are favored prey. In the Queen Charlotte Islands, Northwestern Crow, Steller's Jay, and Varied Thrush are especially targeted species. Very little is known about the bird's diet in winter, but in my experience they seem to hunt waterfowl extensively.

In sum, Goshawk is a prey generalist targeting whatever medium-sized mammalian and larger avian prey happens to be in greatest abundance, but also a versatile, calculating, and determined predator, using the technique best suited to the habitat and prey. Mammals constitute up to 59 percent of the diet, birds 18 to 69 percent. They frequently target gallinaceous species. The Snyders invert the balance, concluding that prey consists "mainly of birds with a scattering of small mammals."

Already packing a knockdown punch with their combination of weight and speed, Goshawks put a little more oomph into their strike by throwing their feet forward so that the forward momentum of the bird's feet is achieved at impact. Most prey is killed by the shock of impact. But if not, the Goshawk is formi-

Perch-hunting is a page out of the Northern Goshawk playbook. It is all but certain that this bird is hungry. With prey numbers diminished by the season, compounded by the bird's youthful inexperience, empty crops are the norm more than the exception among young raptors, their formidable prowess notwithstanding. Jim Zipp

dable in the clinches, tightening its grip repeatedly in a "killing reflex" every time its victim twitches with life (Forbush refers to this as a "death grapple").

STATUS: Certainly humans pose the greatest threat to this bird, although there are accounts of owls—most notably Barred Owl—killing Goshawks. Yet despite its formidable hunting prowess, starvation appears to be the greatest challenge facing the Goshawk. While the prey-impoverished northern environment most certainly honed the considerable hunting skills of this species, that environment remains stingy with its resources and indifferent to the plight of its inhabitants.

The North American population of Northern Goshawk appears stable now that human persecution has been reduced in many places. In Canada *A. g. atricapillus* "is not considered at risk." The remoteness and unpeopled nature of its boreal forest stronghold is, for now, the bird's true saving grace. Forest fragmentation does not favor this species. Summaries from western hawkwatch sites appear "uniformly stable" or show "slight declines" except for a long-term decline in Nevada and recent declines in Washington.

BUTEOS and ALLIES
Twelve species

Common Black-Hawk
Buteogallus anthracinus

ETYMOLOGY: From the Latin *buteo gallus* for "chicken hawk," and *anthracinus* for "coal black."

PROFILE: This large, rather sedentary raptor is our sole representative of this tropical genus. Several sources lament the under-studied nature of this bird, an observation supported by the reigning confusion regarding the classification of several regional forms and their taxonomic standing. One thing seems certain: wherever this tropical and subtropical raptor is found, water is an essential component.

In plumage, adults are superficially similar to the Zone-tailed Hawk, a buteo also found in the American Southwest and at times occupying the same riparian habitat frequented by Black-Hawk. But the similarities between these two tropical species go no deeper than plumage. Two more dissimilar raptors could hardly be forced into comparison. Black-Hawk is a perch-hunter and occasionally a wading bird specializing mostly in the capture of aquatic prey. Zone-tailed is an aerialist targeting an array of terrestrial prey primarily found in dry upland habitats, including mountainous terrain; although, like Common Black-Hawk, it may nest in the trees of riparian corridors.

DESCRIPTION: A large, stocky, short-tailed, long-legged, somewhat lethargic raptor typically seen perched on a low solid branch or rock outcropping just above a secluded, clear, slow-moving

Common Black-Hawk has a very restricted range in the United States and typically nests in riparian corridors along permanent streams. While sexes have similar plumages, it is safe to say that the bird at the nest is a female insofar as males do most of the hunting but females do all of the incubating and attend to the young. Two fledglings are typical. Ned Harris

riparian corridor. Adults are striking: their plumage is overall "sooty" black, with a slight brownish infusion, particularly in the wings. The black tail is bisected by a single broad white band. Lores and legs are bright yellow. Sexes are similar. Juveniles are structurally similar to adults but sooty brown above with a streaked breast, barred thighs, and a thick, dark muttonchop malar stripe. The juvenile's tail also shows multiple wavy dark bands above and below. In flight, the Black-Hawk appears very broad winged, recalling the shape of a Black Vulture. It soars on flat wings, unlike the slimmer Zone-tailed Hawk, which flies with a Turkey Vulture–like dihedral.

MEASUREMENTS

Length: 21 inches
Wingspan: 46 inches
Weight: 1.4–2.9 pounds

A Common Black-Hawk sampler. Adults above, juveniles below. Note the broad, paddle-shaped wings common to both ages. Clockwise from top left: Jerry Liguori, Ned Harris, Jim Zipp, Bill Clark

Females are larger, but dimorphism is not clearly evident.

SYSTEMATICS/SUBSPECIES:

Taxonomy relating to Black-Hawk and related species or forms remains uncertain and perhaps subject to further evaluation. The Black-Hawk superspecies complex includes six recognized species/subspecies, only one of which, *Buteogallus anthracinus,* occurs in the American Southwest as well as inland portions of Central America. *B. anthracinus* is somewhat larger and blacker than Gundlach's Hawk or Cuban Black-Hawk, *B. gundlachii,* which is limited to Cuba and the Isle of Pines.

VOCALIZATIONS:

The call is described by some as reminiscent of a chirping trill of Bald Eagle. But said Mearns of the cry: "their loudly whistled cry is different from that of any bird of prey . . . but is difficult to describe, although rendered with great power."

DISTRIBUTION:

Members of the genus *Buteogallus* range from the southwestern United States to Argentina. In the United States, *B. anthracinus* is confined as a breeder to Utah, New Mexico, and south Texas, with most North American birds breeding in Arizona along rivers draining the Mogollon Rim.

MIGRATION:

U.S. breeders are migratory and are generally absent from breeding areas November through March, with birds returning in April. Little is known about the winter range of U.S. birds except all banding returns from birds banded in Arizona have been from Sinaloa, Mexico.

HABITAT:

North American birds are closely tied to riparian corridors with permanent streams cutting through arid habitat. These riparian woodlands are dominated by mature cottonwoods, sycamores, and walnut and flank placid stretches of permanent clear freshwater rivers rich in aquatic prey—principally small fish, amphibians, and reptiles.

BREEDING:

The home range is described as "possibly smallest . . . of any North American buteonine raptor," with adults apparently returning to the same nesting areas year after year.

Given its sedentary habits and generally "tame" nature, finding Common Black-Hawk would be extremely challenging were it not for the bird's limited habitat and spirited courtship display, whose enthusiasm is much at odds with the bird's reputation for sluggishness. Courtship flights incorporate high soaring, undulating flight, and exaggerated wingbeats, with the wingtips appearing to touch above and below the body. Both sexes apparently display and vocalize; leg dangling and talon touching are elements of the courtship flight.

In the United States, breeding season begins in April. The mostly stick nest is commonly situated in the crotch of a main trunk of a tree located within a grove. Nests vary in size but typically are well shaded, and leafed twigs figure in the construction, which involves both sexes. Nests are sometimes used for several years. Egg laying is commonly in April, with a clutch size of one or two eggs. The grayish white eggs are spotted sparingly with dull or light brown. Incubation is done entirely by the female and takes 32 to 34 days. The male delivers prey, but

the actual feeding of the young is usually done by the female. Young fledge in about 42 days. We lack specific information on young birds' continued association with adults postbreeding, although juvenile birds are "frequently seen" in areas adjacent to active breeding territories.

BEHAVIOR/HUNTING: Common Black-Hawk is typically a passive perch-hunting raptor that favors generally low perches on sturdy limbs surrounded by foliage and overlooking watercourses. It will also use strategic rocky outcroppings and streamside boulders as hunting perches. Prey is typically captured via a short, direct descent that ranges from a "swooping glide" to a "pounce." It also wades in shallow water, occasionally waving its wingtips over and through the water to attract or herd prey into the shallows.

The Black-Hawk's flight is "swift and powerful." The following flight description rendered by G. B. Thomas and quoted in Sprunt is worth recounting since it seems greatly at odds with the bird's reputation for sluggishness: "It excels any of the hawks, kites, or falcons except possibly the Swallow-tailed Kite. The flight is really marvelous, excelling in some particulars even the far-famed Frigate or man-o-war Bird."

PREY: Black-Hawks consume an array of mostly aquatic prey, targeting prey that is most abundant and available. They are especially partial to fish, reptiles, frogs, and crayfish. They also feed on large insects, including grasshoppers and caterpillars.

This sequence of the same bird and nest shows an adult female incubating, attending to what appears to be a single chick at a nest tree in Texas. You can see the distance that the photographer put between himself and the nest, thus eliminating disturbance that might compromise the raptor's nesting success. Greg Lasley

An adult Common Black-Hawk shows the great breadth of its wings. Despite its reputation for sluggishness, Common Black-Hawk is a swift, nimble, and determined flier. Greg Lasley

STATUS: Black-Hawks are uncommon and difficult to find. The U.S. population is estimated to be between 220 and 250 pairs, most of which are found in Arizona. The population is believed to be self-sustaining, but low numbers and habitat vulnerability are grounds for concern. The species is listed as endangered in New Mexico and threatened in Texas. In the more southern parts of their range, this species is more common; in fact, along some Mexican rivers it is the most commonly encountered raptor, with a bird seemingly perched around every bend.

The greatest threat to this species is any human activity that diminishes or degrades riparian breeding habitat. Specific threats include cattle grazing, clearing for agriculture, and intrusion of salt cedars and other invasive plants.

Of course, any long-term climate change that reduces or degrades the watercourses upon which the Black-Hawk is dependent will have an obvious deleterious effect.

Harris's Hawk
Parabuteo unicinctus

ETYMOLOGY: From the Latin *uni* for "once," and *cinctus* for "girdled." This is presumably a reference to the broad band around the tail. This species was formerly but aptly known as Bay-winged Hawk.

PROFILE: Harris's Hawk is a fascinating, handsome medium-large raptor of arid brushlands. In parts of its range, it is a very social hawk whose cooperative manners show many of the social proclivities of a wolf pack.

DESCRIPTION: This is a long-legged, long-tailed, medium-sized dark buteonine of the arid Southwest. Except for the white undertail, the adult's body is dark brown with russet shoulders and thighs. The long dark tail has a white tip. The legs and cere are yellow.

The juvenile is similar to the adult but its dark underparts are streaked with white. (See the photo on page 114.) Ex-cept for the larger size of the females, the sexes are similar.

MEASUREMENTS
Length: 18–23 inches
Wingspan: 40–47 inches
Weight: 1.3–2.6 pounds

Females are approximately 47 percent heavier than males.

SYSTEMATICS/SUBSPECIES: Three subspecies are described: *P. u. harrisi* is found

---

Tense as a sprinter awaiting the sound of the starter's pistol, this handsome adult Harris's Hawk is all business. What's got the bird's attention? Hard to say. Harris's Hawks take an array of avian and mammalian prey, but this would be a very bad time to be a jackrabbit. Jim Zipp

Adult Harris's Hawks. Note the paddle-shaped wings on the gliding bird at the top. In the desert Southwest, Harris's Hawks use saguaro cactus as hunting perches. Top: Kevin T. Karlson; bottom left: Jerry Liguori; bottom right: Ned Harris

in eastern Mexico and much of Central America. *P. u. unicinctus* inhabits South America. *P. u. superior* is found in southwestern Arizona and western Mexico; it was formerly in California, but is now extirpated.

VOCALIZATIONS: Harris's Hawks make a variety of vocalizations. The most commonly heard sound—the alarm or territorial call—is described as a raucous, harsh *raaak.* It also makes a *chirp* call, given in a series of five to ten notes, usually during communal hunting exercises.

DISTRIBUTION: It occurs in the southwestern United States south to southern Chile, central Argentina, Paraguay, and east into Venezuela and the interior of Brazil. In the United States, it is currently restricted to scattered isolated breeding populations in southern Arizona, southeastern New Mexico, and western and southern Texas.

MIGRATION: In the United States, it is a year-round resident. While it may be nomadic, there is no evidence of migration.

HABITAT: Harris's Hawk inhabits sparse woodland or semiopen desert. In Arizona, it mainly frequents palo verde and mixed-cactus habitats. In New Mexico and Texas, it is found in mesquite-oak shrublands and thorn scrub vegetation. Large trees and other structures suited for perch hunting and nest support are an important component. Access to open water is also a possible component of prime habitat. In the Sonoran Desert, saguaro cactus are commonly used as hunting perches. (See the photo on page 112.)

BREEDING: While this species has been known to breed every month of the year, pairs probably form in spring (February and March in Arizona; slightly later elsewhere). In Arizona, nests are built or repaired January through August—a testimony not only to the protracted breeding season but also to the species' proclivity to lay two, even three clutches in years marked by high prey availability. Conversely, birds may forgo breeding in years when prey numbers are low.

In Mexico and Texas, monogamy is the typical mating strategy. In other places, including Arizona, breeding groups of mostly related individuals are typical, with one adult male and one adult female constituting an alpha pair and up to seven sometimes unrelated adults and immatures acting in concert to secure food and protect young. The communal nesting strategy provides a mechanism for a pack-hunting bird to continue this effective foraging strategy while one member of the alpha pair is bound by reproductive necessity to the nest. It may also serve as a population control in ecologically marginal habitat by taking prospective breeders out of the pool. Nonbreeding, attending adults may benefit by being first in line to inherit prime habitat when one or both members of the alpha pair die.

Bulky stick nests are situated in "almost any relatively tall, sturdy structure" and pairs may build or repair up to four nests. Most nests are low, less than 30 feet above the ground. Nests placed in saguaros and manmade structures are often exposed to direct sunlight. In the case of successive broods, the same nest may be used or an alternate structure chosen. Clutch size is one to five eggs, with three or four typical. The incubation period is 31 to 36 days. The alpha female does most of the incubation, but the breeding male and auxiliary males and females may relieve females at the nest. However, the primary role of the alpha male and auxiliary birds is hunting and nest protection. Young are branching at 40 days and fledge about a week later, but they remain in the natal territory for up to three years. Immatures "regularly participate in cooperative hunts with other members of the group."

BEHAVIOR/HUNTING: As has already been indicated, this is a gregarious raptor that, in some U.S. populations, maintains a complex and by no means uniform social structure involving, at times, multiple adults and immature birds throughout

Juvenile Harris's Hawks may remain in the natal territory for up to three years and participate in cooperative hunting endeavors. Left: Brian Small; right: Brian Sullivan

the year, including the breeding season. They hunt cooperatively, with coordinated attacks upon prey often involving multiple individuals.

A dashing raptor, Harris's Hawk combines rapid acceleration, biped locomotion, tenacity, and coordinated effort. As mentioned, the natal group's primary function is hunting but this cooperative hunting strategy continues beyond the breeding season. In fact, in New Mexico, sociality is greatest during the nonbreeding season, September to March. Cooperative hunting has been shown to be more successful than efforts conducted by lone individuals, and hunting success increases with hunting party size. Group members then share their captures.

Harris's Hawks use several hunting techniques well suited for this nimble, fast, strategy-minded hunter. The most typical strategy is the old "sit and wait" technique used by many raptor species and particularly by Harris's Hawks hunting alone. Another typical strategy involves short perch-to-perch hunting, in which a member of the group flies from perch to strategic perch, where it scans for prey.

Cooperative hunting is normally preceded by an assembly ceremony, in which members of the group perch together, sometimes on the same branch. When hunting cooperatively, birds may converge on targeted prey from different directions. One or more birds may penetrate cover to flush out prey, while other members wait in ambush. In the event of long tail chases (often the case with hares) birds initiate a "relay attack," in which the lead pursuer is replaced by another (fresher) pack member. They also employ dual attacks, in which two birds converge nearly simultaneously. This species only infrequently stoops on prey.

PREY: In the United States, this is a more flexible prey specialist than a generalist. Small to medium-sized mammals appear to be the primary prey of Harris's Hawk, but birds are also important prey, especially when mammal populations are low. Specific prey includes desert cotton-tail, eastern cottontail, and black-tailed jackrabbit, along with ground squirrels, woodrats, and pocket gophers, Gambel's Quail, Northern Bobwhite, Cactus Wren, and Northern Mockingbird. Rabbits and hares are nutritional packages large enough to be shared, thus prey well suited to be pursued when hunting communally. This species readily enters vegetation, sometimes on foot in pursuit of prey.

Snyder points out that the species' long toes and talons in combination with its pronounced size dimorphism constitute traits shared by many bird-catching specialists, thus supporting those who hold that birds figure prominently in this species' diet, giving it a survival

In parts of its range, Harris's are social hawks, hunting cooperatively in the manner of a feathered wolf pack. When the birds capture prey, they share the bounty. Jim Zipp

edge when mammalian prey populations are low.

One of this species' most celebrated traits is its penchant for one or more individuals to perch upon the backs of other group members. "Backstanding" may last for up to several minutes. While the foundation of this behavior remains speculative, it nevertheless attests to the highly social and tolerant nature of this species.

STATUS: This species has suffered historic declines in overall population as well as a range retraction. It was eliminated from Louisiana in the early 1900s, and it formerly nested along the Colorado River in Arizona and California. Its distribution in Texas is patchy, but it was formerly "uniformly distributed throughout its range in Texas." Basically, this bird has fared poorly in the face of urban encroachment.

A heavily marked juvenile Harris's Hawk displays the large taloned feet and boardinghouse reach that make it such a formidable predator of medium-sized birds and small mammals. Harris's combines rapid acceleration with a tenacity that leads birds to pursue prey on foot after it reaches the presumed sanctity of cover. Greg Lasley

Red-shouldered Hawk

Buteo lineatus

ETYMOLOGY: *Lineatus* is Latin for "striped," almost certainly in reference to the black-and-white pattern on the wing and the tail of the adult.

PROFILE: This beautiful and at times flamboyant woodland raptor seems ever fated to be discussed in comparison with Red-tailed and Broad-winged Hawks—two species that are themselves rarely discussed comparatively. Arthur Cleveland Bent dedicated much discussion in his *Life Histories of North American Birds of Prey* to what he saw as a competition between the Red-taileds and Red-shouldereds—noting that in Massachu-setts, where one species was common, the other was not. Said Bent: "I have learned to regard them as competitive species, each intolerant of the other, antagonistic and occupying entirely separate ranges." This is a differentiation likely attributable to habitat preference, with the Red-shouldered Hawk better suited to mature forest interior, and Red-taileds specialized to more open or broken habitat.

Maurice Broun, in *Hawks Aloft*, laments: "It has always been a source of wonder to me that these handsome Buteos are so few, so poorly represented in

An adult Red-shouldered Hawk subspecies sampler. From left (top and bottom): an adult Eastern Red-shouldered, B. l. lineatus; an adult Florida Red-shouldered, B. l. extimus; and the very colorful B. l. elegans of California and Oregon. Clockwise from top left: Jim Zipp, Kevin T. Karlson, Brian Sullivan, Kevin T. Karlson, Kevin T. Karlson, Jerry Liguori

our ridge flights. Why should this bird, so like its Broad-winged and Red-tailed relatives (which together make up 67 percent of our flights), be so scarce along our flyway?" Another favorite topic that surfaces in any discussion of the Red-shouldered Hawk includes its spirited and vocal courtship displays.

DESCRIPTION: This is a colorful, medium-sized buteo. Adults show mostly blackish backs and wings infused with white spotting or lines on the folded wing. The black tail is similarly bisected by narrow white bands. The underparts are rufous orange (solid on the breast, barred on the belly). The rufous orange extends along the top of the folded wing to form a colorful sash or extended epaulet (a "red shoulder"). Except for the larger size of the female, the sexes are similar.

Overall browner juveniles show some of the plumage characteristics of adults, including the banded tail pattern and a trace of the russet shoulder slash. Except in California, creamy underparts of juveniles are heavily streaked with brown from the breast to the belly. The juvenile plumage of California birds is much more like that of adults. Florida adults are overall paler (appearing washed out), typically with gray rather than orange heads. Florida juveniles are likewise paler with less streaking below and little to no reddish tones on the head and shoulder. The eyes of juveniles are also paler.

MEASUREMENTS
Length: 15–19 inches
Wingspan: 37–42 inches
Weight: 1.1–1.9 pounds

SYSTEMATICS/SUBSPECIES: Five subspecies are recognized: *B. l. lineatus,* breeding in the northeastern United States and southeastern Canada; the somewhat smaller *B. l. anneni* of the southeastern United States; the pale *B. l. extimus,* a resident of southern Florida; the richly plumaged *B. l. texanus* of east Texas; and the geographically disjunct *B. l. elegans* of California and southwestern Oregon.

VOCALIZATIONS: Said Audubon: "This bird is one of the most noisy of its genus, during spring especially, when it would be difficult to approach the skirts of woods bordering a large plantation without hearing its discordant shrill notes . . . " Leon Augustus Hausman describes the call as a "musical scream" and confides that the Red-shouldered's colloquial name is "Singing Hawk."

DISTRIBUTION: Red-shouldered Hawks are widespread across the eastern United States and southeastern Canada, with their range extending west to the eastern Great

A juvenile Red-shouldered Hawk subspecies sampler. From left (top and bottom): B. l. elegans of California and Oregon; Florida Red-shouldered B. l. extimus; Eastern Red-shouldered, B. l. lineatus. Top left and bottom left: Brian Sullivan; all others: Kevin T. Karlson

Nest building completed, Red-shouldered Hawks, like several other buteo species, garnish nests with a bit of greenery, perhaps to denote occupancy to other prospecting adults. Steve Sachs

Plains. A western population is found west of the Sierra Nevada from southwestern Oregon to Baja California. Northeastern birds from Oklahoma, northern Wisconsin, northern Ohio, New England, and southern Canada are migratory. Other populations are mostly resident.

MIGRATION: Fall migration in the Northeast occurs from early October to late December. Spring migration is from February to April.

HABITAT: Red-shouldered Hawk generally prefers extensive mature forest but seems willing to adapt to whatever forest types are available. Favored habitats include forested bottomlands, flooded deciduous swamp, and deciduous and deciduous-coniferous forest. Western birds favor riparian stands of oak. In winter they are often found in more broken, open, even suburban habitat. In the East, they are often found in the same habitat as Barred Owl.

BREEDING: Courtship begins about the time tree buds begin to blossom in mid-February to mid-April, depending upon latitude. In California, where birds are resident, pair formation begins in February.

Aerial displays are spirited and vocal and worthy of a detailed account. Notes Bent:

These hawks are very noisy and conspicuous at this season, in marked contrast with their behavior at other seasons. Their loud cries of *kee-ah, kee-ah* are frequently repeated as they circle overhead, their wings and tail broadly expanded . . . Frequently they swing near each other and then far apart, or, mounting high in the air, one may make a thrilling dive . . . These evolutions are indulged in every year, even by mated pairs . . .

Nests are often located near water or along some open corridor—a trail, paved road, suburban yard—and birds often use the same nest year after year; in fact, Bent observes, the species is celebrated for its site fidelity. Large, sturdy stick nests, built or refurbished by both adults, are composed mostly of dead sticks, twigs, and strips of bark. Nests are typically located in the crotch of a deciduous tree or where multiple limbs radiate out below the canopy but at least 20 feet above the ground. "Sprays of green leaves are added especially during nesting period."

Nest building or refurbishment may take four or five weeks. A typical clutch is two or three dull white, variable dark brown–marked eggs, sometimes four. Incubation is about 33 days. Fledging typically takes 35 to 45 days, but young may continue to roost at or near the nest.

BEHAVIOR/HUNTING: During breeding season, Red-shouldered Hawks often hunt from forest canopy, dropping upon prey below. In winter, this perch-hunting raptor likes to sit at midheight along the forest edge (where its outline is broken by a latticework of branches), facing some more open habitat, such as a pasture, marsh, vernal pond, or stream.

Prey sighted, the hawk launches itself with accipiter-quick wingbeats and is capable of accipiterlike nimble maneuvers with its relatively short wings and relatively long tail. Juvenile birds in particular may hunt from low perches in the open (fenceposts in agricultural land, swing sets near bird feeders in suburban yards).

PREY: The diet is varied and includes small mammals, birds, amphibians, and reptiles. Crayfish are particularly targeted in some areas, and they may eat large quantities of grasshoppers during outbreaks." In winter, in northern regions, birds figure more prominently in the diet.

Audubon regarded this species as something of a squirrel specialist, although he also lists Red-winged Starlings (blackbird) and wounded ducks as favored prey. Audubon the hunter is presumably credited for an assist with regards to the wounded duck. I have seen Red-shouldered Hawk attempt to capture icterids foraging in mixed flocks, and when luring migrating Red-shouldereds, raptor banders typically enlist the (reluctant) services of House Sparrow or starling to lure birds, considering pigeons too large to interest this species. The talons of Red-shouldered Hawk are considerably smaller than those of Red-tailed Hawk, a bird that has little difficulty dispatching pigeons.

STATUS: While several populations appear to be stable and flourishing, including birds in south Florida, Texas, and California, in my home state of New Jersey the species is designated threatened. In New Jersey—its celebrated site fidelity notwithstanding—I have witnessed a 40-year decline in breeders, with 10 out

Sturdy stick nests are commonly placed in the crotch of a tree. Two or three young are typical. The three advanced juveniles on the top confirm that prey populations were adequate this breeding year. The bottom nest was situated in a suburban Connecticut park near a sidewalk with busy foot traffic. Top: Steve Sachs; bottom: Jim Zipp

The silvery plumage of this adult Red-shouldered Hawk is unique to some male Florida birds, but it is disappearing because of interbreeding with browner birds of several other subspecies.
Kevin T. Karlson

of the 11 breeding territories I am familiar with no longer supporting birds. This population decline has occurred concurrently with a statewide trend toward reforestation and forest maturation (habitat changes generally favoring this species). A reduction in amphibian prey numbers has been suggested as a possible cause of the decline. Habitat loss caused by suburban encroachment may also be a factor. However, I note the one active nest I am currently aware of overlooks a suburban front yard and has been occupied for at least five years. Eastern hawk count data (1974–2000) show "mixed trends," but the population may be "stable overall."

Broad-winged Hawk
Buteo platypterus

ETYMOLOGY: From the Greek *platys* for "broad," and *pteron* for "wing." See Alexander Wilson's observations below.

PROFILE: Said Wilson of his first encounter with the species:

> The Hawk was shot on the 6th of May, in Mr. Bartram's woods, near the Schuylkill [Philadelphia], and was afterwards presented to Mr. Peale . . . It was perched on the dead limb of a high tree, feeding upon . . . the meadow mouse. On my approach, it uttered a whining kind of whistle, and flew off to another tree, where I followed and shot it. Its great breadth of wing, or width

This dramatic shot of an adult Broad-winged Hawk seems much at odds with Audubon's observation that the bird lacked for "spirit." It has also been called "relatively sluggish and tame." Chipmunks almost certainly harbor a different view. Steve Sachs

> of the secondaries . . . struck me as peculiarities. It seemed a remarkably strongbuilt bird, handsomely marked, and was altogether unknown to me. Mr. Bartram, who examined it very attentively, declared he had never before seen such a Hawk.

Audubon was less flattering in his account of the incubating bird he procured from its nest, noting: "I saw that it was new to me, and then felt vexed that it was not of a more spirited nature, as it neither defended its eggs or itself . . . Its eye, directed towards mine, appeared truly sorrowful."

Leon Augustus Hausman is more flattering in his assessment of the bird but hardly more objective: "the Broad-Winged Hawk might very well be called the Gentle Hawk, for of all our birds of prey it is the mildest and least suspicious." Bent calls the bird "gentle, retiring, quiet . . . " and Brown and Amadon say it is "relatively sluggish and tame."

Our regard for birds of prey seems ever tainted by how they react to human intrusion rather than how they comport themselves in nature. Wilson's meadow mouse would undoubtedly have offered a different opinion.

DESCRIPTION: The Broad-winged Hawk is a compact, crow-sized hawk of mixed deciduous eastern forests. It is our smallest buteo, but one that shows all the traits of the genus: a largish head, a robust body, and a short tail with wingtips falling short of the tail tip. The typical adult has a uniformly dark brown back and an all-dark head with barely a hint of a pale supercilium and a dark malar stripe. The bill is small, and the eyes are brown.

The breast is covered by a near solid chestnut bib going to barring on the belly; the base color of belly and undertail is whitish. The blackish tail is bisected by one broad and one narrower pale grayish band that may not be visible on perched birds.

A Broad-winged sampler. Adults above and juveniles below. While typically a forest raptor in migration and in Central and South America, where many Broad-wingeds winter, the birds at breeding sites sometimes perch-hunt from utility lines. Note the variation of underpart markings on these three juveniles. Top middle and top right: Steve Sachs; all others: Kevin T. Karlson

Juveniles are proportioned like adults and similarly dark backed and dark headed but lack the chestnut bib. They are mostly white below, with thick brown streaking down the sides of the neck that grows thicker and more extensive (blotchy) near the bird's midsection, often forming the semblance of a dark belly band on more heavily marked individuals. The juvenile's tail is brown with multiple dark bands. A rare dark morph, which is more common in the western part of the range (rare in the East), has a solid blackish brown body, but has the tail pattern of light morphs.

MEASUREMENTS
Length: 13–17 inches
Wingspan: 32–36 inches
Weight: 11–17 ounces

SYSTEMATICS/SUBSPECIES: Six subspecies are described, only one of which, *B. p. platypterus,* occupies the North American mainland. The balance are West Indies endemics.

Among buteos, this species is most closely related to Swainson's Hawk and Common Buzzard, a Eurasian species.

VOCALIZATIONS: The call is a high, clear, piping, two-note whistle. The first note is short, while the second is higher and held.

DISTRIBUTION: The Broad-winged Hawk breeds across the forested regions of the eastern and central United States (excluding the Florida Peninsula) and eastern Canada. The breeding range extends north across southern Canada west to at least Alberta, north of the prairies and south of the taiga. In the United States, it is widespread in the forests east of the prairies. In winter, it wholly vacates its breeding range. Excluding weakened or injured birds and except for a small number of mostly juvenile birds found in south Florida, from November to March all North American mainland Broad-winged Hawks relocate south of the United States, occupying a winter range that extends from southern Mexico to Peru and Brazil. They also winter in the West Indies.

HABITAT: For the most part, this is a forest buteo that spends much of its life between the lower forest canopy and the forest floor. It nests primarily in large tracts of deciduous and mixed deciduous-coniferous forest, commonly near water, and seems more accepting of younger forest and nest trees than does Red-shouldered Hawk. It favors forest types broadly defined as "humid broad-leafed forest."

In winter, it is found in a variety of (largely forest) habitat types but will hunt the edges of cultivated land as well as plantations and may be seen sitting on utility lines in open habitat, also during migration. Wintering birds are found in a variety of rainforest habitats, including second-growth forest, coffee plantations, and forest borders.

MIGRATION: The Broad-winged Hawk is a celebrated migrant, distinguished by its tendency to fly in large massed flocks. Every fall, the entire North American mainland population relocates to wintering areas mostly south of the United States, including South America. Broad-winged is among the earliest raptor migrants in fall and the latest in the spring. Because the distance the birds cover is great, the

A perch-hunting adult Broad-winged Hawk in typical breeding habitat. The implications of the hunting perch notwithstanding, Broad-winged Hawk is not a cavity nester. Like other buteos, it builds a stick nest. In the Northeast, it favors hemlock groves for nesting habitat. Jim Zipp

migratory periods are protracted—from February into early July in spring, and from August into November in autumn, with most individuals already well south of the United States border by the end of October. Despite the protracted duration of the journey, it is typical for the bulk of the migratory population to pass any given point along the route in a two-week period. Fall counts in excess of 2,000,000 individuals have been tabulated at Veracruz, Mexico. Kevin Karlson experienced

a single-day count of over 700,000 birds in late September 2002.

Broad-winged Hawks migrate along a broad front in daylight, with a dedicated reliance upon thermals to gain altitude at little energetic cost. It has long been suggested that the timing of the Broad-wingeds' migration is linked to its dietary focus upon cold-blooded prey, but it may also be linked to thermal production. A later departure in fall or earlier return in spring would mean fewer hours of daylight. And the sun's lower angle relative to the horizon in North America would mean weaker and less widespread thermal production, making flight more time consuming and less energetically efficient. While broad-fronted in nature, the flood of migrants is directed and concentrated by geography and weather.

A somewhat rain-dampened individual in typical tropical "winter" habitat in Ecuador.
Brian Sullivan

While a forest buteo, Broad-winged Hawks are most celebrated for their migratory flocking behavior. The soaring birds in this migratory kettle are catching an energy-friendly ride aloft within a rising thermal. Elevation gained, the birds stream out in search of the next thermal. On this day in Veracruz, Mexico, in 2000, over 700,000 Broad-wingeds were counted by experienced hawkwatchers from Pronatura, Mexico. Kevin T. Karlson

Broad-wingeds typically avoid crossing large bodies of water, which are thermal-impoverished. Confronting water barriers, Broad-wingeds may concentrate and divert along lakeshores, bays, peninsulas, and narrow land bridges like the Isthmus of Panama. This creates massed concentrations involving multiple flocks of birds, numbering in the thousands in places of key concentrations. This species is also drawn to updrafts along mountain ridges, particularly on days when thermal activity is diminished by cloud cover. The bird's flocking strategy and temporally concentrated migratory period may also assist birds in finding thermals.

In fall, big Broad-winged movements commonly follow the passage of a cold front. The first southbound Broad-wingeds begin their migration in early August, although some mostly juvenile birds may still be seen at northeastern watch sites into November. Across most of North America, however, the bulk of the migrants passes in September. In Veracruz, Mexico, an average 1,904,262 Broad-wingeds are counted every autumn, and seasonal totals have exceeded

Dark-morph Broad-wingeds are rare in the East, more common in the West. This beautiful juvenile is in a full soar, all sails fully spread to get the most out of the thermal. Note the characteristic candle flame–shaped wing configuration. Brian Sullivan

2,000,000 birds. Spring counts at Veracruz average 84,948 and have exceeded 150,000, attesting to a large and healthy breeding population.

In spring, birds may begin their return migration as early as late February, with big movements numbering in the thousands crossing the Rio Grande Valley of Texas in April. Continuing north, usually with the assistance of warm southerly winds flowing ahead of advancing cold-air masses, a few breeding birds may arrive on territory in New England or southern Canada in early April. But most breeders arrive in early May, with some second-year birds still straggling north into early July.

BREEDING: Courtship begins soon after arrival. Most breeding birds are at least two years old, but second-year birds are occasionally paired with an adult. In Kansas, birds arrive between April 19 and 25. In New Jersey, birds arrive from early April to early May. Birds arrive independently, and pair formation is established within a week of arrival. Courtship involves high circling over prospective nest sites and frequent calling.

Typical nest sites are in moist, contiguous deciduous or mixed deciduous-coniferous forests, and nests are frequently near water and/or forest clearings. Unlike Red-shouldered, this species typically builds a new nest every year; however, pairs commonly use the same woodland tract for successive seasons. The stick nests are flimsy. They are "carelessly built and are about crow-sized, often situated in the first main crotch of a typically less than mature deciduous tree (30–90 ft. high)." Birds tend to nest away from human habitation. Primary construction material is dead sticks and twigs. After the nest foundation is completed, the female ferries in chips of bark or a sprig of evergreen to line the nest bowl. Construction takes two to four weeks.

A typical clutch is two or three eggs. Eggs may be white, pale creamy, or slightly bluish, variously spattered with brown, and are incubated wholly or mostly by the female for 28 to 31 days. Young begin fledging at about five or six weeks, but typically remain in the natal territory for an additional four to eight weeks.

BEHAVIOR/HUNTING: A sentinel forager, a Broad-winged Hawk spends a large portion of its hunting time scanning for prey, often from an open perch below the forest canopy or seated on a perch at the forest edge. In migration and in winter, it sometimes hunts from utility lines along roadsides and along forest edge. The bird's demeanor when hunting has been described as "catlike."

PREY: This species is a "prey generalist," targeting insects, amphibians, reptiles, small mammals, and birds. According to Leon Augustus Hausman, caterpillars of large moths are a particularly favored summer prey item. Small mammals and amphibians are the most frequent prey. During the breeding season, nestling birds figure in the hawk's diet. More invertebrates may be consumed on southern nonbreeding grounds.

STATUS: Easily one of the most abundant of the North American hawks. This species may have benefitted from reforestation in the Northeast, but deforestation in Central and South America may limit habitat for wintering and migrating birds. Based upon count data from Veracruz, Mexico, where the entire population of this species passes annually, it appears that Broad-winged Hawk's population is stable or increasing in North America.

Caribbean populations may be threatened by deforestation. In Puerto Rico, the race *brunnescens* is proposed for listing as endangered. Observations from eastern hawk counts from 1974 to 2000 lead Bildstein to determine that the Broad-winged population is "stable or possibly declining but unclear."

Gray Hawk
Buteo plagiatus

ETYMOLOGY: *Plagiatus* is the perfect passive participle of the Latin *plagiare,* or "to kidnap." This species was formerly called Mexican Goshawk.

PROFILE: This handsome, spirited, tropical and subtropical raptor has earned the respect of many and has caused no small measure of consternation among taxonomists. Smallish for a buteo, and imbued with the vim of an accipiter, the

The adult Gray Hawk of the American Southwest and south Texas ranks among our most handsome raptors. Wherever it is found, hunting perches are requisite. Jim Zipp

"Mexican Goshawk" was ranked among the *Buteo* in 1957, removed in 1997, then returned to the *Buteo* ranks in 2015. Few birds of prey are distinguished by such taxonomic diffidence.

DESCRIPTION: Gray Hawk is a small, Broad-winged–sized buteo and one of the woodland buteo group, an assemblage that includes Roadside Hawk, Red-shouldered, and Broad-winged Hawk. One description calls it "intermediate in shape between typical buteos and accipiters, with relatively short wings, longer tail and longer, narrower tarsi than typical buteos."

Adults, with their mostly gray plumage and barred underparts, bear more than passing resemblance to Northern Goshawk (hence the former name, Mexican Goshawk). The head, back, and breast of the adult is uniformly dark gray, and its undertail is white. The gray tail has several black bands. The brown-

The hunting flight of the Gray Hawk is swift and accipiter-like. Adult, left; juvenile, right.
Left: Tom Johnson; right: Ned Harris

Juvenile Gray Hawks typically remain in the breeding territory of parents after fledging. The bird on the right is in classic habitat; the bird on the left shows the bright white cheeks and sparse, crisp, dark spotting on the underparts that are typical of this species. Greg Lasley

backed juvenile, with heavily spotted or streaked white underparts, closely resembles a more contrastingly patterned immature Broad-winged Hawk, but it has a whiter cheek and a more crisply defined face pattern. The back of the juvenile is mottled with white and buff. Adults and young both show a bright yellow cere, yellow legs, and brown eyes. The juvenile's tail has narrow black bands.

MEASUREMENTS

Length: 14–18 inches
Wingspan: 32–38 inches
Weight: 13–23 ounces

The female is noticeably larger than the male, a distinction easily noted when birds are engaged in aerial courtship.

SYSTEMATICS/SUBSPECIES: The Gray Hawk's taxonomy is problematic. Until 2015, it was considered conspecific with the more southern Gray-lined Hawk (*Buteo nitidus*). Underscoring the taxonomic challenges related to this species, the bird was formerly placed in its monotypic genus (*Asturina*), although this bird's close kinship to buteos was always widely recognized. Among raptors, it appears most similar to Red-shouldered

Hawk (*Buteo lineatus*), Roadside Hawk (*B. magnirostris*), and Ridgway's Hawk (*B. ridgwayi*).

VOCALIZATIONS: Displaying birds utter what Sibley describes as a "descending long, plaintive whistle." He also describes the alarm call as a "high, squeaky *KEE-errrrrrrrrr*," which is commonly heard before the bird is seen.

DISTRIBUTION: In the southwestern United States, Gray Hawk is found in southern Arizona, New Mexico, and southern Texas, primarily in the Big Bend region and along the southern Rio Grande. In Arizona, most birds breed along watercourses linked to the Gila River watershed, in Texas along the Rio Grande watershed. Gray Hawk numbers are believed to be increasing in Arizona, yet ongoing and mounting concern for the health of permanent riparian waterway forests extends by association to Gray Hawk.

MIGRATION: In the United States, birds are migratory, departing in October and returning in late February through March (middle to late March in Arizona). A few birds are occasionally reported in breeding areas in winter, and there are winter records for extreme south Texas.

HABITAT: Gray Hawk is a bird of scattered groves and riparian forests, often in semiarid regions. Tall trees associated with permanent streams (primarily cottonwoods) and homesteads near lakes

Opposite: *Gray Hawks commonly nest in tall trees, often along riparian corridors; however, their preferred hunting habitat is mesquite-hackberry thickets.* Greg Lasley

seem important for nesting; otherwise, this bird does well foraging in mature mesquite and hackberry bosques that are open at ground level. Hunting perches are requisite.

Elsewhere in tropical America, this species is not generally found in heavier humid forests and commonly hunts in the same habitat and targets the same prey as Roadside Hawk. Snyder, citing Glinski, advances the observation that in North America, the species appears to require both riparian cottonwood forest for nesting and mature mesquite-hackberry bosques for hunting. The dense nature of mesquite forests provides an evolutionary explanation for the short wings and accipiter-like nimbleness of the species.

BREEDING: Pairs form as soon as birds reach breeding territories in mid-March to early April. Nest building occurs immediately and is especially evident in April. The stick nest, which is frequently located in a large cottonwood, is often concealed by foliage. Both adults participate in nest building, with the male bringing in most of the dead twigs, and the female shaping the nest. The single clutch of one to three white to bluish white (usually unmarked) eggs is deposited early to late May. Only the female incubates, and it lasts 32 to 34 days, with young fledging at about 42 days of age. Adults have one brood per season, and young frequently remain in the breeding territory after fledging.

BEHAVIOR/HUNTING: Gray Hawk is primarily a passive perch-hunter, spending much of its life beneath the canopy, but it also perches in the open when hunting, most notably and nimbly upon utility lines. Prey sighted, it glides to intercept, deftly plucking prey from branches and the ground. Its flight is "swift and Accipiter-like." In forested areas, it typically hunts below the canopy.

PREY: Reptiles, lizards, and snakes constitute 80 percent of the Gray Hawk's diet, but it also takes a variety of birds up to the size of Gambel's Quail. In Arizona, despite the bird's evident ties to riparian corridors for nesting, aquatic prey is an "uncommon component in Gray Hawk's diet," a selectivity that un-

derscores the significance of mesquite-hackberry bosque in proximity to nest sites where favored prey are located.

STATUS: There are thought to be fewer than 100 pairs of Gray Hawks in the United States, with the San Pedro River near Sierra Vista constituting the bird's breeding stronghold. Approximately half of the Gray Hawks breeding north of Mexico are found along the San Pedro's watercourse, making this very obviously a natural area of paramount importance to this and other subtropical birds breeding in the United States.

When closing on prey, Gray Hawks may set their wings and glide. Ned Harris

Short-tailed Hawk
Buteo brachyurus

ETYMOLOGY: From the Greek *brachys* for "short," and *ours* for "tail," even though its tail is not especially short for a buteo.

PROFILE: A small (Broad-winged Hawk–sized) feathered meteorite of tropical and subtropical regions, appearing in a light and dark morph. In the United States, dark morphs are more common, but in Central and South America the reverse is true. This somewhat understudied raptor is an aerial hunter that is easily overlooked by both humans and prey.

The Short-tailed Hawk's North American breeding range is limited to Florida and southeast Arizona. In Florida, light-morph birds, like the one pictured here, outnumber dark morph. Brian Sullivan

DESCRIPTION: The adult light morph is dark brown above, including an all-dark head; the underparts (including the throat) are bright white and unmarked. It may show a touch of chestnut on the sides of the neck just below its dark hood. The feet and cere are yellow. The juvenile is like the adult but the chestnut neck patch is replaced by streaking. Wingtips on perched birds reach the tail tip, as com-

Short-tailed Hawk, like this dark morph, is a fairly common fixture in the winter skies over the southern tip of Florida, much to the consternation of displaying male Red-winged Blackbirds, whose flashing red epaulets are, to this aerial predator, tantamount to a bullseye. Brian Sullivan

pared to the wings of the Broad-winged Hawk, which fall short of the tail tip.

The body of dark-morph birds—except for the yellow feet and cere—is all brownish black. The dark juvenile is similar but shows a dark chest, with the bal-ance of the underparts heavily mottled (i.e., dark but showing touches or a spat-tering of white). In both morphs, the gray tails of adults and juveniles show darker bands, with juveniles showing more and narrower bands. The sexes are similar.

MEASUREMENTS
Length: 15–17 inches
Wingspan: 32–41 inches
Weight: 12–20 ounces

SYSTEMATICS/SUBSPECIES: Two subspecies are recognized: *B. b. fuliginosis* inhabits North America south to Panama, and *B. b. brachyurus* occurs in South America.

VOCALIZATIONS: Sibley describes the Short-tailed Hawk's call as "high, clear *keeeea* long and drawn-out, sometimes quavering." It is often likened to a Broad-winged Hawk's call.

DISTRIBUTION: Short-tailed Hawk is found locally from Florida and central Mexico south through Brazil. In the United States, it is historically limited to the Florida Peninsula, but beginning in the 1980s a few birds appeared in summer in the Chiricahua Mountains of southeast Arizona, where they have apparently bred successfully and been seen annually by many observers (myself included). In Florida, it may breed north to

Short-tailed Hawk the way this aerial hunter is rarely seen—perched. This is a dark-morph juvenile photographed near Miami, Florida, where they now hunt songbirds in typical suburban locations. Larry Manfredi

This adult light-morph Short-tailed Hawk spent quite a long time hovering and gliding over an open field and adjacent hammock in the Florida Everglades. Kevin T. Karlson

the Florida Panhandle, so it essentially breeds the length of the peninsula. In winter it withdraws to Lake Okeechobee and south, but a few birds remain in north to central Florida and the eastern panhandle. Wintering birds are most concentrated in the southern Everglades to the northern Keys.

MIGRATION: Birds migrate to and from wintering areas that lie generally south of Lake Okeechobee March through May and August through June. At Curry Hammock State Park in the Florida Keys, an average of 295 birds are counted during fall migration.

HABITAT: Short-tailed Hawks nest in dense or open woodland stands in either flooded or upland locations. They inhabit mixed woodland (of many types) and savanna. There is some suggestion birds require "extensive forest tracts for nesting." Millsap specifically mentions cypress and bay swamps. Outside of Florida, they breed in a variety of open woodlands. In Mexico, they frequent pine-oak ridges at altitudes of 6,500 feet—habitat similar to that found in the sky island forests of southeast Arizona. Other forest types this species occupies include humid tropical and deciduous. These hawks seem particularly partial to hunting along forest edge, but they also hunt over closed-canopy forest and open country (such as prairies, marshes, and pastures). In winter in southeastern Florida, some birds hunt over suburban areas.

BREEDING: In Florida, most breeding occurs from early February to late March. The courtship display is similar to that of other buteo species, involving "high circling, sky dancing and tumbling." Nests in Florida are bulky, constructed primarily of sticks and Spanish moss. The male provides most of the sticks, but after the eggs hatch the female brings leafy branches to the nest (especially cypress twigs). Bent described one nest in a "very dense cypress swamp." It was in "the top of an immense cypress tree, about 20 feet from the trunk at the end of the largest limb, 95 feet from the ground." There seems a strong tendency for birds to use the same nesting area year after year, but they typically do not use the same nest for more than two consecutive years and commonly build a new nest every year.

Two eggs are the typical clutch, with eggs "dull white . . . usually with brown spots and blotches." Incubation lasts 34 days, with pairs rearing one brood per season.

BEHAVIOR/HUNTING: While it's described as a "rather sluggish, tame buteo," I find this small bird-hunting specialist at home in the sky, where it seems to spend most of its time, gliding high over the forest edge on open, fixed wings, progressing in a precise stop-and-go manner as it traces the outline of the ecotone below.

The Short-tailed Hawk is a consummate aerialist that soars and cruises high over bird-rich, open environs. It is a master of stop-and-go control, but in a stoop it is nothing short of a feathered meteorite. Both juveniles, the left bird is a light morph, the right a dark morph. Left: Jerry Liguori; right: Kevin T. Karlson

Of all other North American raptors, only White-tailed Hawk seems able to micromanage its progress through the air so precisely.

Kiting as it does at great heights amid the avian detritus of the thermal-rich Florida sky—the multitudes of soaring storks, vultures, and anhingas—a single, cruising Short-tailed Hawk easily goes undetected, as many a displaying male Red-winged Blackbird has learned, to its sorrow. Prey sighted, the Short-tailed may parachute down to close the gap or simply fold up and drop in a near-vertical stoop. It typically hunts at altitudes in excess of several hundred feet, and stoops may penetrate the forest canopy, but most avian prey is situated in the tops of shrubs in more open or broken habitats—hence the peril to displaying Red-winged Blackbirds, which seem a particularly favored prey and whose flared epaulet must be to Short-tailed Hawk as galvanizing as the flick of a matador's cape in the face of a bull. This hawk is occasionally seen diving upon birds in flight.

Short-tailed Hawks are generally solitary, but during migration they are sometimes found in small groups.

PREY: While birds constitute over 90 percent of its prey, this species also captures small numbers of rodents, lizards, and insects. Avian prey includes birds up to the size of Sharp-shinned Hawk.

STATUS: Although the population size and trends have not been rigorously studied, we know that this species is never common. Bent offered this bleak historic perspective: "In Florida . . . it [Short-tailed Hawk] always has been extremely rare and local, and now I believe it has almost, if not quite, disappeared from that state." Happily, Bent's assessment was incorrect. While recent population data is sadly lacking, a population count in 2004 estimated about 250 pairs of Short-tailed Hawks in Florida. Recent increased sightings throughout the state—including in suburban neighborhoods—suggest an increase in numbers. Its status in Florida is uncommon to rare, while an Arizona population is very small and geographically restricted but expanding. Elsewhere, it is "uncommon and thinly spread" but "not globally threatened."

Swainson's Hawk
Buteo swainsoni

ETYMOLOGY: Ornithologist Charles Lucien Bonaparte named this buteo for contemporary William Swainson of England and New Zealand. This species, first collected in 1827 near Saskatoon, was initially identified as Common Buzzard (*Buteo buteo*) but later reexamined and confirmed to be a new and different species by Bonaparte, who then named it after Swainson.

PROFILE: A stiletto-winged buteo of open grasslands that spends much of its time aloft and almost a third of its life migrating between the two geographic poles that define its existence—the prairies of western North America and the ecologically similar Pampas of Argentina. This said, the bird's most typical habitat might therefore constitute the thermal-rich airspace overlying the land route that knits the North American prairies and the Argentine Pampas, a distance

An adult light-morph Swainson's Hawk is caught in the act of rousing. This open-country buteo is adept at both cruise- and perch-hunting, keeping ground squirrels close to their burrows. Jim Zipp

of some 6,000 miles. Since they migrate perhaps four months of the year, it might fairly be advanced that Swainson's Hawk lands only to breed, feed, and roost. Its migratory prowess notwithstanding, and owing perhaps to this species' penchant for feasting upon large insects it finds on the ground, Brown and Amadon describe Swainson's as a "rather sluggish, tame buteo."

DESCRIPTION: Swainson's Hawk is a medium-sized, long-winged, and long-tailed buteo whose wingtips reach its tail tip when it is perched. The plumage shows a light morph, a dark morph, and an array of intermediate plumages. "In all plumages the basal half of the tail, seen from above, is whitish." The sexes are similar, but the female is larger.

The adult light morph is uniformly

A Swainson's Hawk adult sampler. From left (top and bottom): adult light morph, adult intermediate plumage, and adult dark morph. Because of a variety of appearances between the consistent light and dark morph plumages, we use the terminology "intermediate plumage" for birds in between the two. Clockwise from top left: Jerry Liguori, Brian Sullivan, Brian Sullivan, Kevin T. Karlson, Jim Zipp, Brian Small

blackish brown above with a dark head and a grayish tail, showing a dark subterminal band. The face, throat, and underparts (except for the chestnut bibbed breast) are white. On perched birds, the white face and petite bill help distinguish it from Red-tailed and Ferruginous Hawk, which occupy the same prairie habitat.

The juvenile light morph shows a pale brown head that sets off a dark eye line and a malar stripe. The eyebrow and the forehead are buffy. The buffy throat is streaked, with the streaking heaviest on the chest, forming a splotchy bib reminiscent of the adult's chestnut bib. By spring, many second-year birds appear pale headed, and their tails are severely abraded after months of ground feeding.

Dark-morph adults are uniformly dark and lack the white face. However, intermediate-plumaged birds do have a white face, and two-toned underparts, with a buff to rufous belly and a darker browner chest (a bib). Juvenile dark morphs are a darker, more heavily streaked version of light-morph juveniles.

MEASUREMENTS
Length: 17–22 inches
Wingspan: 47–54 inches
Weight: 1.3–2.7 pounds

SYSTEMATICS/SUBSPECIES: No subspecies are recognized. Swainson's is most closely related to White-tailed Hawk (*Geranoaetus albicaudatus*), Galapagos Hawk (*B. galapagoensis*), and Red-backed Hawk (*B. poecilochrous*) and may, with these species, constitute a superspecies group.

VOCALIZATIONS: A long, high scream, similar to that of Red-tailed Hawk but clearer and weaker. It also gives a series of whistled notes.

DISTRIBUTION: This species breeds widely across western North America, from the Great Plains north, sparingly to the interior of Alaska, south into the arid grasslands of Arizona, New Mexico, and west Texas, into northern Mexico. It breeds east to the borders of the prairies—Minnesota and northern Iowa, central Kansas, central Oklahoma, and central Texas. West of the Sierras, Swainson's breeds in the San Joaquin Valley of California. The bird's status in Alaska, Yukon, and the Northwest Territories "needs clarification" but there is evidence of nesting.

It winters principally on the grasslands of Argentina. Brown and Amadon

considered birds found elsewhere along the migratory route "casuals . . . (individuals unable to make the long migration)." However, since at least the 1950s, a small number of Swainson's Hawks have wintered in south Florida.

MIGRATION: Migration is this bird's forte. Among North American raptor migrants, Swainson's Hawk is the long-distance champion, a title it shares with Peregrine. It is a complete migrant, with the entire population vacating breeding areas in North America and relocating, for the most part, to wintering areas in Argentina—a round trip that may exceed 12,000 miles. Fall migration begins in late August and extends to late November; spring migration extends from February to mid-April.

Beginning in late August, the end of

A juvenile Swainson's Hawk sampler. From left (top and bottom): light morph, dark morph, and intermediate plumage. Bottom left: Karl F. Lukens; all others: Brian Sullivan

the breeding cycle, Swainson's Hawks "gather in large flocks, wheeling and circling in the air as they gradually drift southward," beginning their journey to the Pampas.

Snyder notes that in late summer and early fall, the Swainson's Hawks in the Southwest often gather in agricultural lands, where they take large numbers of grasshoppers before heading south. Olendorff estimates each bird consumes "thousands of grasshoppers in late August and September . . . Small fat deposits throughout their bodies are glutted for energy source during the long southward flight."

Migrating in large flocks, sometimes called "kettles," these aggregations move generally southward along a broad front over land, mostly at hours of peak thermal activity. However, Kerlinger suggests that flocking may be a particularly useful strategy early and late in the day, when thermals are scarce—birds fan out in a line to increase their chances of intercepting randomly encountered thermals.

Swainson's Hawk is an "obligate flocker," migrating in large assemblages, and may at times migrate with other obligate-flocking species, such as Turkey Vulture and Broad-winged Hawk. Swainson's may locate thermals by random encounter or by actively searching out individual birds or kettling birds rising in thermals ahead. Once in a thermal, members of the flock benefit by watching those individuals who are outclimbing neighbors, so that they can maneuver themselves to take advantage of the sector offering the greatest vertical ascent, near the core of the thermal. At times of peak thermal activity, noon to midafternoon, birds typically fly at altitudes be-

yond the reach of our unaided eye, and it is only when numbers of birds coalesce into a kettle that we note their presence. These clustered flocks (some numbering in the hundreds) are large and dense enough to appear on Doppler radar.

Migration typically occurs along a broad front unless flocks encounter some concentrating mechanism, either a water barrier such as the Gulf of Mexico, or a geographic chokepoint such as the Isthmus of Panama. Here, aggregations numbering in the thousands may be seen. Birds are also concentrated by energetic opportunity, when local weather or geography produces a fortuitous migratory corridor or "street."

Flocks commonly follow along similar flight paths because thermals may occur in "patches, zones, or waves," creating a thermal "street." Smith calculates that birds entering such a street may be able to sail great distances in a "straight line without losing altitude" and without resorting to energetic flight. In the absence of streets, birds typically rise to the top of a thermal, set their wings, and glide to the next thermal, trading altitude for distance along the way. When thermal production diminishes, birds go to roost in large aggregations, in groves of trees where available, or on open ground (including tilled land) where elevated perches are unavailable. Studies of radio-tracked adult birds disclose that Swainson's Hawks were averaging over 118 miles a day.

The broad-front migration continues with little to concentrate or direct birds until easternmost migrants reach the Gulf of Mexico, resulting in thousands of birds passing over Corpus Christi, Texas. Flocks at such geographic chokepoints

A particularly stunning dorsal view of a juvenile Swainson's Hawk taken in Virginia Beach, Virginia, where this western buteo is very uncommon in fall migration. Brian Sullivan

may number from 5,000 to 10,000 individuals. Between 400,000 and 900,000 migrating Swainson's Hawks are recorded at Veracruz, Mexico, every autumn. In spring, counts at Veracruz average 34,537. (This great exodus has been described as "the most impressive avian gathering since the demise of the Passenger Pigeon.")

The flocks reach Panama by late October to early November. Birds reach Argentina in January. It is believed that the birds fast during their entire 6,000-mile journey, although some feeding has been noted before birds leave the United States.

Spring migration begins late February to mid-March, with birds returning to Alberta and Saskatchewan in late April and early May. They spend as much as a month and a half to two months traveling to or from Argentina, so up to four months of every year are spent commuting, during which time they apparently do not feed. The absence of droppings and regurgitated pellets at migratory roosts supports this supposition. A fasting strategy that allows birds to fly over vast expanses of unsupportive forest habitat in large flocks that would otherwise compete for food resources is dependent upon energetically cheap thermal lift. This reliance upon thermals is also what binds Swainson's Hawk to a land route.

HABITAT: This is historically a species of open prairies and extensive grasslands, as well as deserts. It is also found in irrigated alfalfa fields, particularly when crop has been harvested and grasses are the same height as native prairie grasses, making prey more accessible. In winter, it is found where alfalfa has been grazed by cattle and where sunflowers and corn are abundant. The birds sometimes roost on tilled fields, but more commonly in trees. The preferred habitat is mixed to short grassland habitats with scattered trees.

BREEDING: Nest building begins 7 to 15 days after arrival. Swainson's Hawk is a late nester, with birds in Canada laying in the last half of June, and early July in Alaska. In Arizona, it nests earlier; Bent quoted Lieutenant H. C. Benson as having found 41 nests between March 12 and April 18, 1887, near Fort Huachuca. Nests are typically situated in "scattered trees" located in "grasslands, scrub lands," and now, agricultural landscapes. Benson's 41 nests suggest a very healthy population once flourished in the desert grasslands that dominated the region before the introduction of cattle.

Nest trees are frequently isolated, and in 50 percent of cases, nests are freshly built. Otherwise, refurbished nests of this or other species (most notably magpie) are used. Nests are typical of buteos, bulky affairs "constructed of large sticks, finished off with twigs, leaves and grasses." Most nests are in "commanding situations." Brown and Amadon offer nest size to be three or four feet in diameter. Bent records nest heights ranging from 10 to 15 feet, and one nest in Medoc County, California, recorded to be 100 feet high in a yellow pine. Nesting territories are limited by a shortage of suitable trees, as well as competition with other earlier-nesting raptors, most notably Great Horned Owl and Red-tailed Hawk.

A normal clutch is two eggs (rarely three or four) that are mostly white, "only obscurely and palely marked with brown." Incubation takes 34 or 35 days. Earlier estimates of 28 days are now discounted. The young fledge 38 to 46 days after hatching, and 10 days later young may be found well away from the nest but remain in the adults' territory, where they are largely dependent upon adults for food. Egg laying through fledging takes about 73 days. One brood per season is the rule, which is to be expected given that adults are away from breeding territories for five or six months in California, and seven or eight months in Saskatchewan.

BEHAVIOR/HUNTING: Except during breeding season, Swainson's Hawks are highly gregarious, although small flocks of nonbreeding birds (late migrants?) may occasionally be seen together during the summer. They are often seen perched on a fencepost, haycock, or even on the ground, though they prefer a knoll if one is available.

In North America, Swainson's Hawks forage in open grasslands, shrub steppe, and agricultural land. In winter, they are found abundantly in alfalfa fields and cropland. John May offers this account of Swainson's hunting technique: "coursing over . . . open prairies . . . with slow, rather sluggish, circling flight until it sights prey, when it suddenly is transformed into an alert and skillful hunter." Swainson's Hawk "often hunts from perches . . . when hunting pocket gophers, perches near fresh mounds waiting for gophers to push fresh dirt to the surface, then pounces" stiff-legged on the mound and extracts the gopher. Snyder reports that it is a fire follower and it also follows tractors.

Flocks sometimes hunt crickets and grasshoppers on the ground, "appearing from a distance as they hobble about, like half grown turkeys." Birds stand upright, searching the ground ahead, then walk or hop forward and pounce upon insects, securing them with their feet or leaning forward and grasping with their bill.

One May, I found a flock of 30 or so second-year birds hunting for insects in a grassy bowl on the Pawnee Grassland of Colorado and was impressed by the array of techniques. Some were stalkers, walking or hopping. Others stood tall and immobile, searching the grass around them. A few frustrated birds would take wing and fly to a more likely looking spot not

Swainson's Hawk nests are bulky affairs, often situated in isolated trees. Jim Zipp

already occupied by another feeding bird. Prey sighted, the bird would usually lean over and secure the insect with its bill, then transfer the morsel to a foot before halving it and bolting down the prize.

PREY: It is prey that holds the secret to this bird's two-hemisphere strategy for survival. In summer, during the nesting season, it feeds primarily upon vertebrate prey, particularly upon the seasonal abundance of small mammals, including ground squirrels, pocket gophers, and voles, an energetic package that meets the nutritional needs of growing young and justifies the expenditure of time by adults. Other prey includes snakes, small birds, rabbits, and reptiles. Ornithologist Elliott Coues says "their prey is ordinarily nothing larger than gophers." But,

noted C. H. Merriam, "Those I shot after mid-summer all had their craws stuffed with grasshoppers." However, Smith and Murphy claim "insects are only a small portion of the diet of breeding birds."

The winter diet is dominated by insects. In Argentina, the hawk is known as the "locust hawk." Its primary prey is grasshoppers and crickets, prey that is also targeted by nonbreeding (second-year) birds in North America and by birds putting on weight as they prepare to migrate.

STATUS: Hawkwatch counts at Veracruz, Mexico, which approximates the North American population of Swainson's Hawks, have averaged near 675,000 birds from 2011 to 2014, with a high count of 943,346 in 2009.

This adult Swainson's Hawk has evidently strayed into a Cassin's Kingbird's territory. Jim Zipp

A stunning near-adult White-tailed Hawk framed against a Texas sky. Bill Clark

The world population is estimated to exceed 1,000,000 birds, and while serious declines have been noted in California, overall the population appears to be increasing across much of North America.

This species' increasing focus upon agricultural land, most notably alfalfa and other hay, renders it particularly susceptible to changing farm practices. Swainson's Hawk has also shown itself to be particularly vulnerable to some insecticides applied to crops. In 1995, in Argentina, nearly 6,000 Swainson's Hawks were killed when an organophosphate insecticide was applied. Some birds were killed by direct exposure to the spray, others by ingesting poisoned grasshoppers.

White-tailed Hawk
Geranoaetus albicaudatus

ETYMOLOGY: The species name comes from the Latin *alba* for "white," and *caudat'us* for "tailed."

PROFILE: This handsome aerialist is distinguished by its precise stop-and-go control and its very restricted U.S. distribution.

DESCRIPTION: This large and striking buteo of tropical and subtropic regions is typically found in semiarid open country. Arguably our most striking bird of prey, the adult has a gray head and back

Although the prey is indeterminable, this adult White-tailed Hawk has presumably had a successful hunt. Small mammals as large as rabbits are typical prey. Kevin T. Karlson

set off with blackish wings, russet shoulders, and gleaming white underparts. The tail is bright white with a single, broad, black subterminal band. Juveniles are overall blackish brown above. The dark head has a narrow white eyebrow, a white cheek patch, and a narrow white malar stripe (so three white touches upon on a dark head and face). The heavily streaked midsection contrasts with a bright white breast and undertail coverts. The tail is pale gray with a dark tip. Early second-year birds' underparts show vestiges of the juvenile pattern, being bisected by fine dark horizontal barring that contrasts with its white breast. Third-year, or subadult, birds are more similar to adults, but have dark markings on the underparts, and mottling on the underwing coverts, and they lack the

dark trailing edge to the flight feathers that adults have. Sexes are similar.

MEASUREMENTS
Length: 18–22 inches
Wingspan: 49–53 inches
Weight: 1.5–2.7 pounds

SYSTEMATICS/SUBSPECIES: Three subspecies are currently recognized. *G. a. hypospodius* occurs from Texas through Mexico to northern Columbia and western Venezuela. *G. a. colonus* occurs from eastern Colombia to Suriname south to northern Brazil. There is a rare dark morph ascribed to this subspecies. *G. a. albicaudatus* is the southernmost race, and its range extends from southern Brazil to northern and central Argentina.

Closely related to White-tailed Hawk

is the Galapagos Hawk (*B. galapagoensis*), a Galapagos endemic, and the Red-backed Hawk (*B. polyosoma*) of the High Andes.

VOCALIZATIONS: "A high-pitched cackling," likened to the bleating of a goat or cry of Laughing Gull.

DISTRIBUTION: Despite a huge latitudinal distribution, ranging from Texas to Argentina, in the United States the White-tailed Hawk is geographically restricted to the Gulf prairies of southeastern Texas from southern Galveston Bay to the Rio Grande. It formerly bred in Arizona. In Texas, the bird is fairly common but local, with the greatest concentration of breeding adults in the Coastal Bend region.

Adults remain in or near territories year-round. Immatures may wander as

A juvenile White-tailed Hawk sampler. Note the variation in dark plumage on both the flying and perched birds. Also note the different flight profiles of the gliding bird (top left) and soaring bird (bottom left). Clockwise from top left: Bill Clark, Bill Clark, Ned Harris, Kevin T. Karlson

far as Louisiana and gather in aggregations, particularly in the event of grass fires or management burns, which these birds then hunt over, seeking prey dislodged by the flames.

MIGRATION: The White-tailed Hawk is nonmigratory.

HABITAT: In the United States it is found exclusively in the coastal savanna of Texas—a semiarid grassland savanna dotted with bushes, stunted trees, and Spanish bayonet. Elsewhere this buteo is found in semiarid open country but also dry open woodland and moist palm savanna; exclusively shrub-steppe in northern Argentina. Cultivated and fallow fields are shunned, but lightly grazed cattle pasture is utilized. Coastal Texas is an incessantly windy place, and watching this consummate aerial predator exploit the wind, I am brought to speculate whether a strong and dependable wind component might

A juvenile White-tailed Hawk in classic coastal Texas habitat. Lightly grazed cattle pasture is prime foraging habitat for this species. Brian Sullivan

An accomplished aerialist, the White-tailed Hawk spends much of its time quartering across the sky. Brian Sullivan

not also be an important element in the bird's habitat profile.

BREEDING: In Texas, this species selects sites where grass dominates. But the actual nest is commonly placed in woody or succulent vegetation (Spanish bayonet is a very commonly used support). Unlike many other grassland buteos, this species shuns artificial structures. Nests are typically low—5 to 15 feet from the ground or even lower—with sites offering a slight elevation and a commanding view preferred. Nests are good-sized platforms made of twigs with hardly any lining. Nests may be reused but not necessarily every year. Breeding season runs from February through May, with peak laying March 11 to 20.

Clutch size ranges from one to three with two eggs typical. Eggs are "greenish white, blotched with brown or unmarked." The incubation period is 29 to 32 days. Fledging is between 49 and 52 days. The young remain with the adults until the following breeding cycle—about seven months—and continue to be fed by the adults. In Venezuela, juvenile dependence up to 21 months is noted.

BEHAVIOR/HUNTING: White-tailed Hawk is a consummate aerial predator demonstrating a mastery of the air unmatched by any North American species except Short-tailed Hawk. It spends a good deal of its time soaring and gliding. It kites expertly, studying the terrain below, but it also hovers, spiraling or parachuting lower when it sights prey. It frequently attends grass fires, often in small groups of up to 60 individuals. It commonly stoops or plunges in a step-down manner, with the bird descending to narrow the distance between itself and its prey. Then, with wings partially folded, and turning into the wind, and kiting once again, the bird makes its final adjustments before stooping.

Before sunrise and at sunset, they may elect to perch-hunt. Perches include bushes, trees, telephone poles, and the ground.

PREY: The diet is variable, but in Texas small mammals as large as rabbits are typical prey. It also targets small to medium-sized birds, specifically Northern Bobwhite, King Rail, Mourning Dove, Eastern Meadowlark, and Prairie Chicken. Fears that the very rare Attwater's Prairie Chicken constitutes a large portion of the hawk's diet are apparently exaggerated. Reptiles, mostly snakes, are also an important part of the White-tailed Hawk's diet. Other prey includes crayfish and several large insect species.

STATUS: The species was apparently more numerous a century ago. Bent's 1938 work references the Texas population as "a rather common resident . . . plentifully distributed." Twenty years later, Sprunt says, "the White-tailed is far less in evidence now than only a few years ago." He attributes the decline to a "diminution of food supply and alteration of habitat . . . " In particular, Sprunt cites a decline in rabbit numbers.

Probable causes of decline in Texas include brush removal and overgrazing. Populations in Texas are "stable if not increasing," though the species is still listed as threatened. In 1977, it was estimated there were 200 breeding pairs in Texas.

The Snyders note an ecological compatibility between this species and the cattle-grazing practices endemic to the coastal prairies.

A White-tailed Hawk sampler showing (left to right): second year, third year, and adult. Left: Bill Clark; middle and right: Kevin T. Karlson

Zone-tailed Hawk
Buteo albonotatus

ETYMOLOGY: The species name comes from the Latin *alba* for "white," and *notatus* for "marked."

PROFILE: This is a tropical and subtropical buteo whose signature characteristic may be confusion. Early in the 1800s, there was confusion on the part of ornithologists, who had difficulty distinguishing this species from the similarly plumaged but behaviorally dissimilar Common Black-Hawk. But confusion also appears to be part of Zone-tailed's

A soaring adult Zone-tailed Hawk. This bird-catching Turkey Vulture mimic combines ruse with cunning to gain an advantage over avian prey. It is carrying a Cedar Waxwing in its talons, although that is hard to make out at this stage of capture. Brian Small

playbook. This species closely resembles and even associates with Turkey Vulture, a likeness and affiliation that is presumed to give this aerial bird hunter a strategic edge, lulling prey into a false sense of security or at least momentary indecision. Nonhunting carrion feeders, Turkey Vultures are largely ignored by the birds that Zone-tailed Hawk calls prey. Whether the hawk's similarity in shape and plumage and slow, wobbling flight constitutes active mimicry of the vulture is debatable. But reason and evidence suggest that the hawk does gain strategic advantage from its likeness to the benign scavenger.

The evidence in support of mimicry is broad and well reasoned. Unlike most buteos, which have a distinct juvenile plumage, young Zone-taileds have the same all-blackish Turkey Vulture–like plumage worn by adults, so young are advantaged at precisely the time when their hunting skills are rudimentary. Additionally, as noted by Bent, "its flight is lazy and sluggish." Such a speed-impoverished species that targets small, fast-flying open-country birds (such as meadowlarks and doves) in its diet might be expected to need some strategic edge to secure prey.

It should also be noted that nowhere does the range of Zone-tailed Hawk extend beyond that of Turkey Vulture. Also telling is Zone-tailed's limited numbers. While not uncommon, this species is nowhere concentrated. Surprise is contingent upon a tempered application of ruse. Were prey species continually plagued by predatory vulture look-alikes, their nonchalance in the presence of cruising Zone-taileds and vultures would soon change. It has also been noted by multiple observers that Zone-taileds elect to fly among groups of vultures, and Snyder noted increased hunting success when Zone-taileds were thus escorted.

Zone-taileds are not commonly seen perched. This active aerialist spends much of its time aloft.
Brian Sullivan

This adult Zone-tailed Hawk sampler shows various wing configurations. Left: Brian Sullivan; middle and right: Jerry Liguori

DESCRIPTION: The Zone-tailed Hawk is often described as a "medium-sized" buteo, despite measurements that are similar to Red-tailed and Swainson's Hawks. Perched adults appear overall blackish except for several broad, grayish white tail bands. The cere and legs are bright yellow (like Common Black-Hawk's). However, unlike the Black-Hawk, which has a very distinctive juvenile plumage that is held for one year, and except for the tail pattern, juvenile Zone-taileds are overall blackish like adults. In flight, the flight feathers are silvery gray, like Turkey Vulture's. The juvenile Zone-tailed's tail has multiple narrow dark bands, while the adult's bands are broader and fewer.

The bird's strong resemblance to Turkey Vulture has been discussed, but this likeness cannot be overemphasized. Confusion by human observers is not just possible—it is likely.

MEASUREMENTS
Length: 19–22 inches
Wingspan: 48–55 inches
Weight: 1.3–2.4 pounds

Females are considerably heavier than males, a dimorphic peculiarity particu-larly evident among bird-catching specialists.

SYSTEMATICS: This is a monotypic species whose taxonomic position within *Buteo* is uncertain. The first specimen for the United States was collected February 23, 1892, near San Diego by J. G. Cooper, but it was initially and incorrectly identified as Harlan's Hawk, a bird now widely regarded as a subspecies of Red-tailed Hawk, *B. jamaicensis harlani*.

VOCALIZATIONS: Brown and Amadon describe a "feeble screaming," and Sibley says it is "clearer and lower than Red-tailed."

DISTRIBUTION: In the United States, Zone-tailed breeds in Baja California and is fairly widespread in Arizona, north to the Mogollon Rim; it also breeds in southern New Mexico. In Texas it breeds in the Big Bend region to the Davis Mountains; also in south-central Texas. Its breeding range extends south into Mexico and Central and South America, where it is "widespread but rare or local." In South America, its distribution nearly encircles the Amazon Basin, but this species apparently shuns the rainforest ecosystem.

There is a famous story regarding this species that illustrates the hazards of ornithology and the pluck of early ornithologists in the American Southwest. As the story goes, Major Charles Bendire was in the process of securing Zone-tailed Hawk eggs from a nest near what is now Tucson, Arizona, when from his elevated position he noted "several Apache Indians crouched down at the side of a little canyon." Placing the egg in his mouth, he descended to the safety of the ground, his horse, and his shotgun . . . then "lost no time getting to high and open ground."

How the Apaches interpreted this ornithological endeavor is open to speculation. But it is certain the white man's appetite for uncooked hawk eggs must have led to some ribald discussion around the campfire.

Can you tell the Turkey Vulture from the Turkey Vulture mimic? If you are a Montezuma Quail, your life depends on it. Kevin T. Karlson

MIGRATION: In winter, this species mostly withdraws from the United States and north-central Mexico, although some overwintering is reported. In the United States it departs in October and returns February to March.

HABITAT: Zone-tailed Hawk is generally a bird of dry habitats, but beyond that is something of a habitat generalist, hunting over mixed types of forests, including gallery forest, tropical deciduous forest, and pine-oak forest. It is often found foraging over adjacent open country. It is also frequently seen cruising mountain ridges, semibroken scrub, and riparian woodland habitat, where it commonly nests.

BREEDING: In the United States, courtship begins as soon as birds arrive, mid-March to mid-April. Both sexes engage in nest building. In Arizona, this species typically nests high in tall trees, sometimes in cottonwoods along desert streams, sometimes in pines in more mountainous regions. In western Texas, it nests on cliffs approximately 200 feet high.

The nest is a "rather bulky affair of sticks." Most egg laying is from late March to mid-May. Brown and Amadon describe the nest as "coarsely built and rather bulky."

Two egg sets are the rule—occasionally one or as many as three. Incubation is 28 to 34 days, with the female doing most of the incubating. Fledging occurs in 35 to 42 days. Adults continue to tend to young for another four to eight weeks.

BEHAVIOR/HUNTING: Despite their reputation for sluggishness, Zone-taileds spend an inordinate amount of time aloft, or, as assessed by Brown and Amadon, "This was without doubt the most active Buteo and perhaps with the exception of Swallow-tailed Kite the most active raptor, surpassing even the falcons."

Zone-tailed is beyond question an aerial hunter, a coursing hawk, mapping a search pattern in the manner of a harri-er but from much greater heights—130 to 500 feet above the ground. It may stoop in the manner of a buteo when it sights prey or retreat out of sight and approach "in a shallow stoop," using obstacles for concealment.

PREY: That the Zone-tailed Hawk is capable of speed and finesse at close quarters is clearly evidenced by its mostly vertebrate prey, including birds, but also small mammals (chipmunks especially) and lizards, specifically collared and spiny lizards.

Addressing again the question of how a "slow-flying raptor" is capable of

---

Unlike most buteos, Zone-taileds have adultlike plumage when fledged, but young may be distinguished from adults by their finely banded tail and white flecks on the underwing coverts. Fledglings, like the one on the left, have whitish heads. Nests are a rather bulky affair, and two young are typical. Note the prone form of the second bird in the nest. Ned Harris

---

targeting avian prey, including and most notably open-country species like meadowlarks and doves, which the Snyders assess to form "an important part" of the Zone-tailed's diet, the biologists draw attention to the "bird's long toes and claws," that are in size and configuration much akin to other bird-catching specialists like the Peregrine.

Bent's observation that "The zone-tailed hawk evidently feeds mainly on lizards, frogs and small fishes, which it finds along the beds of the streams where it lives," clearly harks back to the early confusion between this species and Common Black-Hawk, a hawk whose diet does indeed favor aquatic fare.

STATUS: This species is rare in the United States. In a 1976 survey, Snyder and Glinski tallied 100 known nesting locations north of Mexico. This species has been known to wander well outside its range, including a record from Nova Scotia in 1914 and two from New Jersey and Massachusetts in September 2014 and 2015.

While Zone-tailed Hawks are nowhere common, this adult (right) next to a juvenile Turkey Vulture was photographed in Cape May, New Jersey, where they are decidedly very rare. This October 2015 bird constituted only the second record for Cape May, and was probably the same bird that occurred the year before at almost the exact same date. This bird moved north in late summer to Connecticut both years, and then migrated back south. Mike Lanzone

Red-tailed Hawk

Buteo jamaicensis

ETYMOLOGY: *Jamaicensis* means "of Jamaica."

PROFILE: Driving along a fairly typical four-lane highway, this one in southern New Jersey, my mind preoccupied with the initial stages of this book, I spied a raptor perched along the flanking woodlands about two-thirds of the way up on what appeared to be an oak. It was a big, burly, pale-breasted buteo with a ragged band across its midsection and its eyes fused to the grassy median.

What made this encounter notable? The very fact that it is not. Millions of drivers motor past Red-tailed Hawks hunting in this fashion every day.

If not the most common and wide-

Because of its namesake trait and wide distribution, Red-tailed Hawk wins the title of North America's best-known raptor. This image captures something of the venatic finesse enjoyed by this versatile raptor. This photo of a first-year western Red-tailed Hawk was taken from a Utah ridge. Jerry Liguori

spread of North America's raptors, it is (Bald Eagle excepted) certainly the best known, thanks in no small part to the adult bird's very apparent and namesake trait, the bright reddish tail brandished by most of this hawk's 16 subspecies. This buteo also has the ability to acclimate itself to habitats modified for our species' multiple proclivities, making it ubiquitous.

For most people, for much of the year, finding Red-tailed Hawks is as easy as commuting to work, thus making it a regular raptorial roadside attraction. It wasn't always thus. Before the eastern forests were felled and human ingenuity and fire suppression brought trees and artificial perches to the prairie landscape, Red-tailed Hawks were somewhat less common than they are today. In fact, for a time, their numbers were halved by misunderstanding. Alexander Wilson, in his *American Ornithology,* mistakenly considered the "American Buzzard" (or juvenile Red-tailed) a distinct species.

Observing that these "pale brown" tailed birds were lacking the adult Red-tailed Hawk's distinctive red tail and also "two or three inches larger," Wilson allowed that the differences between the two apparent species (which, he correctly noted, did occupy the same habitat) might simply be a matter of age.

In this, Wilson was correct. Juvenile Red-tailed Hawks fully acquire the namesake red tails of adults by the second fall of their lives. As for the disparity in size, the length of the wings and tails of juvenile Red-taileds do, indeed, exceed those of adults, making them appear overall rangier in flight.

Wilson's confusion was understandable and perhaps prescient. Confusion (or at least debate) about Red-tailed plumage is a matter that persists today, although the focus has shifted to the differentiation of morphs and forms as opposed to age classes.

DESCRIPTION: This is a large, robust, boldly but variably patterned raptor whose football-shaped profile is often seen balanced upon some conspicuous perch. It is polymorphic, showing a light, dark, and intermediate morph, with western birds showing the most variation. Light-morph

birds are the rule in the East, although there is much variation in pattern.

In size and weight, Red-taileds are always larger than Broad-winged Hawks and (almost always) Red-shouldered Hawks; they are always smaller than Golden and Bald Eagles. Ferruginous and Rough-legged Hawks are larger than all but the largest Red-tailed Hawks.

Red-tailed plumage is highly variable. Differences relate to age, sex, subspecies, and particularly three color morphs—light, intermediate, and dark. Adult light-morph and intermediate-plumaged birds are classically dark (brownish) above and paler below, with underparts bisected by a broad, streaked band (belly band). Mostly dark upperparts are spattered with pale touches, with the lightly spangled scapulars typically forming a mottled V on the backs of many perched birds, particularly juveniles. Intermediate birds show the same plumage pattern, but their underparts are darker (redder on adults, heavily streaked on juveniles) so that the belly band, while broad, dark, and full, is less conspicuous than on light-morph birds.

Dark-morph birds are overall dark (dark chocolate to black), and the body plumage of adults and juveniles is similar.

Only adult birds show the bird's namesake trait: a conspicuously red tail that ranges from chestnut to orange-red to a rose-colored blush. The tails of some adult birds have narrow dark bands. The tail of adult Harlan's Red-tailed is highly variable, but classic birds have a dark-tipped, all or mostly gray tail that may be streaked or infused with red and whitish streaks.

The brownish tails of juvenile Red-tailed Hawks have multiple narrow dark

This Red-tailed Hawk sampler shows an array of plumages. Clockwise from left: adult light-morph Western, adult dark-morph Western, adult intermediate-plumaged Western, juvenile dorsal, adult dorsal, adult Eastern. Top middle: Brian Sullivan; bottom left: Kevin T. Karlson; all others: Jerry Liguori

bands. The red tail feathers of adults are assumed gradually during the juvenile bird's first molt cycle, which typically begins in June of the bird's second (or "after-hatching") year and is complete by October.

It is typical for the underparts of juveniles to have a whiter base layer and a darker, bolder, more contrasting pattern on the underwings and belly than most adult birds (adult light-morph Harlan's excepted). The breasts and underwing coverts of adult birds are commonly blushed with rose or orange tones; belly bands are fainter, even inconspicuous (or, in the case of very faintly marked birds, missing). Albinism is not uncommon in this species.

MEASUREMENTS
Length: 17–22 inches
Wingspan: 43–52 inches (East),
47–56 inches (West)
Weight: 1.5–3.3 pounds

SYSTEMATICS/SUBSPECIES: Among North American raptors, the Red-tailed Hawk has the distinction of boasting the largest number of North American subspecies. Though 14 subspecies are generally cited, as many as 16 are recognized by various authorities. As mentioned, though, such classifications are not above question or future revision. For example, debate continues about the status of Harlan's Hawk, currently regarded as a subspecies, a non-red-tailed "Red-tail." More

A juvenile Red-tailed sampler. Birds do not get fully red tails until autumn of their second year. Clockwise from top left: dark-morph Western, light-morph Western, intermediate-plumaged Western, Eastern, dark-morph Harlan's, and Krider's. Top left, top center, and bottom left: Brian Sullivan; bottom right: Kevin T. Karlson; all others: Jerry Liguori

recently, it has also been suggested that the very-pale Krider's Red-tailed, historically considered a distinct subspecies, might instead be simply a very pale color morph of the Western Red-tailed, *B. j. calurus.*

The subspecies found north of Mexico include:

B. j. borealis. The Eastern Red-tailed occurs from eastern Canada south to northern Florida and west to the Great Plains. This subspecies shows the greatest range in size between males and females.

B. j. calurus. The Western Red-tailed occurs in North America west of the Great Plains. A very richly and diversely marked subspecies, it has light, interme-

diate, and dark morphs. Light morphs are more boldly marked than the typical Eastern Red-tailed. The adult typically has a finely banded red tail and a rufous—not pinkish—wash on the underparts. The juvenile's wings almost reach the tail when it is perched.

B. j. kriderii. Krider's Red-tailed is a pale prairie form with a tail that is nearly white. Observed John Krider of the bird that bears his name, "It is called by Baird the white red-tail. This bird I have found in Winnebago County, Iowa, in 1870. I first observed it flying at a distance and at first took it for an albino, but seeing several of them in company, together, was very anxious to procure one. They were very shy so much so that I could not get near them."

B. j. harlani. Harlan's Red-tailed is a mostly blackish, gray-tailed form that breeds in northern Alberta and British Columbia east of the Coast Range and interior Alaska. It also occurs in a light morph.

B. j. alascensis is slightly smaller than B. j. borealis and breeds from southeastern Alaska to the Queen Charlotte Islands. Peak wintering numbers are found in northeastern Arkansas, central Oklahoma, and Missouri.

B. j. fuertesi is resident in the desert Southwest to northern Mexico.

B. j. umbrinus, in peninsular Florida and the Bahamas, is found only as a light morph, like B. j. borealis, but the tail feathers have dark bars near the shaft.

Another possible race is B. j. abieticola, which breeds in the spruce-fir belt of northern Canada from Alberta to Nova Scotia.

VOCALIZATIONS: The call is a high, thin, slurred two-parted whistle, the first part higher, then dropping in pitch.

DISTRIBUTION: The Red-tailed Hawk is common and widespread. In North America, it is found at any point of the

The Harlan's Red-tailed, which breeds in Alaska and the Yukon, is a non-red-tailed Red-tail. While currently considered a subspecies, the bird has at times been regarded as a distinct buteo species. This is a light morph. Brian Sullivan

year, almost anyplace you are likely to be. Its breeding range extends from central Alaska across northern Canada to Nova Scotia, with the northern limits defined by the northern edge of the boreal forest. It extends south across all of the continental United States into Mexico, parts of Central America to Panama, and the Lesser Antilles. In winter, northern birds mostly withdraw to south of the Canada–United States border and the northern New England states. Declines in autumn hawk count totals in New Jersey and Pennsylvania suggest that more Red-tailed may now be wintering farther north.

MIGRATION: Birds from northern latitudes depart before winter, although they may be absent for only a few months. Migration is broad-front in nature, with birds using thermals for lift and—where convenient—updrafts off ridges. Fall migration is protracted, August into January, with young birds dispersing early and late-season movements often precipitated by blanketing snowfalls that prompt birds to relocate in search of easier hunting. Migrants may be solitary or move in small, loose groups ranging from two to ten birds. Groups are not uncommon, particularly at migratory bottlenecks. Spring migration is very early for birds breeding in middle latitudes, with some birds returning in February, while the bulk of spring migrants pass in March, and stragglers continue into June.

HABITAT: This species demonstrates "the widest ecological tolerance of any buteo." It sometimes occupies unbroken forest habitat, but at all times of year it shows

Opposite: North America's most celebrated Red-tailed Hawk and the only one with a street address. Known as Pale Male, he pays his rent by ridding the neighborhood of Norway rats. Pale Male was hatched in 1990, which makes him 26 years old! The oldest living Red-tailed Hawk was 30 years old in captivity when he died. Lloyd Spitalnik

a preference for generally open habitat studded with elevated natural or man-made perches. Almost any open area (frequently grassy) constitutes suitable foraging habitat; it also likes perches, so forest edge bordering grasslands is ideal. Other habitats include desert and open mature woodlands with little understory. It frequently hunts the center divide of interstates, and airports, agricultural land, marshes (fresh and salt), and prairie grasslands, as well as alpine meadows and tundra bordering or dotted with taiga forest. Becoming increasingly urbanized, birds have nested upon buildings in downtown areas, close to foraging areas provided by city parks.

Since the early 1990s, the bird known as "Pale Male" has resided at 957 Fifth Avenue on Manhattan's fashionable Upper East Side, giving him and his mate the distinction of being North America's only raptors with a New York street address. Pale Male and mates have bred for 23 years at this address. Currently on his third mate, Pale Male regularly hunts in nearby Central Park.

BREEDING: Aerial courtship-like displays may occur at any time of year but become most evident December through March. Nest building may begin as early as December in some (usually) southern locations, but it is more typical in February

and March. This species typically nests in mature trees, often situated near the crown of a taller tree with a commanding view. Both members of the pair engage in the construction of the large stick nests. While birds typically raise a single brood per nesting cycle, two or more nests per territory are typical, and it is common for Red-tailed to lose the previous year's nest to the somewhat earlier-breeding and nest-usurping Great Horned Owl.

Nest construction is fairly rapid, requiring a mere four to seven days. A sprig of greenery placed early on the outside of the structure may denote occupancy. Tree nests are usually situated in the upper canopy of a taller tree; Red-tailed also use artificial platforms and cliffs.

Even here in southern New Jersey, I have seen new nest construction begin as early as December. But upon completion, the nest was immediately appropriated by Great Horned Owl, obliging the Red-tailed to refurbish a different nest a half-mile away, but within sight of their first effort.

These two adult eastern Red-tails, brandishing their namesake trait, are in the initial stages of producing the one to three eggs that are typical of a nesting cycle. Steve Sachs

By kiting—holding into the wind, on motionless wings—Red-tailed are able to fashion hunting perches out of thin air. This bird is an adult intermediate-plumaged western Red-tail. Jerry Liguori

The one to three white eggs sometimes show a buffy wash and are variously marked with dark brown, reddish brown, or purple markings. The female does most of the incubating, with eggs requiring 34 days to hatch. Fledging takes an additional 42 to 46 days but young may remain in the parental territory for another 18 to 70 days. Juveniles begin capturing prey six or seven weeks after fledging but continue to be tended by adults for at least another week. Yet large numbers of juvenile birds are evident in Cape May, New Jersey, from late July to September in numbers that greatly exceed what might be produced by local breeders. Dispersal among juveniles may be lateral, northerly, or southerly, as Cape May observations attest and northwest winds provide.

Where they are resident, pairs remain together year-round and are often seen perching together. Birds from Alaska, Canada, and some northern states vacate breeding areas before winter, relocating south across the United States.

BEHAVIOR/HUNTING: For the most part the Red-tailed Hawk is a perch-hunting raptor that spends a large portion of its day sitting conspicuously atop an elevated perch overlooking open, often grassy habitat. In woodlands, it favors habitat with sparse or broken understory. It also hunts aloft, soaring or kiting over prey-rich habitat.

Prey sighted from perches is usually secured by using a set-winged glide. Prey sighted while aloft is frequently secured by employing a near-vertical stoop, with birds often binding to prey on the ground before flying to a safe and convenient perch to feed.

PREY: This species hunts an array of mostly small to medium-sized prey, favoring generally whatever is most common, whether this is voles, snakes, pheasant, or quail. In winter, in some areas it feeds almost exclusively upon meadow mice (*Microtus*). It is also partial to carrion.

STATUS: The Red-tailed population appears stable or increasing as birds and prey adapt to urban areas that are increasingly becoming "greener" environments. Using hawk count data from 1974 to 2000, Bildstein determined that western migrant totals were mostly stable during this period but showed slight declines after 1998. At eastern hawkwatch sites numbers were variable, but perhaps stable overall.

These three fractious and recently fledged juveniles are actually longer tailed and more slender-winged than adults. Looks like challenging times ahead for voles and other small mammals, fare favored by Red-taileds of all ages. Rob Curtis

---

Ferruginous Hawk
Buteo regalis

ETYMOLOGY: Ferruginous comes from the Latin *ferrugo* for "rust," for the rufous tones in the adult light-morph plumage. *Regalis* is Latin for "royal," in reference to the bird's size and upright posture or bearing.

PROFILE: "The . . . name *regalis* is a very appropriate one for this splendid raptor, the largest, most powerful, and grandest of our Buteos. It truly is a regal bird. Anyone familiar with this species cannot help being impressed with its kinship to the Golden Eagle, which is, for all its vaulted prowess, really just a glorified Buteo. Both species have feathered tarsi, both build huge nests on cliffs or trees and . . . the food, habits, flight, even the two raptors' behavior and voice are much alike."

DESCRIPTION: This is our largest buteo, with a large anvil-shaped head, barrel chest, and legs feathered to the toes. The adult light morph resembles a reddish-backed, pale-headed prairie eagle. Its folded wings almost reach the tail tip when it is perched. Like many buteos, it is dimorphic in size. The namesake rufous touches cover the backs of adults and extend to the wing coverts, flanks, and feathered legs. It has a large bill, a long gape, and large yellow feet. Its unbanded

Buteos and Allies • **173**

A Ferruginous Hawk sampler. Clockwise from top left: adult dark morph, adult light morph, heavily marked adult light morph, juvenile light morph, adult light morph, and adult dark morph. Clockwise from top left: Brian Small, Ned Harris, Brian Sullivan, Jim Zipp, Jim Zipp, Jim Zipp

tail is pale rufous (sometimes gray or white).

The light-morph adult has a pale head with gray cheeks, a rufous back, snowy white underparts, rufous legs, and barred rufous flanks that on some individuals may extend to form a belly band. The immature lacks rufous tones, showing grayish brown upperparts and a paler head. Its underparts are white, like the adult except the legs, flanks, and belly are darkly spotted, not rufous. The pale, grayish tail shows a dusky subterminal band. The uncommon dark-morph adult is stunning; except for its unmarked pale gray tail, it is overall solid dark brown, recalling cinnamon-dusted chocolate. The dark-morph immature is similar to the dark-morph adult but has a barred gray tail with a dusky subterminal band. Intermediate-plumaged birds occur, but are quite uncommon. The legs are feathered to the feet. Except for size, the sexes are similar.

SYSTEMATICS/SUBSPECIES: No subspecies are recognized, but there are two subpopulations, separated by the Rocky Mountains. Behavioral commonality with Golden Eagle notwithstanding, Ferruginous Hawk's ecological twin is actually the Upland Buzzard (*B. hemilasius*) of central Asia. Despite marked plumage differences, Olendorff suggests a kinship between these species dating back to the Bering land bridge.

VOCALIZATIONS: Sibley describes the voice as "a melancholy whistle; lower-pitched and less harsh than other buteos. Juvenile gives high scream."

DISTRIBUTION: Despite a breeding range as big as the western plains and inter-mountain West, the range of Ferruginous is more restricted overall than that of any other buteo in North America. This species is found in dry open country from eastern Washington, southern

Top: *This particularly well lit adult light-morph Ferruginous Hawk showcases the bird's distinctive rufous leggings.* Jerry Liguori

Bottom: *The intermediate-plumage condition of this Ferruginous Hawk is quite uncommon in this species. While Ferruginous Hawks use several hunting techniques, they hover more than most buteos.* Jerry Liguori

Saskatchewan and southwestern Manitoba south to eastern Oregon, Nevada, New Mexico, northwestern Texas, and western Oklahoma.

In winter, Ferruginous Hawk mostly withdraws from northern portions of its breeding range. It winters widely across California, south to northern Baja, western and southern Nevada, Arizona, New Mexico, portions of Utah and Colorado, Nebraska, the western half of Oklahoma, Kansas, and widely across Texas. It also goes south into the desert grasslands of Mexico.

MIGRATION: Northern birds are wholly migratory. Southern breeders may migrate short distances or may be sedentary. Among northern birds, migration begins August to October, with spring return in late February or early March. While routes are not known, it seems birds initially fly southeast before turning south and following grasslands.

HABITAT: This is an open-country specialist, with habitats ideally suited for the historically perch-poor American prairies. Ferruginous Hawk is primarily a bird of grasslands and shrub-steppe. "Badlands," says Sprunt. This species has a particular fondness for keeping its feet on the ground, using hilltops and sloping hillsides for hunting perches. It also commonly nests on the ground. When cliffs or trees are available, however, it readily uses them as perches and nest sites. In winter, birds concentrate around prairie dog towns and cultivated fields that house pocket gophers.

BREEDING: Southern birds may remain paired throughout the year and move to nesting territories in early March. In Utah, pair formation occurs from late February to early March. Ferruginous Hawks commonly use the same nest in consecutive years.

Courtship is not as flamboyant as

This is typical Ferruginous Hawk habitat. Unlike other buteos, this open-country hunter frequently hunts from a perch on the ground. Jim Zipp

Left: *Ferruginous Hawks build massive nests, and while they evidently prefer to nest in trees, ground nesting is still common. The impressive size of nests is perhaps a defense against wildfires that sweep across prairie grasslands.* Jim Zipp

is that of several other buteos. Observes Olendorff: "I have never heard of, or read about a courtship performance of Ferruginous Hawk that I would call extraordinary or acrobatic." Apparently, as far as pair bonding is concerned, this species would rather build than dance. Both members of the pair engage in building or refurbishing the nest. Olendorff notes that "nests are such a fetish to them . . . that two or more are visited and repaired each year." The species' nest-building ardor notwithstanding, refurbishment in some cases is limited to adding new sticks, twigs, and cow dung to line the bowl.

The nest itself is a bulky structure, consisting mainly of massive dead branches, far larger than the branches used by other buteos. Indeed, after the wholesale slaughter of the bison, bison ribs were a common if not primary component of Ferruginous nests. The birds also utilize manmade structures for nest support, most notably transmission towers in open country. The grand size of nests may be a testimony to the energy or ardor that pairs bring to their task, but it is almost certainly a throwback to a time when the prairies were more nest structure–impoverished than they are today, and this species was obligated to construct nests on hillsides often swept by grass fire, as opposed to trees, which the birds evidently prefer today. Where trees are available, Ferruginous typically uses the highest available, and lone trees are preferred. However, even in these structure-rich times, ground nesting remains common. Continued refurbishment results in nests that are both "massive and high"—12 to 15 feet high.

Eggs are white to bluish white, speckled or spotted with reddish brown, medium brown, buffish brown, or light purple. A typical clutch is two to four eggs, which is large for buteos, but clutch size may range from one to eight, depending upon prey availability. Incubation, conducted mostly by the female, is estimated to last 32 or 33 days. When not hunting, the male is often present, and nests are "rarely left unattended." Young fledge in 38 to 50 days, and the young leave ground nests sooner than birds leave tree-borne nests.

Young remain dependent upon adults for several weeks after feeding. Reproductive success is closely linked to densities of prey species. And in years of low prey density, the number of nesting pairs in a region may be half that found in prey-rich years.

BEHAVIOR/HUNTING: In summer, Ferruginous Hawks are typically solitary or found in pairs. In winter they frequently concentrate where large numbers of prey are found (particularly ground squirrels and prairie dogs). Aggregations of 6 to 12 birds are typical around such prey-rich habitats.

It is no easy task surprising prey in wide-open country that supports multiple rodent-targeting raptor species, including Swainson's Hawk, Red-tailed Hawk, Golden Eagle, and Prairie Falcon, as well as the present species. Ferruginous uses several hunting techniques, including low-level attacks from a low perch, with ground-to-ground strikes

enjoying a high rate of success. It also resorts to low-contour hunting flights along slopes and hillsides to surprise prey. This species' bag of tricks also includes high, soaring flight and hovering. It also hunts prairie dogs and other burrowing rodents on foot by waiting at burrow entrances. Ferruginous Hawk commonly perches on the ground in open country, using badger mounds and hillocks when trees or posts are unavailable. Most buteos typically seek more elevated perches.

PREY: This species appears to concentrate its efforts not necessarily where prey is most abundant but where cover is scant. While the talons of this species are quite small for a raptor its size, they are perfectly fitted to the capture of Ferruginous Hawk's primary prey, which are, for the most part, small and medium-sized mammals, including "rabbits, hares, ground squirrels, prairie dogs, with ground squirrels and prairie dogs being the most frequently captured prey." However, in some locations (such as Utah), jackrabbits constitute the favored prey. Small numbers of birds, amphibians, reptiles, and traces of insects round out Ferruginous Hawk's diet. The bison ribs that were historically a common component of Ferruginous Hawk nests were presumably there for structural support rather than nutrition.

STATUS: The present range is little changed from historical accounts, but some range retraction was noted at Canadian breeding areas during the 1900s because of agriculture and proliferation of aspen in prairie habitat. In 1992, the breeding population was estimated at 3,000 to 5,600 pairs.

Rough-legged Hawk
Buteo lagopus

A light-morph juvenile Rough-legged Hawk leaves a somewhat spindly perch. Jerry Liguori

ETYMOLOGY: The Rough-legged Hawk is named for its feathered tarsus, a trait it has in common with Golden Eagle and Ferruginous Hawk. The species name is from the Greek *lagos* for "hare" and *pous* for "foot," so "hare foot"—probably in reference to the bird's feathered shanks.

PROFILE: This is a large, handsome northern buteo of open country, where it spends considerable time aloft, hovering tirelessly, thus fashioning elevated hunting perches out of thin air. Audubon had a low regard for this species, say-

ing of it, "It is a sluggish bird . . . when alarmed flies low and sedately, and does not exhibit any of the courage and vigor so conspicuous in most other hawks." Yet Arthur Cleveland Bent regarded Rough-legged Hawk "a splendid bird, one of the largest and finest of our hawks."

DESCRIPTION: This is a large and lanky, boldly patterned, polymorphic buteo, with adult males and females showing different belly and tail patterns, but otherwise a mix of plumage patterns. Like several other buteos, Rough-legged has both a

It takes more than a light snow pack to daunt this handsome Arctic buteo. This is an adult male light morph. Evident are the fully feathered shanks that are the source of the bird's name; not pictured is the vole the hawk is almost certainly standing upon. Jerry Liguori

light and dark morph. In profile, it appears somewhat long necked and small billed. Feathered tarsi and rather small feet attest to the birds' northern proclivities and focus upon small mammalian prey.

The adult light morph is cold grayish brown above, and heavily and darkly marked below. The adult male has an all-dark breast, "a bib," and a heavily barred belly separated by a pale U-shaped band. The pale tail has multiple narrow bands and a single broad subterminal band. The generally more contrastingly plumaged female has dark streaks on a buff-colored breast (so lacks the male's bibbed appearance) but has a broad, blackish belly band that straddles the bird's darkly feathered legs. The head of the light morph is conspicuously pale. The light-morph juvenile resembles the female, but its broad

subterminal band is more diffuse, not so crisply defined.

The dark-morph bird is uniformly blackish (male) or brown (female). The dark juvenile is like the female but has a pale head. Intermediate-plumaged birds are uncommon to rare, and appear in between light- and dark-morph birds. In all plumages, the tail is tipped with a wide, dark subterminal band.

MEASUREMENTS
Length: 18–23 inches
Wingspan: 48–56 inches
Weight: 1.6–3 pounds

SYSTEMATICS/SUBSPECIES: Rough-legged Hawk is believed to be most closely related to Upland Buzzard (*Buteo hemilasius*) of central-eastern Asia.

Four subspecies are described:

B. l. lagopus occurs in northern Europe from Scandinavia east to the Yenisei River in Russia. It winters in central Europe and central Asia.

B. l. menzbieri breeds in Siberia and its winter range extends from Turkestan east to Manchuria and Ussuriland and occasionally in north China and Korea and Japan. Larger and paler than the nominate race, it is sometimes almost white, usually less heavily streaked, and lacks a breast band.

B. l. kamchatkensis occurs in Kamchatka and the coasts of the Sea of Okhotsk, south to the Gulf of Uda and north Kuril Islands, possibly in the Aleutian Islands. It winters in east-central Asia.

B. l. sancti-johannis occurs in North America. It is generally smaller, darker, and more variable than the other races.

DISTRIBUTION: This panboreal breeder is found between 61 and 76 degrees north latitude, roughly from Anchorage, Alaska, north to Melville Island in Nunavut, Canada. It is North America's only buteo with populations in Europe and Asia. In North America, it is found from the Aleutians to northern Quebec and throughout the islands of the Canadian Arctic Archipelago north to northern Ellsmere Island, and Alaska south and east to Labrador and south to the tree line and southern Hudson Bay. It occupies some of the smaller islands in the archipelago and in the Bering Sea far from the mainland.

In winter this species entirely vacates

A Rough-legged Hawk sampler. Clockwise from top left: adult light morph, adult female dark morph, adult intermediate plumage, adult female light morph, adult dark morph, and adult male light morph. Clockwise from top left: Kevin T. Karlson, Jerry Liguori, Jerry Liguori, Jim Zipp, Brian Sullivan, Kevin T. Karlson

its breeding range, spending the winter from southern Canada to California, southern Arizona, southern New Mexico, Texas, Missouri, Kentucky, and Maryland. It strays rarely to the Gulf Coast.

MIGRATION: Fall migration is late August through December, with most movement occurring from October into early December. Irregular, late-season southbound movements from January to March appear to be triggered by heavy snowfall in northern wintering areas, causing birds to relocate in search of easier hunting conditions. Spring migration is protracted, owing to the distance between breeding and wintering areas and the retarded nature of spring warmup in the Arctic. So it occurs from early February to late May, with peak passage through key hawkwatch locations from early March through early May.

Like many migrating raptors, Roughleggeds are concentrated along coastlines and show some affinity for ridges. Prime hawkwatching locations include Whitefish Point, Michigan, in spring, with an average of 859 birds per season, and Duluth, Minnesota, in fall, with an average of 487 birds per fall.

HABITAT: Rough-legged Hawk breeds in the Arctic tundra. Sometimes, in years of prey abundance, it penetrates south into the boreal-forest/tundra ecotone. It typically nests on cliffs, often cliffs associated with Arctic rivers. In open tundra, nests are commonly situated on sides of outcroppings. In rare cases it nests in trees, and also rarely nests on the ground. It will adopt manmade structures in the absence of suitable natural substrate, including buildings and radio towers.

Nests are frequently appropriated by cliff-nesting falcon in subsequent years.

In winter this species favors open treeless habitat with a grassy component. Prime habitats include prairie, semideserts, pastures, fresh and tidal wetlands, shrub-steppes, cultivated land, pasture, and lakeshores. Habitat use is contingent upon a high density of rodent prey and perhaps minimal snow cover. Successful hunting also correlates well with low ground cover. It roosts communally in conifers, cottonwoods, and other deciduous trees. When hunting, it utilizes perches as low as muskrat houses and as high as the springy tops of tall trees. Manmade structures, including and most notably utility poles, are readily accepted as hunting perches.

Winter and summer evidence suggests that the birds' territorial selection turns upon the availability of prey: they breed where they find it, and they winter where they find it in abundance.

BREEDING: Breeding birds reach the Seward Peninsula from late April to early May. But egg-laying dates vary year to year because of the timing of snowmelt on nest ledges. On Baffin Island, laying dates are mid-May to mid-July.

Courtship is abbreviated, limited to circling and calling, presumably in response to the very short nesting season, leading some to suggest that birds are paired on migration. Both adults participate in nest building, with the male apparently selecting the site and gathering most of the nest material, while the female constructs the nest. Bulky stick nests are usually situated on taluses and steep hillsides near the tops of cliffs and outcrops. Nests are described as a "jumble of sticks cemented together by excrement." Several nests may be located in close proximity, suggesting alternate nest use. Bent offers another illustrative description of a nest in Lapland, examined on June 5, and described as a "mass of dead sticks, about two feet thick, with a layer of solid ice about six inches thick immediately under the new grass lining on which the three eggs were lying."

Clutch size ranges from two to three eggs in years marked by low rodent numbers, and five to seven in good years. Egg-laying dates vary among sites, depending upon when ledges become snow-free. But on the Seward Peninsula, a relatively temperate location relative to the Brooks Range, first eggs are laid in the second week of May. Incubation lasts from 28 to 31 days. Fledging may occur when birds are 31 or 32 days old; however, "most remain in the nest for 40 days."

Juveniles then associate with their parents for the next two to four weeks, with the male providing food. Young apparently remain in the vicinity of the nest until migration, and dependency upon adults may extend into migration. However, note this observation by Lucien M. Turner: "The young appear to be able to take care of themselves as soon as they leave the nest." Such precociousness would have obvious advantages in northern latitudes, where snow and migration may begin as early as September.

BEHAVIOR/HUNTING: This bird is both a perch-hunter and an accomplished, near-tireless aerialist. Conditions may determine which strategy will prevail. Perches are often isolated trees or structures away from a wooded edge. Springy perches, such as the very tops of trees, are perfectly acceptable. In winter, though, it

---

An adult dark-morph Rough-legged Hawk. Showing dark eyes that help to age it as an adult, it seems none too pleased to have its hunting interrupted by yet another snowstorm. Brian Sullivan

---

A juvenile Rough-legged Hawk sampler. Note the pale eyes. Left to right: two light-morph juveniles and a beautiful dark morph from Washington State. From left: Kevin T. Karlson, Jerry Liguori, Brian Sullivan

commonly hunts aloft, sometimes high and in a quartering search pattern over large open country, like a high-altitude harrier. It frequently hovers at moderate heights, less than 500 feet above the ground, head turning side to side as it searches the ground below; then, setting its wings, it glides to the next likely patch, sometimes less than a hundred yards away, and hovers anew. If it sights prey it may descend to close the distance. Then, it typically drops vertically, pouncing on the prey. Most prey is captured on the ground.

In winter, when it's not soaring or hovering, it frequently perches (commonly on the highest point available), mostly erect, and with its wingtips reaching the buteo-short tail tip.

PREY: Rough-legged Hawk is a small-mammal specialist. In summer, it feeds primarily on lemmings and voles. In winter, it supplements its diet with small birds and targets a wider range of mammalian prey, including ground squirrels and rabbits. But voles are particularly favored, and Rough-legged Hawks concentrate where these mammals are found in accessible abundance.

Both Audubon and Wilson accounted the hawk a hunter of ducks, a notion at odds with Rough-legged's small feet and penchant for hovering. I personally know of just one instance of Rough-legged Hawk feeding on a Black Duck, one that it pirated from a Peregrine as the Peregrine fed on the ground, apparently unable to bear the duck away.

STATUS: There is no recent quantitative estimate on population, but Palmer accounted it one of the "most abundant species of raptor in the world." On the 2014 Christmas Bird Count, a winter survey that samples approximately 7 percent of the North American land mass, a total of 4,791 Rough-legged Hawks were counted. This figure includes both adults and juveniles, so it is a population near its numeric high.

Be that as it may, the bird appears nowhere near as common today in the Delaware Bay region as historic accounts allow. Noted John Krider in 1871, reflecting upon the wintering numbers of Rough-leggeds recorded near Philadelphia: "It was many years ago one of the most abundant of the hawk tribe that we had in the neighborhood of Philadelphia.

I have counted as many as twenty at one time in the meadows below the city . . . " It should be noted that Krider's tally does not include dark-morph birds, which Krider regarded as a different species. So his winter count is low by some unknown factor insofar as the historic ratio of light- to dark-morph birds is unknown and may not reflect current ratios, which, in the eastern United States, heavily favor light-morph birds. However, Krider does note, of the bird he called "Black Hawk" (dark-morph Rough-legged), that it could be seen "ten at one time in the meadows below the City of Philadelphia." So dark-morph Rough-legged Hawks were apparently more common in this region 150 years ago than they are today.

Today, writing in the winter of 2014–2015, it is a rare winter when a Rough-legged of any plumage spends the winter in the marshes of South Jersey, where I live, and where both Wilson and Krider collected and studied. This century-long decline may, of course, not relate to population but to a change in wintering distribution brought about by prey availability. Or perhaps it's due to climate change and reduced snow pack north of New Jersey, allowing Rough-leggeds to shortstop their migration and winter farther north than was typical when Krider studied the birds of the region in the latter half of the nineteenth century. Whatever the cause, while it is still common as an Arctic breeder and as a wintering species in other parts of the United States, there has evidently been a considerable reduction in the number of Rough-legged Hawks wintering in the former stronghold of the Delaware Bay watershed in the last two centuries—with the species going from "most abundant" to absent most years.

That this species has been persecuted by humans is incontestable. Even into the twentieth century, pole trapping was practiced in Delaware Bay marshes, and I once spoke to a Port Norris bayman who bragged to me about his prowess at ridding the planet of "Black Chicken Hawks." Happily, the persecution of raptors here and elsewhere is much diminished. The practice of pole trapping has been outlawed since the mid-1960s. Nevertheless, trends at eastern hawk counts lead Bildstein to the determination that annual numbers of Rough-legged Hawk are "evidently declining."

Typical habitat for wintering Rough-leggeds. Just add voles. While it does practice perch-hunting, this buteo is a tireless aerialist able to exploit prey-rich environs beyond the reach of perch-obligate raptors. Brian Sullivan

AQUILA EAGLES
One species

Golden Eagle
Aquila chrysaetos

ETYMOLOGY: The genus name is from the Latin *aguila,* for "eagle." The species name, *chrysaetos,* is from the Greek *chrysos* for "golden" and *aetos* for "eagle." The bird was called *chrysaetos* by Aelian, a Roman who wrote in Greek in the third century A.D.

PROFILE: The Golden Eagle is one of the planet's largest, most powerful, widely distributed, and celebrated birds of prey. While capable of killing prey larger than itself, this Holarctic species is primarily a predator of small to medium-sized mammals and birds. It has been an emblematic symbol of power and statehood going back at least as far as the Roman Empire, and an inspiration to poets and biologists alike.

Only slightly smaller, on average, than Bald Eagle, Golden Eagle nevertheless surpasses North America's other eagle in weight, hunting finesse, speed, and presence. It has even been known to drive the much larger California Condor, North America's largest aerial predator, from carcasses.

In my journalistic efforts to paint an accurate but compelling profile of this majestic bird I was initially and perhaps inexorably drawn to Alfred, Lord Tennyson's poem, "The Eagle":

> He clasps the crag with crooked hands;
> Close to the sun in lonely lands,
> Ring'd with the azure world, he stands.
>
> The wrinkled sea beneath him crawls;
> He watches from his mountain walls,
> And like a thunderbolt he falls.

DESCRIPTION: This is an impressively large buteo-like bird of prey with a poise and bearing that distinguishes it from lesser raptors.

Golden Eagle is overall blackish

This adult Golden Eagle perches regally atop a juniper in Arizona. Gerry Dewaghe

An adult Golden Eagle on the left, a second year on the right. Both birds show the classic buteo-like structure. Left: Brian Small; right: Jerry Liguori

brown, only here and there marred by touches of tawny or white. The bird's most eye-catching (and namesake) trait is, of course, the golden hackles that gild the head and nape with a regal sheen. Seen on young and adults alike, in poor light the golden hackles may seem no more than a veneer; in bright light the crown and nape fairly glow; seen head on, some individuals appear as light headed as an adult Bald Eagle, a species not closely related to this one. The bill is grayish with a dark tip. The feathered legs support large, yellow feet armed with long, dark talons. The sexes are similar, although females average larger than males.

The juvenile brandishes a bright white tail with a broad dark terminal band. It has white at the base of the inner primaries and secondaries that, in flight, shows as a large white wing patch that is visible above and below. The white portions of the juvenile's plumage are gradually replaced by brown over four or five years; however, some adults retain some measure of white in the tail.

MEASUREMENTS
Length: 27–33 inches
Wingspan: 72–87 inches
Weight: 6.6–14 pounds

SYSTEMATICS/SUBSPECIES: Brown and Amadon recognized four subspecies, although some sources cite five or six. However, only one form, *A. c. canadensis,* occurs in North America.

The nominate subspecies, *A. c. chrysaetos,* ranges across northern Europe and Asia.

Another subspecies cited by Brown and Amadon is *A. c. homeyeri,* of Spain and North Africa, which is "darker, duller and smaller than *A. c. chrysaetos* and *A. c. japonica* of Korea and Japan."

VOCALIZATIONS: This species is generally silent. The food-begging call of the young is the most often heard vocalization—a "series of chips, cheeps and high-pitched chitters."

DISTRIBUTION: Golden Eagle ranges widely but not uniformly across North America, Europe, and Asia, south to Mexico and North Africa. In North America, it is primarily a bird of the western and Arctic regions. It breeds from the North Slope of the Brooks Range in Alaska west to the Aleutians, east to northeastern Canada.

Formerly a breeder in the northeastern United States, it was never common. The western North American breeding population extends south to central Mexico and east to the High Plains.

In winter, it vacates the Arctic and northern regions, except for a few birds wintering along the southeastern coast of Alaska. Many birds breeding in the western United States and southwestern Canada are resident but in winter relocate to areas where prey is concentrated. Also in winter, this species is widely but "locally" distributed across the central and eastern United States. In winter Golden Eagle also expands its range eastward to southeastern Saskatchewan, the central Dakotas, central Kansas, western Oklahoma, and western Texas, and south into central Mexico.

MIGRATION: Spring migration is very early, from late February into May, with most birds migrating in March. Fall migration occurs September through December, with peaks in November and early December. In Alaska, most birds begin migrating before the end of September. This species shows an affinity for migrating along mountain ridges, where updrafts are favorable.

HABITAT: In North America it is primarily a bird of the West, found in open, often mountainous, rolling, or hilly terrain. Its primary breeding habitats include

Golden Eagles hunt from perches and aloft. They can often be seen soaring for long periods over western mountains and valleys. Brian Sullivan

"mountainous canyon land, rim rock terrain of open desert, and grassland areas of westsern U.S. Also nests extensively in riparian habitats in eastern Great Plains." In winter it also occupies waterfowl-rich wetlands—both fresh and tidal—as well as more forested areas in the Appalachians. These eastern wintering birds are birds breeding in northeastern Canada.

BREEDING: In temperate areas, pairs remain in the vicinity of nest sites year-round and nuptial displays may be seen at almost any month. Energetic and vocal displays are similar to those of many buteo species. In California, courtship and nest construction occur December to January. In Denali National Park, in Alaska, pair formation occurs as soon as adults arrive in late February to mid-April. Most nests are situated on cliff ledges but are sometimes in trees, or on manmade structures and on the ground.

Pairs typically have multiple nests, which they may use in rotation. As described by Audubon: "It is of great size, flat, and consists merely of a few dead sticks and brambles, so bare at times that the eggs might be said to be deposited on the naked rock." Brown and Amadon, too, commented upon the initial threadbare nature of nests on ledges, noting that when first constructed, they are little more than scrapes with branches around them; however, with time the structures become huge if the site permits. Tree-borne nests are necessarily more tightly constructed at the outset.

Typically, two eggs are laid at three- to four-day intervals, sometimes one, occasionally three. Eggs are white and usually "spotted or blotched with brown, chest-

---

Initial cliff nests are little more than bare earth ringed with branches, but over the course of successive seasons, cliff nests may assume gargantuan proportions. Tree nests may not become as grand, but they are, by necessity, structurally sound from the start. Left: Brian Small; right: Jim Zipp

This is not a good time to be a ground squirrel. Although the size of Golden Eagle's talons allows them to target much larger prey, small to medium-sized mammals are their preferred prey.
Jerry Liguori

nut red and pale gray." Incubation begins with the first egg, resulting in asynchronous hatching. Incubation lasts 43 to 45 days. Typically, elder siblings attack and kill younger nest mates. With fortune, surviving young fledge in 65 to 70 days, and generally remain in the vicinity of the nest for up to two weeks, where they may be tended to by the female.

BEHAVIOR/HUNTING: Golden Eagles employ several hunting techniques, each tailored to the conditions, terrain, and prey. The techniques fall into three broad categories: an aerial attack executed upon prey by a high soaring bird; still hunting from a perch; and contour cruise hunting (which is particularly effective in country with concealing hilly terrain, where prey are likely to bolt into burrows to make their escape.

Watson describes another hunting technique—the "walk and grab attack."

The Golden Eagle uses this technique when prey is secure under cover or, at times, when young animals have taken shelter beneath a parent. It is considerably less lurid but energetically apt and generally less risky than grappling with large animals. Golden Eagles also consume carrion. In fact, carrion may be a particularly important food source in winter.

While Golden Eagles take most prey on the ground, Forbush recounts a pursuit involving a Band-tailed Pigeon and a Golden Eagle. As the observer, F. C. Willard, summarizes, "Fast as the Band-tailed Pigeon is, I have seen it flying its fastest to get away from a pursuing eagle."

High soaring may culminate in the vertical stoop. The stoop is often used when the prey is large flocking birds, such as cranes or geese. But the high soar may also culminate in a "glide attack," a technique that seems well adapted to the capture of ptarmigan. Contour flights also may culminate in a glide attack or a tail chase. Watson also describes a slow descent attack for prey that is less agile (snakes, tortoises). Most dramatic is the "low flight and sustained grip attack" used to subdue large prey.

And while I do not doubt that Golden Eagle is strong and equipped to kill prey as large as full-grown deer, I do point out that most if not all written accounts I am familiar with are secondhand in nature, and that a degree of improbability has always been part of this bird's lore and allure. In point of fact, there is a long list of tabloid-worthy accounts of toddlers being carried away by eagles. At the time of this writing, there is a YouTube video of an infant allegedly being borne away by a Golden Eagle in a park in Ontario, Canada. Although admitted to be a hoax, the video has nevertheless been viewed millions of times. This was not the first time such a filmed hoax has been perpetrated: Thomas Edison also produced a movie that depicted a child being borne away by an eagle.

The sage Edward Howe Forbush, in *Birds of Massachusetts,* concludes in concert "with knowledgeable others" that "old tales of eagles carrying off children probably have little foundation in fact . . ." But he nevertheless includes an account (hearsay) of an attack by a Golden Eagle upon a nine-year-old girl in British Columbia.

PREY: Where they are found in fair abundance, Golden Eagles typically target mammals ranging in size from ground squirrels to hares and marmots. It is estimated that mammals comprise 80 to 90 percent of their diet. They secondarily

HISTORIC PERSPECTIVE

Before Europeans set foot on North America, Native Americans had established a special sacred bond with this species—akin to a messenger of the Great Spirit. According to Abenaki mythology, "The solar deity 'Kisosen,' meaning 'Sun Bringer,' was symbolized as an eagle whose wings opened to create the day and whose wings closed to create the night. Wad-zoo-sen was the spirit eagle that flapped his wings to create the wind." The thunderbird of Southwestern tribes is believed to find its biological source in the Golden Eagle, as a bird that symbolized courage, wisdom, and strength.

Among nonnative peoples, the most iconic representation between native people and Golden Eagles is the Indian headdress or war bonnet, crafted by (probably) the Lakota Sioux and made famous by Sitting Bull's appearances in "Wild Bill" Hickok's Buffalo Bill's Wild West Show and later by Hollywood movies. While headdresses incorporated the feathers of many bird species, those of the Golden Eagle were most prized, as they were awarded only to honor acts of exceptional leadership and bravery. A headdress adorned with Golden Eagle feathers was the Native American equivalent of a uniform bedecked with medals, campaign badges, and more.

Owing to their spiritual connection, the feathers of Golden Eagle "have been compared to the Bible and Crucifix of Christianity . . . Eagle feathers were also used to construct prayer sticks, doctor's rattles and medicine pipes."

An immature Golden Eagle displays the namesake golden hackles. This photo of a first-year bird shows the bird's focused intent and formidable talons. Brian Sullivan

target birds, and less often reptiles and fish during nesting season.

There are numerous, apparently authentic, reports of Golden Eagle killing large mammals. In his thorough treatment of this species, Jeff Watson includes "witnessed" accounts of Golden Eagle attacking and killing pronghorn antelope and red deer and finds credible accounts of predation upon Dall sheep. To this array of prey add "seals, mountain goat, bighorn sheep, coyotes, badgers, bobcat, turkeys, geese, Trumpeter Swan, Sandhill and Whooping Crane, and Great Blue Heron . . . " This species is "occasionally responsible" for losses to domestic sheep during lambing. But authenticated accounts of Golden Eagle predation upon human children are conspicuously lacking.

I have personally seen a Golden Eagle knock a Great Blue Heron out of the air, then follow the stunned bird onto the marsh, where the eagle presumably fed. In Bosque del Apache National Wildlife Refuge, I watched a Golden Eagle stoop into a massed flock of Sandhill Cranes, securing none. And once, while watching migrating hawks in northwestern New Jersey, I observed an adult Golden Eagle stoop upon, bind to, and kill an adult Red-tailed Hawk, which it then carried into the trees on the windward side of the ridge and out of sight. Two hours later an adult Golden Eagle with a fully distended crop suddenly hove into view at close range, presumably the same bird.

Returning to the Red-tail kill. The eagle had been migrating over and through the buteo's territory. The Red-tail was aloft and elected to harass the eagle for its territorial transgression. The two circled and sparred for a time, then the Red-tail appeared to lose both interest and his senses, allowing the eagle to climb above him, from which vantage the eagle stooped, taking the buteo, it seemed, by surprise.

Leslie Brown says this about the eagle's prowess in a stoop: "A Golden Eagle, weighing 7½ to 8½ lbs., should theoretically be able to dive much faster than a Peregrine Falcon weighing 1½ to 1¾ lbs." He calculates that the theoretical terminal velocity in a vertical dive would be "about 180 miles per hour."

Anyone who has seen the size and armament of an eagle's feet can hardly be surprised by the bird's capacity to dispatch even large prey. The question does arise: how, then, does this species accommodate such an array of prey sizes, insofar as a raptor's feet are specialized to its prey? Leslie Brown offers this explanation: "The feet can accommodate themselves to the size and shape of the prey taken, a small animal being crushed in the grip of overlapping talons; while a wide spread of the foot, enabling the bird to seize a large animal, also places the talon points in a position to pierce . . . "

STATUS: Golden Eagle is speculatively considered by Leslie Brown "probably the most numerous large eagle in the world." In North America, despite protection, it remains our most persecuted raptor. In 1988, the adult population was estimated to be 70,000 birds in North America.

In 1997, the North American breeding population was estimated to be 20,000 to 25,000 pairs and the total population (including nonbreeding birds) was estimated at 50,000 to 70,000. At western hawkwatch sites, declining numbers have been noted since 1998. At eastern watch sites, there has been an overall increase in sightings.

Despite protection, death resulting from some human action remains the greatest threat to this species. Human activity has been estimated to account for 70 percent of Golden Eagle deaths. The systematic shooting of Golden Eagles from fixed-wing aircraft appears to have been put in the past; however, incidental shooting does still occur, and unintended trapping and poisoning as a result of baits set out for predator control also extract a toll.

Golden Eagles are also susceptible to lead poisoning resulting from ingested bullet fragments or pellets embedded in carrion or prey. Troubling and difficult to address are fatal collisions between eagles and power lines and, increasingly, with wind turbines, whose newer, more bird-friendly designs purport to reduce the slaughter. Electrocution resulting from birds landing on power lines in rainy weather is another challenge.

Rock climbers sometimes disrupt nesting efforts by dislodging adults and exposing eggs and young to excessive sunlight. But in the balance, North America's Golden Eagles appear to be doing well in the West, and the population's future well-being is largely dependent upon maintaining the bird's prey base and discouraging persecution. In the East, outside Arctic regions, the bird is a rare to uncommon migrant and winter resident.

FALCONIDAE
Falcons and Caracaras

Crested Caracara
Caracara cheriway

ETYMOLOGY: "Caracara is probably a South American native name for the bird, derived from its call, a low rattle."

PROFILE: A raptorial chimera, exhibiting genetic ties and structural or behavioral traits that bind it to all the birds covered in this book—a one-bird poster child for inclusivity.

DESCRIPTION: The caracara is a sturdy medium-sized raptor, showing the head and bill of an eagle, the body size of a buteo, the sturdy legs of a vulture, and

The Crested Caracara, of Florida, Texas, and the American Southwest, is a raptorial polyglot. As large and sturdy as a buteo, it has the head and bill and something of the bearing of an eagle, yet it is placed in the family Falconidae, so it has genetic ties to the falcons. Feeding heavily upon road-killed animals, it also has standing among the vultures, with which it associates at large carcasses. Brian Small

the feet of falcons, the family that it has genetic ties to. Its body is blackish (dark brown in juveniles) with the breast and upper back spangled in adults; the juvenile's is lightly streaked. The large head and thick neck are white in adults, cream to buff in juveniles. The black cap suggests a poorly fitted toupee. The bare face is red on adults, and gray to pink on juveniles. The bill is bluish gray, and the long legs are bright yellow in adults,

Crested Caracara is a strong flier when it's pursuing live prey. Hunting birds make low sweeping flights across open areas, wheeling when they sight prey. Adults top and middle, juvenile bottom. From top to bottom: Ned Harris, Kevin T. Karlson, Brian Sullivan

grayish in juveniles. The white tail is finely barred and tipped, with a broad dark terminal band. The sexes are similar, but the female is larger.

MEASUREMENTS
Length: 21–24 inches
Wingspan: 46–52 inches
Weight: 1.8–2.8 pounds

SYSTEMATICS/SUBSPECIES: Crested Caracara is currently grouped with three other caracara species in the subfamily *Polyborinae,* or in a separate tribe, *Caracaraini,* within the subfamily *Falconinae.*

The true falcons (tribe *Falconinae*) are "sisters" to caracaras. The number of subspecies has varied from zero to four.

Generally northern forms south to Central America, including *C. cheriway* and *C. c. audubonii* of the United States, are considered distinct from forms found in South America.

VOCALIZATIONS: This bird is mostly silent. When agitated, it emits a series of "rattles, cackles and chattering."

DISTRIBUTION: Crested Caracara is widespread in the New World, ranging from northern Mexico and the southern United States south to Tierra del Fuego in South America.

In the United States, it is a resident in central Florida and southeastern Texas, and rare and local to southwestern Louisiana and southern Arizona.

MIGRATION: This is a nonmigratory permanent resident. Said Audubon, who found the species near St. Augustine, where it no longer occurs, "I was not aware of the existence of the Caracara

Eagle or Brazilian Eagle in the United States, until my visit to Florida in the winter of 1831."

HABITAT: The caracara prefers open to semiopen xeric grasslands, also palm savannas, river edges, and especially ranch land. In Texas, it prefers "open pasture and prairies, generally where dotted by oak motes or crossed by creeks and arroyos narrowly skirted by trees."

BREEDING: Caracaras are reported to be "one of the earliest of the raptors to begin nesting in Florida." Nesting generally coincides with the onset of the dry season. In Florida, pairs remain together year-round, often perching together. The earliest date eggs have been reported is September 1, with most Florida birds laying in late January. In Texas, eggs are laid January through March, and in Arizona, they are laid April through June.

The nest is typically in the tallest vegetation or structure, commanding a wide view. In Florida, caracaras overwhelmingly favor cabbage palm. In Texas, they mostly prefer live oak and elm; in Arizona they are invariably in the crotch of a large saguaro. They are also reported to nest on cliffs.

Nests are composed mostly of vines, weed stalks, briars, and twigs, and are described in Bent as resembling "an inverted Mexican hat . . . often very bulky and show successive layers." Structures are also described as "bulky yet woven, well-constructed . . . " "Well constructed" is not a term commonly applied to raptor nests, much less a nest constructed by a

These adult Crested Caracaras are allopreening. This species exhibits very social behavior among its family groups. Jim Zipp

bird with falcon genes. Falcons typically do not construct their own nests.

Both adults participate in nest building. Egg laying begins soon after the nest is completed or may be delayed up to two months.

Clutch size ranges from one to four, but two or three is typical. The base color of the eggs is white or pinkish white, often washed with buff. Eggs are heavily marked with irregular blotches, scrawls, splashes, and spots of darker browns.

Incubation lasts from 30 to 33 days and young fledge in seven or eight weeks. Incubation is shared by both sexes, and typically there is only one brood per season.

The young remain in the natal territory and may continue to be fed by the parents for several months after fledging. They are somewhat gregarious after fledging, with immatures from multiple clutches congregating. These groups may number up to 30 and even include birds in adult plumage.

BEHAVIOR/HUNTING: Caracaras typically forage early in the morning and late in the afternoon. They perch for much of the day. At dawn, they actively search

Nest robbing is part of this accomplished predator's playbook, hence the ire of this Northern Mockingbird. Steve Sachs

Caracaras are gregarious, and they actively practice kleptoparasitism, as this young White-tailed Hawk has learned. The White-tailed has prey in its talons, but the Caracaras are doing their best to appropriate it. Ned Harris

roadsides for roadkill. Sometimes they soar at great altitudes, but more typically they fly below treetop level.

Long and somewhat mistakenly regarded as primarily a carrion feeder, caracara is actually an opportunistic generalist, targeting "any animal matter, alive or dead, that it can catch or find." It frequently forages on foot and runs well. As it walks, it commonly flips over debris or cow pies with one foot. It seeks "live prey by making low, sweeping flights across open places . . . when prey is spotted, wheels around, lands and approaches prey on foot."

Attesting to its finesse as a hunter, I am impressed by these two accounts in Bent: "I have seen a Caracara chase a jackass-rabbit for some distance through open mesquite . . . and while they were in sight the bird kept within a few feet of the animal and constantly gained on it, in spite of its sharp turns and bounds." "Dr. Barbour (1923) has seen caracaras chase large birds and says that Gundlach once saw one chase, tire out and kill a white ibis."

When feeding at carcasses, caracaras are generally dominant over Black and Turkey Vultures, but they are intimidated

The bird on the bottom is asserting its dominance in a posturing display that takes place during courtship and at other times unrelated to breeding, such as dominance at animal kills. Top: Greg Lasley; bottom: Brian Small

by groups of Black Vultures, so they wait on the periphery, content to grab small scraps.

PREY: The list of prey that this species consumes excludes precious little that walks, crawls, flies, or dies, but items expressly mentioned in the literature include grasshoppers, beetles, millipedes, insect larvae, worms, snails, crabs, young alligators, snakes, turtles, lizards, and frogs. Small to medium-sized birds are taken regularly, including Cattle Egret, Eastern Meadowlark, Florida Scrub-Jay, Gila Woodpecker, Gilded Flicker, House Sparrow, Vesper Sparrow, Indigo Bunting, American Kestrel, and Greater Roadrunner. It also frequently takes eggs and nestlings of wild and domestic birds. Mammals include young rabbits, water rat, spotted skunk, striped skunk, armadillo, plains pocket gopher, mice, squirrels, javelina, peccary, and feral pig. It also eats multiple fish species and carrion, ranging in size from opossum to cattle. Caracras sometimes hunt in pairs.

Bent describes a pair apparently setting up an ambush whose objective was a young lamb.

A quick perusal of the prey items suggests that this is a bird that spends a great deal of time on or near the ground. Such

Caracaras spend a great deal of time on the ground. Note the beautiful, subtle color tones to this fresh juvenile, including the pink facial skin. Steve Sachs

is the case. It typically "perches on fence posts, trees or utility poles."

Caracaras also wade in shallows in search of aquatic foods. And they forage behind plowing tractors, and are known to attend fires—stalking behind the fire line, consuming animals caught by the blaze. They are also attentive to nesting parent birds. Caracaras' nest-robbing victims include Northern Mockingbird and Loggerhead Shrike. They also pursue and harry vultures, forcing them to disgorge the content of their crops. Bent reports a similar tactic used on nesting Brown Pelicans returning with prey. And, of course, caracaras also consume carrion and the insects attracted to carrion. Snyder found the bird pursuing much of its prey on foot and likened its hunting technique to another fleet-footed hunter, the Secretarybird of Africa. The Snyders further noted the bird's affiliation with cattle ranches, observing that both the Florida and Texas populations flourish in cattle country.

The variety of prey and foraging techniques paint the picture of an intelligent, opportunistic, accomplished, and determined bird—one that has adapted to, perhaps even benefited from, our species, whose slaughter of wildlife on highways and profligate animal husbandry practices produce a surfeit of food.

STATUS: The U.S. population and range of this species has generally declined in the twentieth century, with the Florida population estimated to number about 300 individuals in 150 territories. In 1987, the Florida population was designated an endangered species by both the federal and Florida governments.

In Texas, the population "generally declined from 1950 to 1980," but since 1980, Breeding Bird Survey data suggest an increase in both population and range. The Arizona population is likely stable, and the species range is probably "as extensive now as it was formerly."

Outside the United States, caracara is regarded as fairly common to locally abundant. It has been suggested that the conversion of forest to cattle lands has benefited this species, an observation consistent with the Snyders' observations (above).

American Kestrel
Falco sparverius

ETYMOLOGY: The species name is from the Latin: *falco* from *falx* for "sickle," and *sparverius,* "pertaining to a sparrow." This is an ill-chosen name insofar as it implies that sparrows constitute a favored prey, which is not the case. The name "kestrel" may derive from the bird's call or perhaps from the call of Common Kestrel (*Falco tinnunculus*), a widespread Old World relative, one of as many as 15 kestrel species found across the globe.

PROFILE: American Kestrel is a delightful, colorful, and diminutive raptor. Ounce for ounce, no raptor packs more superlatives into such a small form. Weighing less than four ounces, American Kestrel is easily North America's smallest raptor, and the colorful male is on everyone's short list for most striking bird of prey. It ranges from sea level to 12,000 feet in North America, and to 14,000 feet in South America. It is found across most of Canada, the United States,

American Kestrels: a male on the top, a female on the bottom. Jerry Liguori

A Kestrel sampler: males above, females below. Note that the immature male in the upper right photo lacks the buff wash of adults, and shows a good deal of dark spotting. Wing shapes appear very different in various flight postures, such as the soaring bird in top center, relaxed gliding bird in top right, and gliding birds in lower center and right. Top left: Jim Zipp; all others: Kevin T. Karlson

Mexico, and Central and most of South America. American Kestrel ranks as one of the New World's most widespread raptors and, in the United States, perhaps the most common, too.

For 300 years ornithologists have been lavish with their praise of American Kestrel. It has been called "the prettiest and jauntiest of our Hawks, yet no prig" and "most light-hearted and frolicsome." Summarizes Audubon: "We have few more beautiful hawks in the United States than this active little species and I am sure, none half so abundant . . . Everyone knows the Sparrow-Hawk . . . "

Given the bird's newfound ability to expand into urban areas and to quickly colonize recently deforested areas (such as land cleared for grazing or agriculture and burned forest tracts), it may be that

anyone not yet familiar with American Kestrel soon will be.

DESCRIPTION: The American Kestrel is a small, long-tailed falcon, about the size and somewhat the shape of Mourning Dove (albeit larger headed), sharing with the dove a penchant for perching on utility lines. The male and female show markedly dissimilar plumages. The female is rufous brown above (on the back and wings) with narrow dark barring; her underparts are whitish and overlaid with rufous streaks; her brown tail has multiple narrow black bars. The back of the male is rufous with black barring, and the rufous tail is unbanded except for a broad black terminal band. The wings are gunmetal blue. His pale breast and belly are washed with orange and have black spots. The heads of both males and females sport bluish gray caps and a boldly patterned face, showing a bold blackish malar stripe or "mustache," plus an ear patch or sideburn. Juveniles are similar to adults when fledged, so they are sexually dimorphic even as juveniles—a quality not common among birds of prey.

MEASUREMENTS
Length: male 9 inches; female 10 inches
Wingspan: 21–22 inches
Weight: male 3.4–4.5 ounces; female 3.6–5.3 ounces

SYSTEMATICS/SUBSPECIES: Kestrels as a group are widely distributed across the globe; in fact, there are few places on the planet that cannot boast a representative of this colorful tribe. American Kestrel has 13 subspecies, two of which occur in the United States and Canada. *F. sparverius* occupies most of North America. The slightly smaller *F. s. paulus* is found from South Carolina to Florida.

VOCALIZATIONS: Kestrels call loudly and stridently when they are disturbed. The call has been phonetically rendered *kleee, kleee, kleee* and *killy, killy, killy.*

DISTRIBUTION: This species breeds from near tree line in Alaska and Canada south to Tierra del Fuego in South America. It is largely absent in heavily forested areas, including in Amazonia. Except in Canada and some extreme northern portions of New England and the Great Plains, it is a permanent resident. Northern birds winter south across the southern United States and through Mexico to at least Panama. Males winter farther north than females, and males are also more

common in more marginal habitat—for example, wooded or heavily vegetated habitat.

MIGRATION: Northern birds are highly migratory, with some failed breeders starting south in late July. Fall migration peaks in September and October, with stragglers continuing into early December. In spring, most migration occurs from late March to mid-May.

Kestrels migrate along a broad front, with concentrations noted at lakeshore and coastal locations as well as along the front range of the Rockies in spring. Kestrels are generally solitary, although they may migrate in small, loosely knit and variously spaced strings of two to eight birds. During migration, it is not uncommon to see multiple birds perched along utility lines about a pole's distance apart.

HABITAT: Kestrels can be found in almost any open habitat supporting open ground or short vegetation. They are absent in unbroken forest and in open treeless northern tundra, but they do nest in tree-lined riparian corridors on the tundra's southern edge. They are very partial to agricultural land, including vineyards, meadows, sports complexes, power line cuts, and other disturbed habitat, including highway divides. They also forage in the desert and alpine tundra with rocky outcroppings. They have recently been noted moving into urban settings, but thus far seem indifferent to most suburban environments.

BREEDING: In North America, Kestrels breed March to June. The male selects the breeding territory, and after the female joins him, the birds engage in a

"prolonged period of pre-laying activities." Like other falcons, they build no nest but adopt some generally protected or sheltered confine, very typically a nest cavity excavated by a large woodpecker species (such as a flicker). They also nest on cliffs and will appropriate the nests of corvids. They readily utilize manmade structures, such as barns and even occupied buildings that offer a protective nook or cranny. They also readily adopt artificial nest boxes erected in properly open habitat. A cavity-bearing lone (often dead) tree standing in open habitat seems ideally suited for this species.

Clutches are large, typically four or five white or pinkish eggs that are usually speckled and spotted with purplish pink or reddish brown, sometimes more heavily marked with small blotches, though on the whole this species' eggs are generally paler than those of most other falcons. With clutches of up to seven eggs, American Kestrel has one of the largest clutch sizes among birds of prey. The female does most of the incubation, which takes 27 to 32 days.

Fledging occurs in 29 to 31 days. Birds may double-brood. Young leave the nest about 30 days post fledging.

BEHAVIOR/HUNTING: Kestrels hunt from elevated perches; where hunting perches are limited, multiple birds may hunt from the same small tree. In the absence of perches, they hover-hunt by facing into the wind and flapping rapidly, generally 20 to 40 feet above the ground. They typically use both the perch-hunting and hovering methods in concert when hunting, searching first from a perch to conserve energy, then sallying out and hovering when they sight prey. They may then take prey in a vertical pounce or in a stooping glide. Most prey is captured on the ground, although Kestrels will at times capture prey in the air, particularly dragonflies.

PREY: Prey ranges from earthworms driven to the surface by rain to small birds, reptiles, and small mammals. In summer Kestrels often target large insects, particularly grasshoppers and crickets. In winter, they consume more small rodents and small birds; however, despite the implications of the name *sparverius*, small sparrow-sized birds are not the bird's preferred fare. Unlike the Merlin, this small falcon is a mouser. This said, in urban areas, it targets the ubiquitous House Sparrow (*Passer domesticus*).

STATUS: This was formerly one of the most abundant raptors in North America. In the 1990s it was estimated that there were 1,200,000 breeding pairs in North America. Since then, substantial declines in populations of American Kestrel are apparent across much of

Insects, including grasshoppers and crickets, figure prominently in the Kestrel's diet. On the left, a hovering bird is about to pounce on prey while carrying a grasshopper in its mouth. The Kestrel on the right has retreated to the sky to eat its cricket prey. Left: Rob Curtis; right: Kevin T. Karlson

North America. Beginning in the 1980s, the bird's numbers at eastern hawkwatch sites faltered, with declines now reflected across North America.

Breeding Bird Survey results show annual declines in American Kestrel across the continent, ranging from –1.7 percent to –2.7 percent between 1983 and 2005. Christmas Bird Count data corroborates this, showing annual declines of –2.3 percent between 1983 and 2005.

The Kestrels' decline is as sudden, dramatic, unexpected, and arguably as dire as the decline of the Peregrine half a century ago. Like the initial stages of the Peregrine's decline, the cause of American Kestrel's decline is, as yet, unknown. Speculation quite naturally leads to the introduction of some chemical agent, such as an agricultural pesticide. Western declines may relate to factors associated with drought conditions. Other possible causes include the increased conversion of grasslands and agricultural land to suburbia, as well as new intensive farming practices, which reduce prey-rich edge habitat. Predation by Cooper's Hawks, whose population has increased as Kestrel's has declined, is also sometimes mentioned as a possible causal agent.

I note from autumn observations conducted at Cape May, New Jersey, that migrating Northern Flicker (*Colaptes auratus*) numbers have also declined markedly and proportionally during this same period (since the 1970s). This woodpecker's excavated cavities meet American Kestrel breeding standards. In point of fact, the only breeding Kestrels I am aware of in New Jersey are now using artificial nest boxes exclusively. Competition for existing nest sites with European Starlings, who occupy the holes prior to the Kestrels' return, is also a

Opposite: *The male American Kestrel ranks among the most stunning of North America's birds.* Kevin T. Karlson

factor. As regards the impact of increased numbers of Cooper's Hawks, I note that Northern Flicker, too, is a species frequently targeted by Cooper's Hawk.

One thing seems certain—raptor populations, however healthy, are ever susceptible to changes in their environment. In fact, the plight of American Kestrel takes on greater poignancy when set against the backdrop of the present general health and stability of the populations of most of the species covered in this book.

In time, we will understand the cause of the Kestrel's decline, and I hope the understanding will come in time to address it. Until then, increased nest box programs seem the best course of action. What landowner would not want the "prettiest and jauntiest" of our hawks in the neighborhood? Only crickets, grasshoppers, and small rodents might object to such an initiative.

Merlin
Falco columbarius (Linnaeus)

ETYMOLOGY: The scientific name is from the Latin: *falco* from *falx*, for "sickle," and *columbarius* for "a pigeon keeper," possibly a reference to the presumed prey of this species, or perhaps to its resemblance to a pigeon in flight. The common name "Merlin" harks back to *esmerillion,* the Old French name for this species.

PROFILE: Says Wilson about the species, "This small hawk possesses great spirit and rapidity of flight," which is in full accord with the description found in *Birds of North America*: "The Merlin is a small,

dashing falcon that breeds throughout the northern forests and prairies of North America." None who have watched this bird-catching specialist in flight are unimpressed. Falcon authority Tom Cade calls it a "doughty little hunter."

About the size of an American Kestrel, Merlins appear overall more robust and shorter-tailed and are considerably heavier, with the added ballast consisting mostly of muscle, if the bird's superior speed and ability to subdue medium-sized (mostly avian) prey is any measure. As handsome as it is accomplished, its face is highlighted by a pale supercilium and a single dark mustache. It looks nefarious and comports itself accordingly, dispatching birds in flight with alacrity and finesse—or, if called for, tenacity. Merlin is as determined in pursuit of prey as it is accomplished. When a Merlin bears down on a shorebird culled from the flock, a fatal outcome seems all but assured. So expert is this feathered interceptor, I cannot personally recall a single instance when I've seen a hunting adult male Merlin fail to secure prey. Imagine an aerial hunter that captures prey in the air nearly as easily as robins pry worms from suburban lawns.

Only in the summarizing of this observation of Merlin's hunting success do I realize how remarkable this is. Most birds of prey come nowhere close to batting a thousand in their hunting efforts. In fact, as regards most species, I'd estimate that close to half of all capture efforts end in failure. From Osprey to Red-tail to Cooper's Hawk, empty talons are not the exception, and a hawk's typical recourse, having lost the balance-tipping element of surprise, is to then seek another victim.

The Merlin is a small, dashing falcon that breeds throughout the northern forests and prairies of America. This adult male taiga Merlin was migrating through Cape May, New Jersey, a location that records multiple hundreds of Merlins between September and November. Kevin T. Karlson

Not so Merlin, whose failed first effort is often followed by a redoubled second. Some hidden reservoir of untapped speed seems ever the bird's trumping response to thwarted ambition. The Merlin kill I remember most involved an adult male that chose to target migrating Tree Swallows in the sky over Cape May. The hundred or so swallows gathered in a defensive ball. While they could outclimb the heavier falcon, the open sky offered no place to hide, and as evasive strategies go, "up, up, up, up, up" has both physical and strategic limits. The falcon's tactical response was to halve the flock repeatedly until what was left was an isolated bird. Then, tapping into that hidden reserve, the Merlin accelerated, quickly closed upon the fleeing singleton, and seized it. Swallows are fast, agile fliers. The Merlin simply outmastered it, first in strategy, then in speed, and, finally, in maneuverability and determination.

Other authorities rate the overall hunting success rate of Merlin much lower than I, a disparity that might relate to habitat or prey. While most observations of this species are made on the breeding and wintering grounds, most of my own observations have occurred at a migratory concentration point where prey is likely to be inexperienced young passerines out of their element, often caught over water, and perhaps exhausted by a night of migration. Additionally, in this setting, the tactics of predator and prey have not been honed by successive, daily contests, and the results may be biased by the attrition of less capable contestants.

DESCRIPTION: The Merlin is a somewhat pigeon-sized and -shaped raptor but less chesty, more athletically trim than a domestic pigeon. It is larger headed and shorter tailed than the American Kestrel. Females and juveniles are chocolate to gray-brown above, and heavily streaked below. From a distance, non-adult males appear dark overall, except for a whitish throat. The single weak mustache distinguishes it from the Kestrel, which sports two crisply defined dark slashes set upon a whitish face, and from the Peregrine, whose single bold mustache mark is wider, darker, and more crisply defined. Adult male Merlins are bluish above, with the hue ranging from blackish blue in birds from the coastal northwest to steel blue in birds hailing from the prairies. The whitish underparts are streaked below, darkly and heavily on females and juveniles, and more rufous on adult

males. Their dark tails are scored by multiple narrow pale bands and tipped with a white terminal band.

MEASUREMENTS
Length: male 9–11 inches;
female 11–12 inches
Wingspan: male 21–23 inches;
female 24–27 inches
Weight: male 4.5–6.6 ounces;
female 6.4–8.3 ounces

For comparison, the female American Kestrel weighs 3.6 to 5.3 ounces.

SUBSPECIES: Nine Merlin subspecies are generally recognized, three of which are in North America. *F. c. columbarius*, the widespread Taiga Merlin, breeds primarily in subarctic northern forests from Alaska to Newfoundland, and winters widely across the United States, the Caribbean, and Mexico south to northern South America. *F. c. suckleyi,* or the Black Merlin, is a mostly resident subspecies that breeds in western British Columbia and has a winter range that extends to northern California. *F. c. richardsoni*, the so-called Prairie Merlin, is a very pale race that breeds in the Great Plains. For the most part it withdraws south in winter, although a few birds remain in urban areas where nonmigrating prey remain abundant.

VOCALIZATIONS: Merlins are generally silent, except when they are nesting; then, when they are excited, they make a rapid series of strident notes: *kee, kee, kee . . .*

DISTRIBUTION: This is a Holarctic breeder, with populations in both the Old and New Worlds, breeding primarily in

This Merlin sampler shows (top and bottom) North America's Taiga adult male, Taiga female, and Black Merlin. Top right: Tom Johnson; bottom middle: Brian Sullivan; all others: Kevin T. Karlson

northern boreal forests as well as tundra in North America. Across most of its range, it winters wholly south of its breeding areas. In North America, it is found as a breeder from western Alaska, east across boreal regions of Canada to the Maritimes and Newfoundland. On the West Coast, it breeds south to Washington and in the prairies to Wyoming. In the East, southern range expansion has brought birds to southern New York State and northern Pennsylvania.

In winter, Taiga Merlins evacuate their breeding range and apportion themselves across much of North America south of Canada and New England, and south to Mexico, Central America, and northern South America. In the East, they winter coastally as far north as New York City and south to Florida and Cuba. They also spread along the Gulf Coast, particularly where smaller shorebirds concentrate. Black Merlin are mostly year-round residents, although some relocation occurs within the breeding range as birds adjust to seasonal changes in prey.

Wherever this species winters, an abundance of flocking birds seems requisite, be they shorebirds, larks, House Sparrows, starlings, blackbirds, or other flocking species.

MIGRATION: In the fall, the Taiga Merlin migrates from August to early December, with peak movements noted in September and October. Peak counts at some coastal locations may exceed 80 birds per day, but as a migrant Merlin is much less common away from coastal locations and lakeshores. Spring migration is early

March to early May, but some males may return to nest sites in late winter.

Unlike the Kestrel, the Merlin is a solitary migrant. Juvenile birds are particularly ill disposed toward raptors of any size intruding into their airspace.

The heaviest concentrations occur in coastal locations, with most movement noted between noon and dusk, when birds typically fly lower to hunt. Given clear skies and good thermals, birds often migrate very high, but given poor flying conditions, may hug the terrain and fly low over water. Some birds evidently migrate at night, but whether this is by choice or because birds simply find themselves caught offshore at sunset is unclear. Over land, most migration ceases before sunset, and birds typically spend the last two hours of daylight hunting.

HABITAT: When they are breeding, Merlins are partial to semiopen forested habitat (to facilitate hunting), and they typically nest adjacent to forest openings. They are also commonly found near rivers, lakes, and bogs, and on islands in large lakes and burned-over areas. They do not build their own nest, but appropriate a suitably large nest made by other birds in a previous season; however, at the northern edge of their breeding range they may commonly nest on the ground. In winter, they are primarily found in open habitat, especially coastal flats and marshes (where small shorebirds concentrate) as well as on treeless plains and agricultural lands where larks and other small flocking land birds are found.

BREEDING: Males return to their nesting areas in late winter or early spring, and females join them several days to weeks later. Pair formation occurs mid-April to May in Alaska, and earlier farther south. Pairs typically use the same nesting area year after year, but not necessarily the same site.

Like other falcons, this species does not build a nest but appropriates an old (usually corvid) nest. They use conifers or deciduous trees, and birds select in favor of nests that are higher and also offer concealment and easy access. While not typically cavity nesters, Merlins do nest on ledges and on the ground (most typically on sloping ground). They lay five or six reddish brown, brown-blotched eggs in late April to late May. They deposit at two-day intervals. Incubation lasts 30 days. The male provides most of the food, while the female does the actual feeding. Fledging occurs about 29 days after hatching. Quite vocal, the fledglings remain near the nest and are tended by the adults for up to four weeks.

Hunting young reportedly target dragonflies and playfully pursue potential prey and other raptors. This penchant for "play"—or harassment—and a dedicated focus upon dragonflies as prey continues as juveniles begin their first southbound migration.

BEHAVIOR/HUNTING: Merlins typically take an elevated perch to locate prey, which is often distant, necessitating a calculated approach. But if prey is close, encumbered, or caught in the open (such as over open water), the attack will be swift and direct. Merlins may also encounter prey while engaged in flight (this is typically how juveniles find and engage

After fledging, juvenile Taiga Merlins prey heavily upon dragonflies, which they capture and often consume on the wing. This accomplished hunter has one in each talon. Chris and Chad Saladin

dragonflies during migration). This species also practices cruise-hunting, with falcons flying rapidly and unseen below concealing vegetation or terrain. The Merlin is tenacious in pursuit, and fleeing birds are either overtaken in flight or compelled to gain altitude, where the Merlin then executes a "ringing-up maneuver" in which the prey is forced higher and higher while denied the safety of the ground below. The maneuver continues until the prey is exhausted or the Merlin gains a strategic advantage and closes. With prey encountered during cruise-hunting, the falcon adjusts the angle of attack and accelerates.

While the Merlin always captures prey from the air, that prey may at times be plucked from branches; it is then carried in the falcon's talons to a perch or the nest, already dead by decapitation. Dragonflies, however, are frequently consumed on the wing, small birds less commonly so. In Cape May, New Jersey, on days marked by good Merlin flights and high densities of dragonflies (which are also migrating), the gossamer wings of insects fall like ticker tape in the late afternoon as birds hunt.

PREY: The Merlin is a hunter of small to medium-sized birds, and it heavily targets woodland species in summer. But it also takes prey as large as Golden-Plover, pigeons, and small ducks. Most of the falcon's prey (80 percent) weighs less than 1.5 ounces. In winter, in interior grasslands and agricultural lands, it especially targets Horned Larks. In coastal areas, Dunlin and Western Sandpipers are perennial favorites. In migration it is fairly opportunistic, but any small to medium-sized bird or bat caught over open water is certain to garner a hungry Merlin's attention. Dragonflies are an important food source for young in September.

As a general rule, Merlin targets the most abundant avian prey species in the area, which, in urban areas or in the vicinity of feedlots, may be House Sparrows. Bohemian Waxwings also constitute an important winter prey item in northern urban areas. Cade estimates a single Merlin captures and consumes 800 to 900 birds per year.

STATUS: Collision is, predictably, the number one killer of this speedster. Other causes implicated include shooting, poison, and cat predation. Despite attrition, the population is stable and increasing, with range expansions into urban areas in the prairies and in the Northeast.

In coastal areas, Merlins target flocking shorebirds. This female in Cordova, Alaska, has a Western Sandpiper. Kevin T. Karlson

Aplomado Falcon
Falco femoralis

An adult Aplomado Falcon with a Golden-fronted Woodpecker. Brian Sullivan

ETYMOLOGY: Part of the common name comes from the Spanish *plomo,* or "lead," for its lead-colored plumage; the species name *femoralis* pertains to the thighs, a clear reference to the bright orange feathers on the upper legs.

PROFILE: The Aplomado Falcon was once extirpated as a breeder in the United States, but is now reestablished in the coastal grasslands of the Texas coast. One can only marvel and envy Lieutenant Harry C. Benson, 4th United States Cavalry, who in 1887 reported finding five Aplomado Falcon nests in the vicinity of Fort Huachuca, Arizona.

By 1951, when Herbert Brandt published *Arizona and Its Bird Life,* this colorful, long-tailed, long-legged falcon had been extirpated. Resident where it occurs, pairs remain together and hunt cooperatively in pursuit of mostly avian prey.

DESCRIPTION: This is a strikingly plumaged, medium-sized, long-tailed and long-legged falcon, capable of high speed in direct pursuit of prey as fast as pigeons and doves. Where prey and habitat dictate, it resorts to mannerisms that are accipiter-like.

About Cooper's Hawk–sized, this handsome hawk of Neotropical savannas is distinguished by dark gray upperparts, a white throat and breast, an orange to buffy orange (juvenile) vent, and an undertail separated by a black band or cummerbund across the belly. Its long, dark tail has multiple narrow white bands. The bold, almost theatrical head pattern sports a dark crown and a white supercilium, which meet to form a collar on the hind neck. The head pattern is further distinguished by a broad, black eyeline and a short, black mustache. Except for size, the sexes are similar.

Juvenile birds are blackish brown above, with a buffy base to the breast and face where adults have white; juveniles also have streaked breasts. In flight, the profile recalls a large American Kestrel.

MEASUREMENTS

Length: male 14–16 inches; female 16–18 inches
Wingspan: male 31–33 inches; female 47–50 inches
Weight: male 8.4–10.7 ounces; female 12–16 ounces

VOCALIZATIONS: Brown and Amadon describe this species' voice as "a high-pitched kacking of the usual falcon type." Sibely describes the notes as "faster and higher than Prairie or Peregrine." It utters a single *chip* call to initiate paired hunting on the part of the as-yet unengaged partner. The call seems to "coordinate collaborative activities."

SYSTEMATICS/SUBSPECIES: This species is probably most closely related to the Bat Falcon (*Falco rufigularis*) and the Orange-breasted Falcon (*Falco deiroleucus*), although some evidence suggests a closer alliance with Peregrine Falcon (*Falco peregrinus*).

Three weakly differentiated subspecies are recognized. *F. f. septentrionalis* occurs from the southwestern United States south locally through Mexico. *F. f. femoralis* occurs in South America at low altitudes. *F. f. pichinchae* is resident in the temperate zone of the Andes from southwest Colombia to Chile and northwest Argentina. This subspecies

---

This grassland falcon is commonly seen sitting atop a conspicuous perch. The juvenile in the center is flanked by adults. Note the leg bands on all of these birds. A reintroduction program in its historic territories in south Texas has been quite successful, with many breeding pairs raising young every year on hack towers and natural nest sites. From left: Tom Johnson, Greg Lasley, Greg Lasley

is "darker in color and larger" than northern subspecies.

DISTRIBUTION: The Aplomado Falcon is found locally from Mexico to Tierra del Fuego, and is resident through most of Central and South America, but possibly withdraws from Patagonia and higher elevations during austral winter. It is classified as a winter resident or vagrant in western Mexico. It historically bred in the southwestern United States. The last documented natural breeding in the United States was in New Mexico in 1952. It occurs from sea level to above 13,000 feet in the Andes Mountains. Wild birds wandering up from Mexico are still sometimes reported in border regions of the United States. The bird's historic range in the United States, as delineated by Bent, "extends north to . . . Tucson and Tombstone, Arizona; New Mexico (Eagle, Apache, and Rincon); . . . East to Texas (Ft. Stockton, Pecos, and Brownsville)."

A reintroduction program from 1985 to 1989 involving captive-bred birds released in south Texas appears to be succeeding, with increased sightings and documented nest success at historic breeding sites near South Padre Island. In 2007, another round of reintroduction efforts was initiated in New Mexico.

MIGRATION: This species is nonmigratory through the central part of its range, although it probably retires from Patagonia and high altitudes during the southern winter.

HABITAT: The Aplomado Falcon favors lightly forested or open country. In the United States it is a resident of coastal prairie and desert grasslands with scattered yuccas and mesquite. In South America it also inhabits shrub-steppe and is able to tolerate a range of climates, from moist tropical lowlands to desert savanna, as well as alpine habitats in the Andes.

The Aplomado Falcon thrives in lightly forested open country. Its reputation for sluggishness may be related to its crepuscular feeding habits as well as its success as a hunter, but few other raptors can match its explosive direct flight when it pursues avian prey. Note the Kestrel-like proportions of the bird in flight. Brian Sullivan

The flight of the Aplomado Falcon is both buoyant and swift, and its wingbeats are stiff like American Kestrel's. These are first-year birds. Greg Lasley

BREEDING: This species' breeding habits are very poorly known. Owing to its extensive range, the onset of breeding ranges widely, but it typically coincides with the dry season. In Mexico, pairs deposit eggs mid-February to late March. Birds do not build their own nests but, like many falcons, appropriate the nests of corvids or other raptors, and occasionally use bromeliads. Historically, in the United States it has favored Chihuahuan Raven nests. Eggs, typically two to four, are white to pinkish white and profusely marked with speckling, spots, and blotches of light brown or chestnut red.

Incubation takes 31 to 32 days. Fledging occurs four to five weeks post hatching. Juveniles commonly remain together after fledging. Paired adults appear to remain together year-round and hunt cooperatively.

BEHAVIOR/HUNTING: The Aplomado Falcon spends much of its time on conspicuous perches, such as snags, posts, and telephone poles, often in shadows, preening or peering about, and comparatively little time hunting. This sedentary proclivity may be the foundation of the bird's reputation for sluggishness and may relate to both the crepuscular nature of its hunting pattern as well as the bird's evident success as a hunter: only successful hunters earn the privilege of inactivity. Brown and Amadon described this species as "extremely graceful and rapid in flight, though more listless than Merlin or Peregrine."

As a hunter, the Aplomado Falcon is something of a hybrid generalist, relying upon both falcon-like speed and accipiter-like cunning and tenacity, depending upon the situation and prey, capable of securing prey both in the air and on the ground. Responding to the bird's reputation for "sluggishness," this description by Major Allan Brooks is elucidating and exonerating:

> [T]his graceful Falcon is not much in evidence until a prairie fire is started on the wide coastal plain, when they quickly arrive, sweeping gracefully backwards and forwards, in front of the advancing flames and deftly capturing the large green locusts that are driven to flight. These are eaten on the wing, the falcon rising in the air as it picks its prey to pieces . . .

I take particular note of the use of the word "graceful," a label not often applied to nonkite raptors.

This capable hunter seems to have a technique for every occasion: another observer likens the bird to a Sharp-shinned Hawk, employing a "stealthy manner of hunting for its prey beneath the thick foliage of the woods, flying near the ground or perching in secluded places from which it would launch an attack." If the situation calls for pursuit, this falcon is fully capable of flying down prey as fast as pigeons and doves in open country in the manner of a Peregrine or Merlin. Such direct pursuit is described as the Aplomado's preferred method of pursuing birds in open country, but it also snatches prey from the ground, including small mammals and reptiles. It is also reported to "soar at dusk, catching and eating insects on the wing."

Pairs hunt cooperatively, with one bird hovering and waiting while the other acts as driver or beater, sometimes diving into cover, where it may then pursue prey on foot.

When the harried prey is flushed, the mate, waiting overhead, engages. Aplomado Falcon is adept at hovering and rarely stoops from a soar. Mated pairs feed simultaneously from kills, with the female clutching the carcass and offering "small bits of food to the male." These cooperative hunting efforts are twice as successful as solo efforts.

Not above kleptoparasitism, pairs collaboratively relieve Kestrels, harriers, and kingfishers of prey ranging from rodents to crayfish and fish (which is not your typical falcon fare).

PREY: Aplomado Falcons eat mostly birds and insects, most of which they capture in the air, though they capture some on the ground. They also take some reptiles (lizards) and small mammals (including bats). But make no mistake—Aplomado is primarily a bird-catching raptor, with insects constituting only a small portion of its diet.

STATUS: This is a federally endangered species. It was extirpated as a breeder in the southwestern United States and northern Mexico by the 1950s for unclear reasons. Suspected causes include the degradation of native grasslands from overgrazing, fire suppression, and conversion to mesquite.

Also implicated as a cause of decline was the widespread use of DDT. The Snyders suggest that perhaps the overzealous efforts of egg collectors might also bear responsibility for the decline of this species which—given the evident beauty of the eggs, their value to collectors, and the salaries paid to low-ranking military officers—would be understandable.

The open coastal grasslands of south Texas are ideal habitat for the Aplomado Falcon. Brian Sullivan

While the historic status of this species is "impossible to determine because of inadequate or corrupted data," Major Bendire (writing in 1892) accounted the bird "fairly common" in the vicinity of Fort Huachuca, Arizona. But by the turn of the century (1900) "this shy little falcon seems to have forsaken Arizona as a breeding area, the cause of which is another desert mystery."

Given the bird's endangered status and efforts taken to restore the northern population, as well as modern efforts to restore native grasslands, there is room to be optimistic about the bird's future in the American Southwest. Deforestation in South America may also prove beneficial to Aplomados.

The species reintroduced into coastal Texas appears to be doing well, with 700 adults released and 244 young fledged since 1995.

Gyrfalcon
Falco rusticolus

ETYMOLOGY: Etymologists differ with regards to the root of "gyr." Suggestions have included German *ger,* for "spear," Latin *gyro,* for "circle," and *geier,* for "greedy." The species name *rusticolus* (Linnaeus) is Latin for "a rustic," and is likely a reference to the bird's remote breeding habitat.

PROFILE: Cade calls this the "largest and most majestic of the long-winged hawks." It is the northernmost diurnal raptor, with a circumpolar breeding range extending to 82 degrees north latitude. Admired for centuries and well studied, this Arctic falcon continues to surprise and inspire us. In the words of Emperor Frederick II in his treatise on falconry, "the Gyrfalcon

As Emperor Frederick II observed in his treatise on falconry, "the Gyrfalcon holds pride of place over even the Peregrine in strength, speed, courage." This Gyr's somewhat diminished prey could hardly quibble with this assessment. Jerry Liguori

holds pride of place over even the Peregrine in strength, speed, courage . . ."

Few would question the prowess of this bird trained in Medieval times to hunt prey the size of cranes and swans from the fists of emperors and kings. This bird is capable of flying down waterfowl in level flight, so there hardly seems reason to gainsay the bird's tenacity or speed. Ask any surviving ptarmigan—if you can find one.

Some birds, especially adult males, apparently remain on territory year-round. An unknown but presumably large number of far-northern breeding birds evidently choose to winter out on the ice, far from land. Using the winter pack ice as a supportive base and ranging tens, even hundreds, of square miles out over open ocean in search of prey, coming to land, as pelagic birds do, only to breed, makes Gyrfalcon the only known marine raptor. Some individuals in a study population of 48 radio-tagged individuals appeared to have no obvious home ranges and traveled continually during the nonbreeding season, spending up to 40 consecutive days at sea. One juvenile female traveled 2,825 miles, over a 200-day period, spending over half that time over the ocean between Greenland and Iceland.

Despite their nomadic predilections, few individuals wander south of 55 degrees north latitude.

DESCRIPTION: The Gyrfalcon is a large falcon, with great variation between sexes and plumage, with several distinct color morphs noted that range from black to gray to white. (While once considered distinct subspecies, differences among these plumage types are now believed to be feather deep, and plumage types are known to grade into each other across the bird's extensive range.) Gyrfalcons are mostly larger and more robust than Peregrines and somewhat pot-bellied.

Forsman notes that the gray morph and dark morph are identified by broad yet falcon-shaped wings with rounded tips, a fairly long but broad tail, and a heavy body. The feet are "heavy and strong, with toes rather thicker and decidedly shorter relative to the legs, relative to Peregrine," an adaptation that may

Hunting Gyrfalcons use several techniques, including a flap-and-glide combination (top and center photos) used for low contour hunting as well as soaring or quartering flight (bottom photo) punctuated by a stoop. Top to bottom: Jerry Liguori, Jerry Liguori, Brian Small

advantage Gyrfalcon in the "handling of large mammals" and perhaps advantage a falcon that habitually perches on ice. The cere and feet are yellow on adults, and pale or bluish on juveniles. The widespread gray-brown morph's "upperparts appear uniformly grayish or grayish brown with slightly paler tail." The mustache stripe is fairly indistinct.

The white morph of this species is typically described as "unmistakable." The overall white ground color has variously patterned upperparts with fine blackish markings (grayish brown markings on white or buff in juvenile birds).

MEASUREMENTS

Length: male 19–21 inches;
female 22–24 inches
Wingspan: male 43–47 inches;
female 49–51 inches
Weight: male 2.2–2.9 pounds;
female 3.1–4.6 pounds

In August 1833, on a trip to Labrador, Audubon secured both members of a nesting pair and found the female to weigh 3 pounds 2 ounces and her mate 2 pounds 14 ounces. Audubon's female was apparently on the small side.

SYSTEMATICS/SUBSPECIES: No subspecies are currently recognized by the AOU, but plumage types of gray, dark/brown, and white are distributed throughout the bird's Arctic range. While morphs are widespread, some are more heavily represented in certain geographic regions than others, with birds from Arctic Canadian islands and northern Greenland "mostly white, those from southern Greenland dark or intermediate." In Northwest Territories, birds are 50 percent white and 50 percent dark. The gray morph is variable and the most widespread color morph. The white morph may be more common in colder areas and perhaps among those birds now known to winter on the pack ice.

VOCALIZATION: The alarm is a hoarse *kwah kwah kwah* . . . "lower, gruffer, with more trumpeting quality than Peregrine."

DISTRIBUTION: The Gyrfalcon breeds throughout the Arctic biome, locally from approximately 79 degrees north to 55 degrees north. A few birds may winter somewhat regularly south to British Columbia, Alberta, Saskatchewan, and Ontario, and occasionally farther south. Birds that venture outside the normal winter range tend to be female and juvenile.

Those birds breeding below 70 degrees north are thought to be largely resident and remain in the vicinity of the nest site throughout the Arctic winter, providing prey is available. However, it has recently been established that a large number of high-Arctic breeding Gyrfalcons winter at sea using the pack ice far from land as a base from which to launch attacks upon wintering seabirds.

MIGRATION: Movement outside breeding areas begins in late August. Arrival on the winter territory is typically in October and November. In spring, in coastal Northwest Territories birds are observed as early as March and April. Most migration is coastal in nature. Montane and inland populations may be more likely to migrate, but Gyrfalcon can "persist as resident," wherever flocking ptarmigan numbers remain supportive.

HABITAT: Gyrfalcons breed widely across Arctic and alpine tundra, "often along rivers and seacoasts." They occasionally breed south to the tundra-boreal forest ecotone. Cade delineates three basic breeding habitat types: maritime, riverine, and montane.

Because it thrives where guano accumulates, the orange lichen behind this white-morph Gyrfalcon's Arctic perch attests to years of occupancy. Some particularly favored Greenland nest ledges have been occupied for close to 3,000 years. Brian Small

BREEDING: Gyrfalcons breed from sea level to at least 4,500 feet. Breeding sites are contingent upon the combination of a suitable nest site and the abundance of prey, with the breeding distribution of Gyrfalcon strikingly similar to that of Rock Ptarmigan. Most nests are located upon "precipitous cliff faces." Like other falcons, this species does not build its own nest but excavates a shallow scrape on cliff ledges or usurps the nest of another species. Nests of ravens and Rough-legged Hawks are often appropriated, and nesting in tree-borne nests as well as those on human structures is docu-mented, with tree nests apparently more common in the Palearctic.

Breeding is broadly March through July, but insofar as low Arctic breeders are resident throughout the year, some males may begin displaying over nest sites from mid-February to early March, when females arrive. Pairs demonstrate a high degree of fidelity to territories but multiple nest sites are common, and rotation is typical, with alternate sites situated mere feet to several miles from favored sites. Favored ledges are those offering a shielding overhang, and carbon dating of guano at Greenland nest sites have disclosed occupancy dating back between 2,360 and 2,740 years ago. Nest sites are not particularly high, in Alaska averaging 50 feet above the cliff base (with a range of 6 to 200 feet).

Eggs are usually laid on bare substrate or accumulated debris; however, raven nests are often appropriated. The old nests of Rough-legged Hawk are generally still snow covered when Gyrfalcon begins nesting. A typical brood has three or four eggs (two to seven in years marked by food extremes). Incubation begins with the penultimate egg and lasts 35 or 36 days. Both sexes incubate, but the female is the primary incubator. The male supplies all the prey for the first two or three weeks and most prey overall. Young fledge at seven or eight weeks, mid-July to early August, and are tended by adults for at least a month.

Unlike some other Arctic raptors, the breeding of Gyrfalcon seems unaffected by the population cycle of lemmings; however, this species' breeding success is most certainly affected by ptarmigan numbers. Cade, however, notes that lemmings are an important prey item for recently fledged Gyrfalcons and that rodent predators like jaegers become a food source for Gyrfalcons during lemming irruptive years.

BEHAVIOR/HUNTING: Gyrfalcons typically do not hunt in the vicinity of the nest, but it is highly presumptuous on the part of prey-sized birds to consider the vicinity of the nest a "safe zone."

Gyrfalcons use several hunting methods, calibrated to terrain and prey. These are a high, quartering search followed by a stoop, which often culminates in a tail chase; low contour flying, employing a flap and glide; and soaring over ridges and valleys, in a style similar to that of Golden Eagle. These techniques may be used in combination and in succession.

Once a Gyrfalcon sights prey, there

Left: An immature gray-morph Gyrfalcon stands on the Arctic coastal tundra of Prudhoe Bay, Alaska. Right: A stunning white Gyrfalcon finishes dinner. Over much of its range and for most of the year, this means birds. Rock and Willow Ptarmigan are particularly targeted species.
Left: Kevin T. Karlson; right: Lloyd Spitalnik

This very robust juvenile dark morph was photographed by Ray Schwartz in a cemetery in New Haven, Connecticut, somewhat south of the birds' typical winter range. It has a starling in its talons. Courtesy Kevin T. Karlson

are four modes of pursuit. For prey on the ground spotted at a distance, the falcon flies close to the ground, using terrain to mask the approach in hopes of taking prey by surprise. Barring this, the falcon pursues the prey in a tail chase over long distances, exhausting it, ultimately forcing it to go aloft or ground itself. The falcon is more likely to knock or drive the prey to the ground than to snatch it in the air. The third mode is hovering, if the prey is in cover, and the fourth is a direct climb to gain altitude on birds, using a steep climb rather than the ringing-up manner of a Peregrine.

"Ridge hopping" is a common hunting tactic wherein the Gyr hunts low over one ridgetop, passes directly across an intervening valley, then hunts low along the crest of the flanking ridge, perching, perhaps, to scan for prey. Gyrs take most prey on or near the ground.

PREY: Gyrfalcons eat chiefly birds. Both Rock and Willow Ptarmigan are particularly targeted all year, but especially in winter and spring, before migratory birds arrive. Birds range in size from small passerines (such as longspurs) to ducks and geese. Gyrs also take some mammals, ranging in size from rodents to hares. Birds in coastal areas take fewer ptarmigan and more seabirds and waterfowl. Pairs at higher altitude take more mammals.

In winter Gyrs selectively target Ring-necked Pheasant, Greater Sage-Grouse, and assorted waterfowl.

STATUS: Eugene Potapov has calculated the potential breeding range of the Gyrfalcon to encompass 4,600,476 square miles—a vast amount of habitat. Assuming an average density of 1.5 pairs per 620 square miles, a projected world population of Gyrfalcons approximates 11,106 pairs. Tom Cade used more conservative density estimates and calculated 7,000 to 9,000 pairs. Potapov also calculated minimum and maximum estimates based upon population estimates provided by biologists for eight countries boasting high breeding densities. These are Iceland, Norway, Sweden, Finland, Russia, the United States (Alaska), Canada, and Greenland. He arrived at a total population of between 7,880 and 10,990 pairs, estimates that bracket his projection and are more in accord with Cade's estimates.

Estimates for Canada and the United States put the North American population between 2,925 and 3,875 pairs (with most birds occurring in Canada). These are astonishing figures; yet most avid birders may spend their lives never seeing one of these grand Arctic falcons. By using any of the estimates presented, this species hardly lives up to its reputation for being rare.

Peregrine Falcon
Falco peregrinus

ETYMOLOGY: The Latin *peregrinus* is for "foreign, wandering." Albertus Magnus (1206–1280) offers this explanation for the bird's name: it constantly moves from one place to another (an erroneous observation). "The mediaeval falconers so named the bird because the young were not taken like eggs from the nest but caught in their passage from the breeding place."

PROFILE: This is a bird made for and of superlatives. From its huge, wind-seining feet to its fathomless dark eyes and its hemisphere-vaulting wings, this is a bird that inspires.

Noted Audubon: "The flight of this bird is of astonishing rapidity." Said Wilson,

> This noble bird had excited our curiosity for a long time. Every visit which we made to the coast, was rendered doubly interesting by the wonderful stories which we heard of its exploits in fowling, and of its daring enterprise . . . It was described as darting, with the rapidity of an arrow, . . . Even the wild geese were said to be in danger from its attack, it having been known to sacrifice them to its rapacity . . . If we were to repeat all the anecdotes which have been related to us of the achievements of the Duck Hawk, they would swell our pages at the expense, probably, of our reputation.

Opposite: *Following a successful reintroduction campaign, Peregrine Falcons have returned to historic eastern nest sites. This adult pair was photographed in Connecticut.* Jim Zipp

Today thousands of visitors continue to travel to coastal locations to see this bird of high praise and find fascination in its passage. A good day's flight in Cape May, New Jersey, may exceed 100 birds. However, the planet's greatest Peregrine movement passes through the Florida Keys where, in 2015, 4,559 migrating Peregrines were tallied at the Florida Keys Hawkwatch at Curry Hammock State Park—a total that includes a one-day record total of 1,506 birds recorded on October 10, 2015. From Tom Cade's account of this bird in his *Falcons of the World,* I quote, with thanks to him, Roger Tory Peterson's observation lifted from the pages of *Birds over America:*

> Man has emerged from the shadows of antiquity with a Peregrine on his wrist. Its dispassionate brown eyes, more than those of any other bird, have been witness to the struggle for civilization, from the squalid tents on the steppes of Asia, thousands of years ago to the marbled halls of European Kings in the seventeenth century.

Thus proclaimed the dean of American bird watching, nearly a century and a half after Alexander Wilson's account and just before man and bird engaged in an epic and unforeseen tragedy that would humiliate us and threaten the bird's place in our future.

I hope there will be a time when an account of this celebrated falcon can be written without invoking the specter of DDT. Sadly, the moment to separate the bird from that legacy of hubris and human unmindfulness has not yet arrived. I would greatly enjoy being the first to make this separation, but to do so would cheat the bird of its heritage—sad as this chapter might be. For at least the span of my generation, the letters DDT and Peregrine will be irrevocably bound and serve as a warning to future generations that even calculated changes wrought upon the environment are never done with impunity.

DESCRIPTION: This is a large to medium-sized falcon. As noted by John Krider: "They vary much in size—the male (also called a tercel) is much smaller than the female (known as the falcon) and the plumage of the adult bird different from that of young." Audubon chose to depict the birds with prey calibrated to size. The male mantles a Green-winged Teal, the female a Gadwall. The "Duck Hawk's" reputation as an accomplished slayer of waterfowl is not without foundation.

Structurally, the Peregrine is large-headed, with a robust body whose muscular girth when perched is masked somewhat by the length of the wings that nearly reach the tip of its long tail. The bird's bright yellow feet are enormous for its size, the trait that gave rise to the bird's early name, "Great-footed Hawk," the name favored by both Wilson and Audubon. By the second edition of the *AOU Checklist of North American Birds,* it was known as Duck Hawk, a name the species held until late in the twentieth century, when it was replaced by the current name. I once had the temerity to point out to Roger Tory Peterson that the feet of the birds in his Peregrine portrait were too small. "Yes," he agreed, then added, "but if you draw them to their proper size, people don't like it." I note as I write these words that Roger's image and his Peregrine print sit catty-corner above my desk, his white Gyrfalcon painting behind.

A Peregrine sampler. From left, top and bottom: adult ventral, adult dorsal, and juvenile. Note the golden crown on the juvenile, indicative of a young tundra Peregrine. Clockwise from top left: Jim Zipp, Jim Zipp, Kevin T. Karlson, Kevin T. Karlson, Steve Sachs, Steve Sachs

The adult is slate gray above, the head capped with a blackish helmet whose single broad mustache extends from the bird's blackish brown eye almost to the breast. The throat and breast are white with some light spotting and sometimes washed with rufous or pink. The balance of the underparts is heavily barred. Juvenile birds are similar to adults but brown above and also show a bold, well-defined, wide, dark mustache. The throat is whitish but the balance of the underparts is heavily streaked, so much so that the underparts of distant juveniles may appear wholly dark.

The similarly sized and proportioned Prairie Falcon is overall paler, and grayish brown above and spotted below. The Prairie Falcon's mustache is less prominent, and when it is perched, its wingtips fall short of the tip of the tail. The mustache on the smaller Merlin is even less distinct, showing little contrast against the Merlin's darker face. The Gyrfalcon appears overall more robust, particularly more pot-bellied than the Peregrine, and the wingtips fall well short of the tail tip.

MEASUREMENTS

Length: male 9–11 inches; female 11–12 inches
Wingspan: male 21–23 inches; female 24–27 inches
Weight: male 4.5–6.6 ounces; female 6.4–8.3 ounces

SYSTEMATICS/SUBSPECIES: Nineteen subspecies are recognized worldwide, three of which are native to North America:

F. p. anatum breeds from southern portions of the Arctic tundra to Mexico, except for the Pacific Northwest. It formerly bred in the eastern half of the United States but was extirpated by DDT.

F. p. tundrius breeds across the Arctic tundra regions from Alaska to Greenland. This is generally the palest subspecies. Juvenile birds typically show a pale, tawny to golden crown.

F. p. pealei (Peale's Falcon) breeds from Aleutian Islands to coastal Alaska south to the Pacific Northwest. It is generally the darkest subspecies, with the head and broad mustache giving birds a hooded appearance.

DISTRIBUTION: This species has one of the widest natural distributions on the planet. It breeds on every continent but Antarctica, as well as many oceanic islands. In North America, it ranges across the Arctic, north to the islands of the Canadian Archipelago, south to the edge of the taiga forest. It also breeds coastally from the Aleutians to southern California and in the Rockies and Cascades. It formerly ranged widely across the eastern United States. The second edition of the *AOU Checklist* (1895) observes: "Breeds locally throughout most of its United States range." Noted John Krider 1879: "I have often met this bird as far east as Maine, and as far west as Minnesota, along the Mississippi River, and have not been able myself to find its nest . . . "

Following their extirpation in the 1960s, there was a large-scale reintroduction effort in the 1970s. In the East, reintroduced breeding birds are today mostly relegated to urban areas, with some renesting now occurring on traditional nest ledges, as well as on platforms erected in coastal locations. Reintroduced birds are the product of a mix of genetic stock.

The Peale's subspecies is largely resident, but Arctic birds are wholly migratory, with wintering birds retreating into an "enormous" winter range. They are found in open, prey-rich habitats in the Midwest, south through the West Indies and coastal portions of Mexico and Central and South America to central Argentina and southern Chile.

MIGRATION: This is a celebrated coastal and offshore migrant, with some birds (especially adult males) migrating entirely offshore, day and night. In fall, concentrations occur along seacoasts. Over forested habitat, birds are attracted to river corridors and sparsely vegetated ridge tops. At the Curry Hammock State Park Hawkwatch in the Florida Keys, 2,858 migrating Peregrines have been counted in a single season. More recent data shows continued increases in numbers at Curry Hammock, with 4,010 birds counted in 2013; 4,216 in 2014; and 4,559 in 2015. A single-day count on October 10, 2015, recorded an amazing 1,506 birds, surpassing the previous single-day count record by over 800 birds!

Fall migration is from early September to mid-December, with most birds migrating from late September to mid-October. In spring, many birds appear to migrate through the center of the United States after staging along the Texas coast. Spring migration ranges from mid-March through mid-June, with peak migration April through May.

HABITAT: This is a hawk of open places: open sky and open, unencumbered terrain. In North America, the greatest breeding densities are now found in Arctic regions. In winter and during migration, coastal habitats seem favored, including beaches, coastal marshes, open wetlands where shorebirds and waterfowl abound, mudflats, and mangroves bordering shorebird-rich flats. But almost any open, featureless terrain rich in prey species—most notably waterfowl, shorebirds, pigeons, and doves—may hold wintering Peregrine. In the Northwest, where Peale's Falcons are permanent residents, the winter and breeding habitats are the same, although prey species often differ seasonally. In summer, birds heavily target cliff-nesting alcids, and they may hunt little else.

For all Peregrines, cliffs and bluffs are an important component of prime nesting territories and, historically, in the East and elsewhere, they particularly favor cliffs overlooking broad rivers (such as the Palisades, overlooking the Hudson River in New York, and the bluff-rich Colville River in Alaska). Cliffs bordering large lakeshores and coastal locations are also prime nest locations. Increasingly, manmade structures vie with more natural nest locations and have enabled Peregrines to nest in places formerly unoccupied. These structures include communication towers in abandoned DEW-line installations in the Arctic; water towers, bridges, and skyscrapers in urban areas; as well as "hack boxes" specifically designed and positioned to accommodate hacked (released) birds and their descendants. Peregrines also sometimes use old nests situated in spruce trees growing on tundra eskers.

On the nest ledge. Like other falcons, Peregrines do not build nests but deposit eggs on bare substrate or in the nests of other raptors or corvids. Incubation takes about 34 days. Young fledge in five or six weeks but continue to be tended by adults for an additional five or six weeks. Top and center: Jim Zipp; bottom: Steve Sachs

In the Arctic, Peregrines occupy the same cliffs used by Gyrfalcons, ravens, and Rough-legged Hawks.

BREEDING: Like other falcons, this species does not build a nest, so it is obligated to deposit its eggs on some existing platform close to prime hunting habitat (typically open but at least prey-rich). It favors cliff ledges and crags, but it also adopts old nests of large birds (including raven and heron) in large open tree cavities. The birds have also been known to nest on riverbanks and steep slopes, and even on the ground, in patches of heath surrounded by bog. Peregrines are increasingly adopting manmade structures.

Peregrines breed from February to July, depending upon latitude. In places where birds remain year-round (the Aleutians, Mexico), birds may sit side by side on nest ledges as early as January.

Birds excavate shallow scrapes in pliable substrate two weeks to two months prior to egg laying. Courtship continues until egg laying. Apparently, Peregrines do not mate for life. Males show a high degree of fidelity to nest sites, but females are fluid and appear to select in favor of preferred nest sites. Preferred sites are elevated for protection from ground predators and for the view over prime hunting habitat, very often overlooking a river or lake. The male begins the scrape but the female often finishes it.

A typical clutch is three or four eggs, occasionally five or six. One could hardly do better than quote the description of Peregrine eggs offered by Derek Ratcliffe in his treatise on this species:

> The eggs of the Peregrine are among the most handsome laid by any bird. Whilst the prevailing color is the characteristic red-brown of the genus *Falco*, the range of variation in Peregrine eggs is very large. At first sight, it appears there are three types of pigmentation. The surface of a fresh egg has variable amounts of bright red-brown markings . . . Beneath the surface markings is a more diffuse and often more continuous "ground color," varying from a typical biscuit brown to brick red or paler shades of pink, fawn, buff and cream.

If eggs avoid predation, the eager hands of egg collectors, and breakage under the weight of the incubating female, they hatch in 33 to 35 days. Birds fully cloaked in their juvenile plumage fledge in five to six weeks. Young and adults roost and remain about the cliff for a few days, seldom visiting the nest ledge. Both parents continue to bring prey to their young for about five or six weeks. Prey is exchanged in flight. Perhaps this functions as a training exercise, preparing young for the time they become one of the natural world's most accomplished aerial interceptors.

BEHAVIOR/HUNTING: The level cruising flight of a Peregrine (40 to 55 miles per hour) is not particularly fast and is, in fact, slower than the top speed of many prey species, including pigeons and assorted ducks. During pursuit, however, the level speed of a Peregrine may exceed 100 miles per hour—fast enough to outpace all but the swiftest prey.

Peregrines most commonly intercept prey in flight. They may launch an attack from a perch (cliff, tree, manmade structure) or from the ground, or while soaring or engaged in active flight. They sometimes hunt insects, small mammals, and nestlings on foot. They have been known to follow hunters and farm machinery to intercept flushed prey. Audubon asserted that the bird would come to the "report" of a fowling piece (gun). They also hunt bats at roosting cave entrances.

Peregrines capture prey using several

Tag, you're prey. Why raptors like this adult male Peregrine select the individual they do out of a flock may relate to some vulnerability or infirmity demonstrated by the prey, or it might be that this particular Rock Pigeon had a distinctive plumage pattern that made it easy to target amid the panic. Chris and Chad Saladin

techniques, the most celebrated of which is the stoop, in which a Peregrine, having gained superior height, uses gravity and body mass to quickly close on prey in a dive that ranges from vertical to a tempered 20 degrees. The speed of a Peregrine's dive has long been a matter of wonder and debate. One calculation of the terminal velocity of a diving falcon was 223 miles per hour.

Pre-ornithological and now debunked presumptions that impact is made with the keel or wings notwithstanding, a Peregrine strikes with its feet. Refuted Alexander Wilson, "this cannot be the fact, as the breast bone of this species does not differ from that of others of the same tribe, which would not admit to so violent concussion."

So the strike is made with the feet, but how? Noted Wilson, "ducks which

Cedar Waxwing: it's what's for dinner. Peregrines also take avian prey as large as waterfowl. Adults often pass food to young fledglings in the air. Chris and Chad Saladin

Widely regarded as the fastest living thing on planet Earth, the Peregrine has a dive—called a "stoop"—that may exceed 200 miles per hour. Jim Zipp

are struck down, have their backs lacerated from the rump to the neck. If this be the fact, it is proof that the hawk employs only its talons." So an open, not a closed foot. More recently, "high speed cinematography confirmed that all four toes are splayed at impact." After contact the feet are immediately closed into a fist.

At other times, Peregrines simply grab prey in the air. The size of the prey, the composition of the substrate below, and the relative speed of the falcon and prey at impact probably determine whether a Peregrine binds to its prey or sends it tumbling, to be retrieved in the air or after it hits the ground or water. Prey that survives the falcon's strike is killed by decapitation.

Another celebrated hunting technique this bird employs with great success is a form of three-dimensional herding, known among falconers as "ringing up." Peregrines employ this method to capture prey flying at altitudes greater than the Peregrine and also to close upon and exhaust pursued prey that attempts to escape by climbing. Ringing up is an apt description, as birds engaged in this hunting maneuver continuously climb toward prey by flying in a series of ascending circles that simultaneously force prey to climb and block any effort on the part of the prey to dive and seek shelter in whatever habitat might be below. Climactically, the Peregrine ultimately climbs above its prey, then executes a series of shallow, harassing stoops that serve to exhaust the prey, which is captured in the air or—if the prey dives for cover—pursued as the falcon stoops. If the stoop is unsuccessful and the prey levels out, the falcon pursues, using accelerated, powered flight (a tail chase). Peregrines commonly consume captured prey on a perch or on the ground, but some prey is consumed by birds on the wing, especially during migration.

I once observed an adult female with a flicker in her talons turn into the wind and, flapping rapidly, rise vertically until nearly out of sight. Then, lunch in tow, she headed southeast out over the Atlantic. Next stop, West Indies, perhaps?

Peregrines also practice cruise or "contour hunting": flying fast and low, they use topographic features and vegetation to conceal their approach and attempt to surprise prey, which, once flushed, they overtake and capture. I once saw a juvenile Peregrine capture a migrating

Superior speed and taloned feet do not guarantee success. But as this flicker in the talons of this juvenile Peregrine attests, the youngster has gained a measure of hunting skill to go with a Peregrine's evolutionary refinements. Rob Curtis

DDT

The eggs are not just coveted by collectors—they constitute one of the Peregrine's few vulnerabilities. Despite assorted persecutions and changes to their environment, Peregrine numbers remained generally stable until the 1940s and '50s when, suddenly, populations in the United States and Europe began experiencing a high degree of nest failure. It was determined that a number of eggs were breaking under the weight of incubating females and that females were even consuming egg shells. In time, as the alarm over increased nest failure burgeoned, it was established that it was the introduction of a synthetic organic insecticide into the biosphere that was disrupting the reproductive capacity of Peregrines and other birds of prey by inhibiting calcium formation, resulting in untenably thin-shelled eggs. Developed in 1939 by a Swiss chemical firm, "dichlor-diphenyl-trichlor-ethane (abbreviated for obvious reasons to DDT) was widely used by United States and British armed forces to combat malaria-carrying mosquitoes during World War II. After the war it was used by farmers to control crop-eating insects, and by many communities intent on reducing nuisance levels of mosquitoes in burgeoning suburban and coastal neighborhoods.

In summer in my neighborhood in northern New Jersey, the DDT-fogging truck was as punctual, prevalent, and anticipated as the ice cream truck. Ice cream bars in hand, we would chase the fogger down the street, playing hide-and-seek in the billowing, sweet-smelling cloud.

Unbeknownst to science, the chemical substance—while applied in levels that were not immediately lethal to birds—could pass from affected prey to birds that consumed them and accumulate at increasingly higher levels in fatty tissue in the form of DDE, a biological breakdown product of DDT. It wasn't until 1961 that the link was made between DDT and eggshell thinning, thanks largely to the efforts of British scientists Norman Moore and Derek Ratcliffe.

In the United States, the EPA ordered a ban on DDT in 1972, but not before all Peregrines nesting in the eastern United States were extirpated and Arctic populations halved. Western Peregrine populations, too, evidenced sharp declines. Today, Arctic populations have in many places returned to pre-DDT levels, and western populations are recovering. The empty nest ledges of the eastern *anatum* linger as a dark tribute to human unmindfulness. The loss of this subspecies has been mitigated somewhat by the widespread reintroduction of Peregrines spearheaded by the Cornell Lab of Ornithology and Dr. Tom Cade in the 1960s.

Some of these released birds, whose genetic lines are a mix of Old and New World Peregrine subspecies, have found their way to historic nest ledges. More have established in urban areas, drawn to the wealth of manmade cliffs as well as a reliable surfeit of the Peregrine's favorite prey—large, meaty pigeons.

Sharp-shinned Hawk using this technique. What made the encounter notable was what transpired next. Slowed and preoccupied by her burden, the falcon was immediately set upon by a Northern Harrier that came up from behind and below. Reaching out with harrier-long legs, she ripped the still-struggling Sharp-shinned from the falcon's grasp.

Peregrines also occasionally "run,

If this adult Peregrine were a tundra bird instead of one of the reintroduced and nonmigratory resident birds, it would be enjoying the touch of tropical sun instead of falling snow. On the other hand, this probably passes for a nice day in coastal Greenland, even though it was a winter day in Cleveland, Ohio. Chris and Chad Saladin

hop and flap after invertebrates, rarely reptiles and small mammals." They also take fledgling birds in this manner.

PREY: An aerial specialist, the Peregrine captures a large and diverse array of mostly avian prey, ranging in size from passerines to geese and herons. Prey weight range for females is 3½ to 4 pounds. In migration, Peregrines forage over open ocean, often far from land, and when they are migrating over the forest, they take prey in the air. They target some prey species more heavily than others, most notably those that engage in aerial courtship displays (such as Wilson's Snipe and ptarmigan) or show conspicuous "flash patterns" in flight (such as Red-winged Blackbirds and flickers). Not coincidentally, these species are also denizens of open country.

Doves and pigeons are preferred wherever they occur. While a species-specific accounting of Peregrine prey does not exist for North America, Cade estimates that 200 species would "not be out of order." Prey also includes some mammals—predominantly bats, but also small rodents.

STATUS: Prior to World War II, there were an estimated 7,000 to 10,000 occupied territories in North America. By 1998 (26 years after DDT was banned), the number of active nest sites in North America approached complete recovery.

Prairie Falcon
Falco mexicanus

An adult Prairie Falcon. Want to make something of it, Bub? Jerry Liguori

ETYMOLOGY: The species name *mexicanus* is for "Mexican," something of a misnomer, as the bird's breeding range falls mostly in the United States.

PROFILE: The Prairie Falcon is a large desert falcon, master of the skies where distance is measured by the horizon and the air tastes like flint. An "irascible, excitable bird . . . " "Not as courageous and 'noble' as Peregrine." Counters Cade: "In aerial performance it is a match for the peregrine in most respects, and its rather aggressive and high-strung temperament produces an altogether capable and determined hunter . . . "

DESCRIPTION: This is a large, long-tailed, pale brown falcon of open, arid western lands. Similar in size and shape to the more widespread and familiar Peregrine, to which it is closely related, Prairie Falcon is more square-headed, with almost owlishly large eyes (which may advantage the bird, whose largely desert prey may be more active at dawn and dusk). The cheek is scored by a single malar stripe, which is narrower and less defined than that of the Peregrine. The whitish underparts are spotted in adults, streaked in juveniles. The sexes are similar, but the females are larger.

MEASUREMENTS
Length: male 14–16 inches;
female 16–18 inches
Wingspan: male 36–38 inches;
female 41–44 inches

Weight: male 0.9–1.4 pounds; female 1.5–2.1 pounds

SYSTEMATICS/SUBSPECIES: The Prairie Falcon was traditionally regarded as a member of the "desert falcon group," which includes Gyrfalcon, Lanner, and Saker, but DNA analysis "suggests a closer kinship to Peregrine."

No subspecies are recognized. But Anderson and Squires report several color phases.

VOCALIZATIONS: The Prairie Falcon's sounds are similar to the Gyrfalcon's array, but more subdued. Sibley accounts Prairie Falcon's vocalizations as similar to Peregrine but higher. Anderson and Squires concur: "Prairie Falcons scream in a high-pitched voice."

DISTRIBUTION: Cade says that the Prairie Falcon "has the most restricted breeding distribution" of the North American falcons; however, this breeding range encompasses much of the western United States, from the High Plains west to California, central Oregon, and central Washington, north into southern British Columbia, Alberta, and to the southwest, with the northern limit of the breeding range reaching southeastern British Columbia, southern Alberta, southern Saskatchewan, and northern North Dakota. The southern limit is defined by Baja California; southern Arizona; southern New Mexico; eastern Voahuila, Mexico; and western and northern Texas. In winter, it vacates much of its Canadian breeding range and higher elevations. The states with the highest populations are Idaho, Wyoming, Utah, Montana, and California. Cade notes that the birds are "quite unevenly spread within this range." Adults show a high degree of fidelity to nest sites, but where nest sites are abundant, pairs usually do not use the same site in

A mated pair of adult Prairie Falcons on the cliffs in the Klamath National Wildlife Refuge in Oregon, the male on the left, female on the right. Kevin T. Karlson

consecutive years. Yet prime sites show a high rate of occupancy.

Birds in Utah are reported to winter near nesting areas, but Canadian birds vacate their natal areas. The winter range extends east into the American prairies to Minnesota, northwestern Iowa, central Missouri, and most of Texas, as well as Mexico. But for the most part, the winter range is mainly in the Great Plains and the Great Basin.

MIGRATION: Prairie Falcons' migration is not as proscribed as that of many raptors, and may move more in response to prey availability than the calendar. Nevertheless, in the Goshute Mountains of Nevada, birds are noted at raptor-watch locations August 23 to November 1. There, an average 28 migrating Prairie Falcons are tallied every autumn.

Wintering birds are present in Utah October to March. Birds retire to higher altitudes to avoid summer heat; with colder weather, they descend from the mountains. Spring arrival and onset of breeding correlates with the emergence of hibernating ground squirrels.

HABITAT: Brown and Amadon say Prairie Falcon is "primarily a bird of treeless areas . . . Arid plains and steppes of interior North America . . ." It also inhabits alpine tundra. Cliffs and bluffs are essential components of its breeding habitat. It is often seen perched on utility poles and high-tension towers. On boulders or other natural perches, its color fuses so well with the landscape it is frequently heard before it is seen. It shares nest cliffs with ravens and, more grudgingly, with Golden Eagles, Great Horned Owls, and Red-tailed Hawks. It does not require a

Opposite: Prairie Falcons prefer cliff nests that offer a degree of protective overhang. These three advanced young constitute a typical clutch. Young leave the nest 29 to 47 days after hatching, then seek out areas where food is abundant. Jim Zipp

water component and is not coastal in nature as is Peregrine, but watercourses are frequently the source of the cliffs upon which the bird breeds.

In winter, birds move to lower areas, where there are concentrations of larks. Specific habitats include "desert grassland, dry farms, wheat fields, irrigated croplands, cattle feedlots," that support populations of starlings and other grain-eating birds.

BREEDING: The breeding cycle begins as soon as the adults return to the nest site. Dates vary with latitude and altitude, but generally it is late February through March. Incubation begins when the clutch is nearly complete. Egg laying coincides with the time when young ground squirrels are becoming active aboveground.

Prairie Falcons nest primarily on cliff faces but also in trees and on power line structures. But the most common nest sites are in cavities, ledges, crevices or potholes on volcanic buttes, sandstone canyons, bluffs, and isolated rock outcrops. Most cliff nests have some degree of overhang, and Prairie Falcon frequently reuses nests of other species (raven, Golden Eagle). Most scrapes are located on the upper half of cliff faces. The nest is a shallow depression or scrape, either on soft, bare substrate or in an appropriated nest and usually on south-facing cliffs.

A typical clutch is four or five white to

Two adult Prairie Falcons engage in a food pass. Note the size difference between the male (above) and the larger female. Steve Sachs

pinkish white eggs, usually overlaid with a "speckling or spotting of reddish-brown or brown, buff purplish pink, sometimes more heavily marked . . . " The relatively short incubation period lasts 29 to 31 days. Young leave the nest 29 to 47 days posthatching. After fledging, the falcons drift into areas where food is abundant.

BEHAVIOR/HUNTING: The "most common strategy is a swift, direct flight that ends with a long, low-angle stoop at prey."

To understand the Prairie Falcon's hunting techniques, it is first important to understand that during the breeding season, ground squirrels are the dietary mainstay. In winter, the falcon's diet switches over to birds, particularly Horned Larks, which flock in numbers in habitats where many Prairie Falcons winter.

During sunny or windy weather, Prairie Falcon may soar at altitudes above their cruise-hunting height, and after sighting prey, dive at a 30- to 60-degree angle, leveling off as they near the ground and gliding the remaining 10 to 300 meters. They sometimes perch-hunt, in combination with an accipiter-like hedge-hopping approach that takes advantage of cover; this species is also observed to hunt in a low, slow harrier-like manner. They take most prey on or near the ground. If the Peregrine is a boxer, the Prairie Falcon is a brawler.

I was taken by this colorful description by Major Brooks of the Prairie Falcon's style and ruggedness when attacking small mammals: "In striking at these [ground squirrels, marmots, and jackrabbits], it descends like a bullet at a long low angle, and if the animal is missed it may ricochet along the ground for some distance, striking again and again, a puff of dust marking each unsuccessful effort."

STATUS: The pesticides that devastated Peregrine populations in the middle of the twentieth century left Prairie Falcon populations relatively unscathed, although variable amounts of pesticide residue were found in Prairie Falcon eggs. Today, the bird is accounted "widespread and common within its breeding range . . . with a total breeding population estimated at 5,000 to 6,000 breeding pairs." Underscoring the health of the population is the legal annual harvest of birds in 19 states for falconry.

Low and fast is the Prairie Falcon's forte. Brian Sullivan

NEW WORLD VULTURES

Three species

Black Vulture

Coragyps atratus

ETYMOLOGY: *Coragyps* is from the Greek *korax,* for "raven" and *gyps* for "vulture." The Latin *atratus* is for "clothed in black" as for mourning.

PROFILE: This smallish, somewhat compact New World vulture enjoys a broad geographic range throughout the Americas; while its range in the United States is expanding, it is still mostly restricted to the southeastern and Mid-Atlantic states.

Like the Turkey Vulture, with which it associates, the bird has traditionally been ranked among the diurnal birds of prey. In places where human sanitation mechanisms are lax—including, historically, cities and towns in the southern United States—these birds perform a valuable sanitation function.

While New World vultures are not properly classified as "raptors," as their weak feet are incapable of grasping prey (the defining characteristic of the *raptare*), they do have many of the gross characteristics of the Old World vultures, which are raptors in functional and genetic fact.

Opposite: *Not ranked among the planet's most endearing denizens, Black Vulture is nevertheless an efficient scavenger and sometimes predator. The unfeathered head permits the bird to delve deep into the fetid confines of large carcasses.* Brian Small

---

DESCRIPTION: The Black Vulture is a large bird of prey, slightly larger than Red-tailed Hawk but smaller and more compact than the Turkey Vulture. It is overall dull black, with a dull gray unfeathered head; legs and feet are whitish, caked as they are in excrement. Standing birds appear to crouch or slouch. The whitish outer primaries show only as a trace along the edge of the folded wing. It looks more menacing than Turkey Vulture and is in point of fact more aggressive, more nimble afoot, and more predatory than its larger cousin. Sexes are similar, and immatures resemble adults.

MEASUREMENTS
Length: 23–28 inches
Wingspan: 55–63 inches
Weight: 3.8–5.1 pounds

SYSTEMATICS/SUBSPECIES: Three subspecies are recognized. *C. a. atratus* occurs in eastern North America. *C. a. brasiliensis* occurs mostly at low altitudes, from central Mexico to Lima, Peru, and southern Brazil, east to Bolivia. *C. a. foetens,* of western South America, is resident in the Andes from northern Ecuador to northern Bolivia.

VOCALIZATIONS: Black Vulture lacks a syrinx but is capable of piglike grunts and hisses.

DISTRIBUTION: Widespread, Black Vulture is a permanent resident through most of South America and across all of Central America. In North America, it is primarily a resident of the southeastern United States, but it also occurs in southern Arizona, west Texas, eastern Oklahoma, southern Missouri, southern

Overall more compact than the Turkey Vulture, the Black Vulture spends much of its time aloft searching visually for carrion or the telltale descent of other vultures to lead it to carrion. Unlike Turkey Vultures, Black Vultures do not locate prey by smell. Kevin T. Karlson

Illinois, southern Indiana, central Ohio, south-central Pennsylvania, and New Jersey south to the Gulf Coast and Florida. It has also been recorded in summer in southeastern New York and southern Maine.

Writing in the early 1800s, both Audubon and Wilson noted Black Vulture's southern proclivities and (then) its absence in the Northeast. Now, however, owing to a range expansion that began in the mid-1970s, Black Vulture is a common resident of both eastern Pennsylvania and all of New Jersey, its population in places exceeding that of Turkey Vulture. This expansion has, perhaps, been aided by the explosion of white-tailed deer numbers in the Northeast, coupled with increased roadkill of deer and other animals resulting from the evolution of the automobile-driven suburban culture that evolved just after World War II.

MIGRATION: Over most of its range this is a nonmigratory, resident species, although some northeastern breeders do appear to retreat south in November and December, with migration noted in Cape May, New Jersey. There is also some evidence of fall migration through Panama.

HABITAT: Black Vultures generally forage over open unforested habitat but typically roost and breed in woodlands. On sunny days, unless they are feeding, they are usually seen soaring very high, often higher than Turkey Vultures, which locate prey (at least in part) by smell, an olfactory edge Black Vultures lack. Some authorities suggest that Black Vultures watch Turkey Vultures and rely upon them to locate carrion by smell, then drive the Turkey Vultures away from the carcasses through overt aggression or sheer force of numbers. However, in South Jersey, I commonly see Black Vultures foraging before Turkey Vultures leave the roost. As thermal-oriented as Turkey Vultures when traveling long distances, Black Vultures are quicker to resort to powered flight so are able to leave roosts earlier than the more thermal-dependent Turkey Vultures.

BREEDING: Pairs remain in close contact year-round, apparently mating for life. Prior to nesting, pairs spend time perching together near prospective nest sites. A typical nest site is a place that offers a degree of seclusion and concealment (such as a hollow log, blown-down root structure, rocky crevices, caves, thickets, and, very commonly, abandoned buildings surrounded by woody growth). Birds appear to select areas away from human disturbance.

Audubon claimed Black Vultures never lay more than two eggs. Eggs are gray-green or creamy white to buff, or with sparse small blotches of deep reddish brown and markings sometimes

Benediction for some road-killed animal? No, wing drying or thermoregulation on a cold morning. Brian Small

concentrated at the larger end. Incubation, shared equally by the parents, lasts 38 or 39 days. At eight weeks, young can leave ground nest cavities, but fledging takes 10 or 11 weeks. After fledging, adults and young commonly share the same roost, and the young may continue to be fed by adults for as much as eight months.

BEHAVIOR/FORAGING: Black Vultures spend much of the day aloft or perched in the vicinity of carrion. They roost and feed communally, often in association with Turkey Vultures. In winter, typical roosts are in mature trees or man-made structures, often on a hillside so that early morning foraging expeditions can be conducted downhill in a gravity-friendly glide, thus avoiding the need to wait until thermals form. Black Vultures are believed to make roosts the center of their social and communications strategy. Birds returning to the roost with distended crops might expect to garner the watchful attention of unsuccessful birds when they leave the roost the following day.

Monitoring the next guy (whether at the roost or soaring aloft) seems to be central to Black Vulture's foraging strategy. Sharing is not a detriment when the carcass is a meat package as large as a white-tailed deer.

Most authorities account this species a scavenger, but it is also predatory, targeting weak or young animals. In cities, it has served a useful function as a sanitary engineer as it is often found foraging in landfills, "slaughterhouses, which are their favorite resort," and, in historic times, hospitals. Notes Wilson:

In towns and villages of the southern states, particularly Charleston and Georgetown, South Carolina, and in Savannah, Georgia, these birds may be seen sauntering about the streets; sunning themselves on the roofs of houses and the fences; or if the weather be cold, cowering around the tops of chimneys. They are protected by law; and may be said to be completely domesticated, being as common as the poultry, and equally familiar.

Wilson also labels the birds "indolent, loitering for hours in one place." While questioning the birds' domesticity, I do not doubt its acclimation to urban environments, since this nonchalance is seen in Black Vulture today in many southern American urban centers.

FOOD: Its diet includes offal, but this bird's numbers seem highest where there are large numbers of domestic animals whose births or deaths are grist for the bird's mill. Recounted here in full is an account by Alexander Wilson, who was evidently much impressed by his encounter with feeding Black Vultures near Charleston, South Carolina:

February 21, 1809. Went out to Hampstead this afternoon. A horse had dropped down in the street, in convulsions; and dying, it was dragged out to Hampstead and skinned. The Ground, for a hundred yards around it was black with Carrion Crows [Black Vulture]; many sat on the tops of sheds, fences and houses within sight; sixty or eighty on the opposite side of the stream. I counted at one time two-hundred and thirty-seven, but I believe there were more . . . I ventured to within thirty yards

A Black Vulture flanked by adult Turkey Vultures. While smaller than Turkey Vultures, Black Vultures tend to dominate at carcasses. When assembled in numbers, they are known to make even caracaras wait their turn. Kevin T. Karlson

of the carcass where three or four dogs and twenty or thirty vultures were busily tearing and devouring . . . I remarked the vultures frequently attack each other, fighting with their claws or heels, striking like a cock with open wings, and fixing their claws on each other's head.

More predatory than Turkey Vulture, this species has been known to kill young piglets and other young livestock. Notes Alexander Wilson, "It is said that the Black Vultures sometimes attack young pigs, and eat off their ears and tails; and we have even heard stories of their assaulting feeble calves, and picking out their eyes. But these instances are rare . . ."

However, a South Jersey landowner of my acquaintance attributes significant loss to Black Vulture, allowing that Black Vultures routinely capture and kill piglets ranging in age from one day to two weeks. He confides that the favored technique is for one or two vultures to reach under the outdoor sheds that shelter the mother and suckling pigs from the elements, then, grasping the piglet by the legs, ears, or snout, drag it into the open and proceed to consume it, starting with the ears, eyes, lips, and anus (his observations are in accord with Wilson's above). This feeding action quickly draws a host of onlooking vultures, who join in a feeding frenzy, quickly eviscerating and dismembering the hapless piglet. He confides that this predatory behavior has been ongoing since the 1980s (soon after Black Vultures became established as breeders in Cape May County, New Jersey).

STATUS: Black Vulture is accounted the most numerous vulture in the Western

Hemisphere. The health and growth of the population is attributed to the bird's close association with humans. As we flourish and modify the environment to meet our needs, this bird increases. Despite a modest population decline in the southeastern United States, the overall U.S. population is increasing and expanding north and east. The highest population densities occur in Florida, south Texas, central Mississippi, southern Louisiana, central Tennessee, and southwest Alabama. Birds seem particularly numerous where animal husbandry is practiced on an industrial scale.

Turkey Vulture
Cathartes aura

ETYMOLOGY: *Kathartes* is Greek for "a purifier," and *aura* is the South American name for the bird.

PROFILE: Owing to its large size, distinctive V-for-vulture wing configuration, low cruising flight, symbiotic relationship with our species, and its very extensive range (southern Canada to the tip of South America), the Turkey Vulture may be the most familiar and easily recognized bird species in the Americas.

Feeding almost exclusively upon carrion, this aerial scavenger rarely kills the prey it consumes. While it is not, strictly speaking, a raptor (a bird that grasps its prey), it commonly associates with other birds of prey. Almost eagle-sized in flight, it shows much the same shape and soaring mastery as Golden Eagle.

Despite widespread familiarity, and acclaim for its powers of flight, human regard for this carrion-eating species has long been two-sided. While most birds of prey will deign to eat carrion both at need and, in some species, as a matter of dietary course, vultures are often castigated for their dietary focus upon dead animals. Our dual regard for this species is wonderfully expressed by Alexander Wilson:

> The Turkey-buzzards are gregarious, peaceable, and harmless; never offering any violence to a living animal, or, like the plunders of the *Falco* tribe, depriving the husbandman of his stock. Hence, though in consequence of their filthy habits they are not beloved, yet they are respected for their usefulness; and in the southern states where they are most needed . . . are protected by a law . . .

It seems ironic that a species that gets its meat plastic wrapped and pre-cut into meal-sized portions should be so critical of another carrion feeder.

My personal regard for this species is akin to that of Maurice Broun, who said of Turkey Vulture in *Hawks Aloft*: "It is always pleasant to watch these great dark birds as they lazily, gracefully tack back and forth along our ridge, demonstrating their effortless conquest of the air currents." And in deference to those who think otherwise, I find Turkey Vulture a physically attractive bird—not only impressive in flight, but at close quarters, too, where the adult bird's red-flushed head, somber eyes, and horn-colored bill are visually arresting.

DESCRIPTION: Females are very slightly larger on average. In flight, Turkey Vultures are all dark (blackish) except for a

Turkey Vultures like this adult feed almost exclusively upon carrion, which they locate by sight and smell. The white on the feathers is droppings acquired at the roost. Steve Sachs

silvery grayish trailing edge to the under-wing. In good light, the body is shown to be blackish brown, with feathers some-what loosely arrayed. The unfeathered head of adults is bright red, and the hook-tipped bill is yellow to ivory. Juveniles have bare, grayish heads and dark bills. In flight, distant and high-flying birds appear to have long, broad wings with slotted wingtips, long tails, and small heads. Even when the birds are soaring, their tails are commonly not fanned.

MEASUREMENTS

Length: 23–38 inches
Wingspan: 55–63 inches
Weight: 3.8–5.1 pounds

SYSTEMATICS/SUBSPECIES: The first ca-thartid (New World Vulture) appeared about 60 to 50 million years ago during the Eocene. Curiously, the first fossil re-cords of the New World vultures were unearthed not in the Americas, but in France. This particular species' ancestors

In flight, Turkey Vultures hold their wings in a pronounced dihedral. Adult left, juvenile right.
Left: Kevin T. Karlson; right: Jim Zipp

originated in the mid-Pleistocene, so 40,000 to 10,000 years ago. These proto–Turkey Vultures were somewhat larger than today's birds. Today's Turkey Vulture is very closely related to Lesser Yellow-headed Vulture (*Cathartes burrovianus*) of Mexico and Central and South America.

As many as six subspecies are recognized:

C. a. septentrionalis breeds in eastern North America from the upper Midwest to southern New England and eastern Canada south to Florida, Texas, and the Gulf States. In winter, many northern breeders withdraw into the southeastern states, with some birds regularly wintering as far north as northern New Jersey.

C. a. meridionalis breeds in western North America east to southern Manitoba and south-central Texas. It winters in Central America and South America

south to southern Brazil and Paraguay, but some southernmost breeders may be resident.

C. a. aura breeds in southern California, southern Nevada, Arizona, New Mexico, and south Texas south to Costa Rica; also in the Greater Antilles. It winters from Mexico to Panama.

C. a. ruficollis occurs in Panama and tropical lowland South America through Uruguay and northern Argentina.

C. a. jota occurs in the Andean region from central Columbia south to Patagonia and the Falkland Islands.

VOCALIZATIONS: Turkey Vultures are typically silent, but when disturbed they may make a low-pitched nasal whine as well as a short staccato clucking—possibly a food call. Hissing and grunting sounds are also ascribed to this species.

DISTRIBUTION: Turkey Vulture has one of the greatest ranges of any New World bird species. It breeds from southern Canada to Tierra del Fuego and even the Falkland Islands. However, breeders are not uniformly apportioned across North America. It is described as "absent or very local in portions of the Great Plains." During the last half of the twentieth century, this species evidenced a distinct northward range expansion and population increase, including greater numbers of wintering birds in the northern portions of its breeding range. This change correlates to the great increase in white-tailed deer populations, as well as rising winter temperatures.

In my youth in northern New Jersey (1950s–'60s), this species was absent in December and January, typically returning as a migrant in the first week in February. Since the 1970s, however, they are a year-round resident throughout the state, and their northern breeding range extends north and west to Saskatchewan.

MIGRATION: The extent and timing of migration varies according to the sub-

The feet of New World vultures are ill-suited for grasping, a shortfall that evidently applies to perches as well as prey. Jim Zipp

Wheeling within a thermal, these migrating Turkey Vultures shed their loathsome qualities. Kevin T. Karlson

species, with eastern birds less migratory than western populations. Fall migration is broadly August to November, with peak numbers noted in early September through early October in the West and Midwest, late October into December in the East. But some winter arrivals reach Florida in early October. Birds continue to migrate through Panama into late November. Audubon, writing in the early 1800s, noted that "A very few remain and spend the winter in New Jersey and Pennsylvania . . ." However, as noted, the birds are now a common wintering species throughout this region.

In spring, nonwintering arrivals typ-ically reach New Jersey on or about February 2. In the Midwest, birds typically arrive several weeks later. In the West, they arrive in early March to early April. They migrate most commonly on days with little to moderate cloud cover (so days with good thermal activity). They travel in small groups, typically of 10 to 50 birds; however, in celebrated concentration points like Veracruz, flocks numbering in the thousands have been noted. In fall, the mean average season total at Veracruz is 197,299 birds; in spring at this same site the seasonal average is 162,652. In spring, at Braddock Bay, New York, a hawkwatch site on the south shore of Lake Erie, an average 11,404 vultures are tallied.

Turkey Vultures mix with other flocking raptor migrants, particularly Broad-winged and Swainson's Hawks. Both Bald and Golden Eagles may also join vulture flocks.

Unless winds are favorable and exceptional elevation has been gained, Turkey Vultures are reluctant to make water crossings in excess of a dozen miles. However, given optimal thermals and a light headwind, birds have been known to make the 12-mile crossing of Delaware Bay from Cape May, New Jersey, to Cape Henlopen, Delaware.

While a thermal-centric migrant, this vulture also takes advantage of favorable ridge updrafts, particularly on days when thermal production is scant. It generally waits until midmorning to begin its migration (unless favorable updrafts exist), and birds cease migration by late afternoon, when thermal production wanes.

HABITAT: Turkey Vultures appear to prefer a mix of forest and open areas (grasslands, wetlands, agricultural land, power line cuts). They roost communally (often with Black Vultures) in mature deciduous trees and conifers (particularly in winter). They also readily use manmade structures, such as water towers and communication towers. Typical numbers range from a dozen roosting birds to over 100, with one roost in vulture-rich Florida setting a record with 4,000.

Those wishing to see representative North American vulture habitat from a vulture's perspective are invited to go online and search for Andrew Wyeth's painting *Soaring,* which I believe is the only time this celebrated American landscape artist ever worked a living bird into his work.

BREEDING: Apparently monogamous, Turkey Vultures show a high degree of fidelity to attractive nest sites.

In the southern United States, they breed from mid-March to early April, with both members of the pair circling and perching near potential nest sites, which may be in rock outcrops, or among boulders and shallow caves. They use favored nest sites repeatedly. They also nest in prostrate hollow logs, on the ground beside stumps, as well as in thickets of palmetto, cactus, chaparral, and shrubs. Also, and increasingly, they nest upon elevated human structures, including abandoned houses and barns, although isolation from human disturbance appears to be an important component of chosen sites.

The clutch of two or three eggs is laid on the bare substrate, with no effort at nest construction. Eggs are gray-green to creamy buff, with large dark brown to reddish brown to lilac splotches. Incubation by both adults begins with the first egg, which hatches in 39 to 41 days. Fledging takes 10 or 11 weeks, although ground-nesting young may move from the nest site by eight weeks. This species has one brood per year, and young are fed by parents while they remain at the natal site. Soon after fledging, young relocate to communal roosts. It is not believed that young migrate with their parents.

Turkey Vultures feed on the ground, most commonly where the dead animal is located, but they may pull smaller prey to the sides of roadways or into protective confines if other vultures are present.

Vultures do not build nests but deposit their one to three eggs on the bare substrate of some sheltered place. This nest in Connecticut was in a shallow cave. Young fledge in 10 or 11 weeks.
Jim Zipp

BEHAVIOR/FORAGING: Roosting birds may become active at the first touch of sunlight, spreading their wings benediction wide, commonly with their backs to the sun. Some authorities maintain that the display is intended to dry night-dampened feathers, others that it is an effort to thermoregulate. For whatever reason, the birds soon fold their wings and typically wait until a breeze stirs the wind to rise, or thermals to perk, before leaving the roost to forage. Birds use the minutes before departure to preen.

I am familiar with one winter roost in a very upscale portion of Somerset County, New Jersey, that is on a hilltop overlooking an interstate highway rich in roadkill deer. The birds lift off soon after sunrise and, using gravity to advantage, glide to the highway with a minimum of flapping. Gorging themselves on the night's tribute of roadkill animals, they then catch the day's peak thermals at or shortly after noon and return to roost well before sunset in preparation for the next day's replay of this daily pattern.

In this age of plentiful deer and high highway mortality, I have often wondered whether it is not limited foraging time (caused by shortened hours of daylight) and the low angle of the winter sun that sets the northern limit of this soaring bird's winter range. Carrion seems not to be in short supply in New England, but hours of productive thermal production may be insufficient for birds to feed and return to roosts in an energy-efficient manner.

Graceful it might be, but purposeful, too. Turkey Vultures search for carrion by sight and smell. Unlike most birds (including Black Vulture), the Turkey Vulture has a refined olfactory detection package, so is able to locate carrion hidden beneath the tree canopy by smell alone. This is one of the reasons the birds often fly at modest heights and tack back and forth, hunting, as setters do, by coursing back and forth, searching for scent. They show a preference for fresh carrion, but if a large carcass is intact, they gain access through the anus, genitals, mouth, or nostrils.

PREY: Prey ranges in size from small mammals to large ungulates. And while moribund is the preferred state of prey, there are accounts of vultures tossing down small stranded live fish. Young vultures, in particular, frequent landfills. When cattle and sheep are giving birth, vultures relish the afterbirth. They are also partial to the entrails from field-dressed large mammals.

STATUS: Turkey Vultures are "widespread and abundant." Despite human threats that lead to injury and mortality, this species appears to have thrived under the changes brought upon the environment over the past 200 years, and in North America its range is expanding. Once considered a carrier of disease and persecuted by shooting, trapping, and poisoning, vultures are now mostly ignored or admired by most people except where roosting birds concentrate in residential areas, and where their droppings mar the roofs of homes and parked automobiles. Like its relative the California Condor, this species is susceptible to lead poisoning resulting from birds ingesting bullet fragments embedded in animals or gut piles they feed upon.

California Condor
Gymnogyps californiansus

ETYMOLOGY: *Condor* is Spanish and probably stems from the Inca *cuntur,* their name for the Andean Condor, *Vultur gryphus.* The genus name comes from Greek—*gyps* for "vulture" and *gymnos* for "naked," a clear reference to the bird's unfeathered head.

PROFILE: A real-life phoenix and our grandest soaring bird, the Condor is living testimony to our species' evolving responsibility for the environment. But for most of the twentieth century, and for largely human-related reasons, this bird's population was in rapid decline.

Majestic birds deserve majestic settings, such as this California Condor in the Grand Canyon. Ned Harris

Writing in 1923, William Leon Dawson, believing that the days of the California Condor were numbered, and knowing that his words might well serve to eulogize this magnificent bird, was eloquent bordering upon poetic in his account of California Condor: " . . . for me the heart of California lies in the Condor country. And for me the heart of mystery, of wonder, and of desire lies with the California Condor, that majestic and almost legendary figure, which still haunts the fastnesses of our lessening wilderness . . . I am not ashamed to have

fallen in love with so gentle a ghoul . . . "
Nor am I.

This magnificent vulture is the largest soaring bird in North America, its wingspan more than two feet wider than that of the Golden Eagle, and it weighs twice as much. Dependent upon large mammal carcasses for food, during the Pleistocene, the great age of mammals, the species was widespread across North America, but by the time Lewis and Clark met up with one in 1804–05 along the banks of the Columbia River, the condor's range had retracted to the West Coast, extending from southern British Columbia to northern Baja.

Fossil records of this species have been uncovered in Florida and near Buffalo, New York, attesting to its former much more extensive North American range. Splendid and resilient as it was, after Europeans reached the West Coast, the bird's population entered into a swift, steady decline. The end, happily, was not the extinction expected by Dawson and others, but a phoenix-like revival. This was thanks to a hardened resolve on the part of scientists and the public, who chose, instead of extinction, a determined and dynamic artificial propagation and reintroduction program that has, since its inception in the 1980s, shown both success as well as persistent challenges to be addressed. That I am able to write about this great bird of prey in the present tense, in the twenty-first century, is almost as improbable as the flight of Icarus and as trumping as the rebirth of a phoenix.

DESCRIPTION: A huge, plank-winged vulture, dwarfing all other birds in North American skies. Adults are mostly black,

with soaring birds displaying white wing linings. Also evident are long, splayed fingers (outer primaries), a short wedge-shaped tail, and a bright orange head and neck. In addition perched adults have a white bar bisecting the folded wing, a horn-colored bill, and reddish eyes. Juveniles have mottled underwing linings, a gray head, and a grayish bill.

MEASUREMENTS
Length: 43–50 inches
Wingspan: 98–118 inches
Weight: 8.2–14.1 pounds

Says Dawson about the Condor's wingspan:

> In efforts to express grandeur of the bird's presence and its impressive size, the Condor's wing-spread has often been exaggerated . . . "a bird that measures ten feet, laid on its back and marked at wing tips without really stretching the bird is an exceptionally large bird." Nine feet is a fairer average. Whether there have actually been specimens which would go eleven feet, we are not prepared to say.

SUBSPECIES/RELATED SPECIES: This is a monotypic species. Its closest living relatives are the Andean Condor (*Vultur gryphus*) and King Vulture (*Sarcoramus papa*). Larger but extinct Pleistocene forms may have represented a subspecies.

VOCALIZATIONS: Condors are usually silent. Their repertoire is limited to hisses and grunts.

DISTRIBUTION: By the twentieth century, the California Condor's range was limited to the coastal ranges of California from

An adult California Condor poised for flight. The huge birds rely upon a bit of a pitch to get airborne. Ned Harris

Monterey to San Benito Counties, east to the western slope of the Sierra Nevada, with breeding apparently limited to Los Padres National Forest in Santa Barbara, as well as Ventura and extreme northern Los Angeles Counties. The last free-flying (wild) birds were removed from the wild in 1987 and placed in protective custody. Beginning in 1992, captive-reared birds, the progeny of wild Condors taken into protective custody, were reintroduced to southern California, later Baja, and in 1996 into the Grand Canyon (where there are historic records of the species).

MIGRATION: There is no indication of migratory behavior.

HABITAT: For breeding, Condors are able to occupy a variety of habitats, from chaparral to forested mountains. They forage for the most part over open grasslands as well as sea coasts. Their most important habitat requirements are ample food supply and dependable air currents to support extensive soaring. Elevation of some sort may be important for birds to get airborne, including even modest slopes that augment a running start.

BREEDING: Initial pairing occurs in late fall and early winter; thereafter, pairs remain together for multiple years. Beginning in January and February, pairs visit multiple potential nest sites within their territory. These include crevices in a cliff or under rocks and boulders. Openings may be barely large enough to admit birds. The substrate is bare soil, gravel, or a rocky floor. One very famous nesting effort involved a pair that chose to nest high in the cavity of a giant sequoia in 1984. Condors lay but a single egg per nesting effort and typically breed once every three years. This very low reproductive rate certainly contributed to the Condor's decline. Incubation is 53 to 60 days and fledging occurs 163 to 178 days later. Young are wholly dependent upon adults for six months and partially dependent for perhaps another half-year.

BEHAVIOR/FORAGING: Condors typically forage only when air movement (thermals or updrafts) is conducive to extended soaring flight. On the ground, they are capable of rapid running and hopping. Notes Audubon, quoting J. K. Townsend: "in walking they resemble a Turkey, strutting over the ground with great dignity; but . . . when two are striving to reach a dead fish . . . the stately walk then degenerates into a clumsy sort of hopping canter, which is anything but graceful."

"Condors take fastidious care of their persons. They are fond of water, and after a bath will hang out their wings to dry. This operation over they primp and preen themselves by the hour." Condors spend as much as 15 hours a day at their roost site. Yet their home ranges are huge, and birds may travel up to 150 miles in their daily activities in search of an unpredictable food supply, primarily carrion.

In the 1980s, the foraging area used by the remnant California Condor population was roughly 20,000 square kilometers, with some breeding birds ranging up to 108 miles from nest sites. Capable of long periods of starvation, they can "easily survive 1–2 weeks without ingesting

Thanks to the condor restoration program, North America's grandest soaring bird is once again a fixture in California skies. Brian Sullivan

food." Visual hunters, their typical soaring search pattern is conducted "several hundred meters above the landscape, either singly or in irregular groupings." As noted by Audubon, "The Indians, whose observations may generally be depended upon, say that it ascertains the presence of food solely by its power of vision . . ." While Condors like their carrion fresh, not putrefied, they are typically not the first carrion feeders at a kill, but instead clue in on the skills of other carrion feeders, such as vultures, Golden Eagles, and ravens. Even then, Condors do not descend to food "until an hour or two after the first Condor appears in the area."

At kills they are highly gregarious. When gathered, they generally dominate at a carcass, but despite their superior size, Condors are subservient to Golden Eagles. They feed almost exclusively upon soft tissue, ingesting little hide.

FOOD: Exclusively a carrion feeder, Condors forage mostly upon the carcasses of large terrestrial mammals, although many early accounts mention the bird feeding upon salmon and marine mammals. In modern times the birds have relied heavily upon dead cattle and stillborn calves as well as deer and other large, dead wild mammals, including feral pigs.

STATUS: This is one of the planet's most endangered species, with a total population of just over 400 birds, including adults and young in the wild and in captivity.

Since its discovery, the Condor was never common. Noted Townsend in Audubon, the "California Vulture, cannot . . . be called a plentiful species, as . . . it is rare to see more than two or three at a time." While Townsend's observations were made at the northern limits of the Condor's range, well away from its principal breeding areas in southern California (where many more individuals might have been seen even into the twentieth century), Townsend's observation of Condor numbers is nevertheless apt. However, the bird's principal challenge was not simply low numbers; it was high mortality coupled with the species' very low reproductive rate. Most authorities now agree that (at least historically) shooting was the main challenge confronting the bird. Simply stated, the massive birds made too tempting a target in a place and cultural environment where almost every male carried a firearm.

Also implicated as a cause of mortality was unintended poisoning caused by birds ingesting strychnine-laced carcasses set out for predator control (specifically coyote and bear). Yet another contributing cause of the Condor's decline was ritual sacrifice performed by Native Americans, whose impact upon the species was likely less than that exacted by scientific collecting or egg collecting. As summarized by Dawson, in the 1890s and in the early years of the twentieth century, "when the word went out that the condor was 'getting scarce,' every bird stuffer and every junk-pile dubbed museum saw to it that it got its share. The zoologists rallied to the fray, and the less scrupulous among them, not content with one or two specimens, set out to get all they might while the getting was good."

But in the 1980s, Snyder and Snyder, intently studying the now severely reduced population, discovered a wholly overlooked but potentially devastating

Smaller than a Piper Cub but larger than an eagle, California Condors may travel up to 100 miles in a day in search of carrion. Two adults are shown. Brian Sullivan

agent of the Condor's destruction. That agent was lead poisoning, resulting from Condors ingesting bullet fragments embedded in the soft tissue of the animals they consumed—animals shot by sportsmen but not retrieved—or lead fragments embedded in the discarded gut piles of field-dressed animals. Of four dead Condors recovered by the Snyders in the 1980s, three were victims of lead poisoning, and the fourth was killed by a cyanide coyote trap. Whether strychnine was an agent leading to the decline of this gastronomically rugged vulture is contestable, but cyanide is unarguably lethal. Other documented causes of Condor deaths include collision with utility lines, drowning in water tanks, and miring in oil.

While the historic causes of the decline are open to debate, the final rapid decline of the Condor at the end of the twentieth century is well documented. "In 1982 there were a mere 21 California Condors left on earth. By 1983 the number had fallen to 19; 15 in 1984 and 9 in 1985—an unsustainable decline." Unless something was done to halt the decline, it

seemed unlikely that condors would outlive the millennium. Happily, something *was* done.

ROAD TO RECOVERY

The decision to embark upon an aggressive captive-breeding program marks one of our species' great environmental turnarounds. The road to recovery was effortful, hands-on, and multifaceted, involving the U.S. Fish and Wildlife Service, the California Department of Fish and Wildlife, the National Audubon Society, the Bureau of Land Management, the Zoological Society of San Diego, the Los Angeles Zoo, The Peregrine Fund, and independent biologists, whose joint efforts were coordinated by a Condor recovery team. This team concluded in 1976 that the best chance for the Condor's survival was a captive-breeding plan, which began with the taking of wild nestlings in 1982. From 1983 to 1987, many additional Condors were taken captive, mostly as eggs, in an effort to induce the wild birds to multiple clutch. Later, when it was determined that the captive population was genetically deficient, the last free-flying adult birds were also captured and joined the captive flocks, which, in 1987, included 27 individuals (13 males and 14 females)—all the California Condors left on earth. Between 1988 and 1991, there were no free-flying California Condors in the wild.

The goal of the Condor release plan is to have two geographically distinct, self-sustaining populations, each with 150 wild birds and a minimum of 15 breeding pairs. At present, there are three release sites in California, and one each in Arizona and Baja, Mexico, and while the stated objectives have yet to be reached, the project has met with encouraging success. Since 1996, The Peregrine Fund (one of the recovery plan's principal architects) has released 162 Condors. In addition, many of the Arizona and Utah population have attained breeding age and have produced thus far 25 wild-hatched young in the vicinity of the Grand Canyon.

The captive-breeding strategy proved successful. By the late 1990s, production at the San Diego Zoo, the Los Angeles Zoo, and The Peregrine Fund, in Boise, Idaho, was close to 20 offspring a year. This success led to the initial release of birds back into the wild in 1992 in the Sespe Condor Sanctuary in California—the birds' historic retreat. These first released birds and those that followed were "completely dependent" upon a clean food subsidy to keep birds lead-free. The release was not without challenges (released birds were evidently attracted to or imprinted upon people), and beginning in 1993, birds were moved to a more remote location in Santa Barbara County. By 1996, birds were also being released in Arizona. The first hatching of a Condor in the wild occurred in 2014. It did not survive.

The total world population of Condors stands at more than 400, including wild birds and those held in captivity. The Peregrine Fund is optimistic that the goal of 150 individuals and 15 breeding pairs is attainable and that if the threat posed by secondary lead poisoning can be controlled, the California Condor has "the potential to eventually thrive." Lead poisoning continues to plague the birds, and mortality due to lead poisoning is approaching levels found in wild birds before the reintroduction program. Of 104 Condor mortalities since 1996, 54 percent have been linked to lead poisoning. Despite offerings of lead-free carcasses, and efforts to get hunters to use nonlead bullets, these wide-ranging scavengers are still locating lead-impregnated carcasses or viscera.

Today, perhaps the best place to witness the success of the reintroduction program, and see a wild, free-flying California Condor in an environment whose grandeur matches the bird, is the South Rim of the Grand Canyon. Here, birds continue to be drawn to the hosts of human visitors, not because of imprinting, but because this carrion-feeding vulture is genetically hotwired to be where large mammals are gathered and death is an imminent companion. Were it not for the emergency medical services available and scores of park rangers admonishing visitors to stay away from the canyon rim, this strategy would undoubtedly pay energetic dividends for Condors. Our species might be the dominant ecological force on the planet, and capable of making ecologically sound decisions, but when it comes

Eureka. This juvenile condor was photographed September 18, 2014, on the rim of the Grand Canyon. Wearing no bands or bling, it is most certainly a bird raised in the wild. Ron Mattson

to self-preservation, *Homo sapiens* are not necessarily in the upper percentile of the planet's denizens.

The California Condor may outlive us yet.

It is not inconceivable that as the dust settles upon what once was Los Angeles, a pack of coyotes may gather in Hancock Park to gnaw the last bit of gristle off that last human rib cage desiccating in the California sun, while a California Con-dor perched near the edge of the La Brea Tar Pits sits quietly, biding her time. In the final analysis, it is not superior speed, cunning, tenacity, or coordinated effort that wins the day; it is patience and perseverance. As a species whose patience has been honed by centuries, California Condor seems well positioned and disposed to write our species' epitaph. In the end, all things knit by flesh are equal in the eyes of carrion feeders.

Threats to Birds *of* Prey

1. Sadly, despite legal protection, illegal shooting continues to be a threat to raptors. While some shootings are premeditated and prompted by ignorance about birds of prey and their importance to the maintenance of a healthy ecosystem, others are simply thoughtless acts of violence.

As a hunter, I am compelled to assert that despite earlier misconceptions, hunters today are very conservation-minded and almost unanimously supportive of birds of prey. Hunters don't kill hawks—brigands with guns kill hawks, and it is an insult to responsible hunters to be blamed for the misguided actions of ignorant and lawless individuals with guns. The elevated regard hunters have for raptors is based upon respect for them and the environment. As co-hunters, we naturally admire and strive to emulate the skills of our feathered kin.

2. Another widespread threat to birds of prey is electrocution. This happens when

Opposite: *Quitting time for caracara. Nothing for this accomplished scavenger to do but wait for the morning tribute of road-killed animals scattered along Texas highways.* Greg Lasley

rain-sodden birds perch on power lines, and their wings touch parallel lines, thus making a lethal connection. The threat is particularly acute in large birds of prey. Perches elevated above power lines help birds avoid contact.

3. Collisions with elevated wires, including barbed wire fences, levy a toll. Despite their vaulted powers of sight, birds of prey do not always see narrow strands of wire cutting across their path.

4. Collisions with wind turbines kill birds. Both hawks and wind turbines are attracted to the same wind-rich environments, too often with lethal consequences. Power companies are aware of this challenge and strive to minimize the danger, but our growing emphasis upon renewable energy sources means more bird strikes and more effort and resources needed to address this grave new threat. Our species' needs must always be balanced by a respect for the impacts our efforts have upon nature. If our relationship with birds of prey has taught us nothing else, it is this. Newer turbine designs that incorporate larger, slower blades and even bladeless designs may offer a solution, or at least a reduction in bird strikes.

Mistakenly blamed for wrongdoings, birds of prey like this Turkey Vulture are sometimes the victims of senseless acts of violence. This particular bird, photographed in New York State along the Palisades cliffs, was seen repeatedly over the course of two years. Steve Sachs

The systematic slaughter of hawks was practiced in many places. These Northern Harriers were shot and pole trapped on New Jersey's Delaware Bayshore sometime in the first half of the twentieth century under the mistaken belief that they posed a threat to waterfowl. Happily, harriers and other birds of prey enjoy full protection under state and federal law, and scenes like this have been relegated to the dustbins of history. Photos courtesy of the collection of Bayshore Center at Bivalve

5. Collisions with automobiles is another danger. Birds of prey often hunt roadsides and highway center divides. Wholly focused upon prey, they may fly into the path of oncoming vehicles, or they may be struck and killed while consuming prey on roadsides. In addition, food thrown from car windows attracts birds and mammals, whose roadkill carcasses then attract hungry birds of prey and other predators. Please hold your unwanted french fries until you find a proper receptacle.

6. Window strikes are a problem where bird feeders are placed close to large windows and patio glass doors.

7. Lead poisoning, caused when birds ingest bullet fragments or shotgun pellets, has led to the banning of lead shot for waterfowl hunting and lead bullets in places where endangered birds of prey (most notably California Condor) are found. But lead affects all predators who ingest it, endangered or not. And because lead is inexpensive, it is still widely used by most hunters in most hunting situations, despite the fact that lead alternatives exist. These would be sold more widely if hunters raised their voices in the name of raptor protection. Bullets made of non-

toxic metals are offered by a number of manufacturers in an array of calibers. Their ballistics performance compares well to bullets cast from lead.

In the absence of strong leadership on this issue, it is incumbent upon hunters as individuals to take the lead and adopt a conservation stand based upon hunting with nontoxic bullets. Remember, copper is what you were shooting with your old Daisy Model 99, and it worked fine for you. As an added incentive, copper bullets do not fragment when they enter an animal, leaving a toxic trail of tiny particles along the bullet's path. Lead is toxic to humans, too.

A ban on lead bullets must necessarily extend to varmint shooting as well as large game animals. Many birds of prey target prairie dogs and ground squirrels and will feed from carcasses. Happily, lead-free ammunition is now available in

---

Birds of prey commonly use utility poles as hunting perches, particularly on the tree-impoverished prairies, where this light-morph Ferruginous Hawk breeds. The problem is that long-winged raptors may touch electrical lines with open wings, completing a circuit that results in electrocution and death. Rain-soaked birds are particularly vulnerable. Brian Sullivan

Secondary poisoning, caused when raptors ingest rodents that have consumed anticoagulant rat poison, is a growing concern. While there is no way of knowing whether the Norway Rat in the bill of this adult Red-tailed Hawk is so contaminated, this particular bird, known as Pale Male, did lose a mate to just such secondary poisoning, and other birds of prey have been similarly afflicted. Lloyd Spitalnik

.22 LR rim fire as well as the ever-popular .223 round, a favorite among varmint hunters.

8. Rock climbers and adventurous hikers are often drawn to challenges, posed by cliffs that may be occupied by nesting raptors. Such intrusion during the nesting season—roughly January through July—disrupts incubation by flushing brooding adults, thus subjecting nestlings to prolonged exposure to direct sunlight in hot weather. Later in the season, it may cause young birds to attempt to fledge before they are able. On public lands, please heed access closure signs, recognizing the sensitive nature of cliff-nesting birds of prey. The cliff will be

there after the breeding season and, with your compliance, so, too, will nesting raptors the following year, adding to your enjoyment of what is very apparently a prime natural area.

9. Inexplicably, in this post-DDT age, chemical insecticides continue to pose a hazard to birds of prey, mostly beyond the borders of the United States and Canada. In 1995–96, nearly 6,000 Swainson's Hawks wintering in Argentina were killed by the application of an insecticide known as monocrotophos, an organophosphate compound.

10. There is mounting concern about secondary poisoning by raptors that ingest rodents that have eaten over-the-counter rat poison that contains anticoagulant agents. Hawks, owls, and other animals that consume poisoned rodents are then similarly affected, dying of internal hemorrhaging or liver failure. One high-profile death involved Lima, one of Pale Male's mates, whose liver was found to contain multiple anticoagulant agents. The Cornell College of Veterinary Medicine has confirmed the deaths of 39 birds (mostly raptors) in this way since 2011. Me? I swear by the good ol' knuckle-cracker rat trap.

11. The routines of raptors may also be disrupted by ardent admirers and photographers. Resist the temptation to approach birds so closely that they are forced to flush, disrupting their hunting and exposing smaller raptors to larger raptors and harassment by mobbing birds such as crows and jays. When raptors fix their eyes on you and stare, you are close enough. Resist the temptation to approach closer. Nesting raptors are particularly sensitive to intrusion. The nest shots found in this book were specifically requested to meet the needs of this project and required restraint and days of preplanning to minimize stress upon breeding birds. Most professional photographers avoid raptor nests and encourage others to follow this example.

You and raptors are much better served by your keeping your admiration at a respectful distance. There are many places you can go to see and photograph great numbers of raptors in their natural environment with exciting intimacy and no stress to birds. For directions to a hawkwatching site near you, go to the Hawk Migration Association of North America website (www.hmana.org).

12. The removal of young raptors from their nests is illegal. Do not do it, no matter how noble your intentions. Falconry has been called an "art," but it is more nearly a commitment, with few people in this day and age willing or able to dedicate the time, experience, and resources necessary to keep birds healthy, well exercised, and at a proper weight. Yes, this ancient sport is a way of gaining great intimacy with birds of prey, but without proper training and commitment, your well-intentioned efforts to capture and cage a wild bird will almost certainly end in failure, possibly in fines, and, worst of all, the unnecessary death of a raptor.

Things You Can Do to Help Birds *of* Prey

1. Keep your distance. Don't love them to death. In your efforts to get a better view or a closer shot, do not press them until they flush. No doubt you have been inspired by the images in this book. Know that they were taken by professionals who may have spent days setting up their shots to minimize disturbance. Many raptor photographers avoid nesting raptors entirely—a prudent policy that you should emulate.

2. If you feed songbirds in your yard, you will inevitably attract bird- and rodent-eating raptors. Place your feeders well away from large plate-glass windows and doors. And remember that by feeding birds, you are not causing birds to be killed by hawks, you are only causing them to be killed where you will see them.

3. Raptors need habitat. Promote the protection of open space in your community.

4. Give your financial support to organizations that work for the betterment of birds of prey and natural habitat preservation. This includes support for local bird and wildlife rehabilitators, in whose hands thousands of injured raptors are given a second chance to live and breed.

5. Be certain that the welfare of raptors and their prey is part of every local land- and water-use decision. Remember, birds of prey are the bellwethers of a healthy environment. Their presence is your assurance that the natural balance is being maintained and that our environmental safety net is secure where you live.

6. Share your enthusiasm for birds of prey with others. Be an ambassador—take friends and family members to natural areas near you.

Notes

INTRODUCTION

PAGE

11 *"there was nothing left but the bones"*:
Krider 1879

Osprey

23 *would have been named after Tereus*:
Choate 1973
Greek halos for "sea" and aetos for "eagle":
Ibid.
Accipitriformes, the family Pandionidae:
AOU Checklist 1998
eagles, hawks, and Old World vultures:
Poole 1989
to a depth of one meter: Ibid.
These include a dense oily plumage:
Ferguson-Lees and Christie 2001

24 *"and some pure yellow oil"*: Wilson 1814
"digest tough scales and bones": Stone,
Butgas, and Reiley 1978 in Poole 1989
the bird plunges into water: Snyder and
Snyder 1991
Measurements: Clark and Wheeler 1987
larger than males: Poole, Bierregaard, and
Martell 2002

26 *which comprises eight species*: Ibid.
Rocky Mountains, and Pacific Northwest:
Snyder and Snyder 1991
from the Carolinas to Florida: Poole,
Bierregaard, and Martell 2002
the 22nd of September: Wilson and
Bonaparte 1814
"a nest of these birds on one's farm": Ibid.

28 *"vigorous-winged"*: Ibid.

29 *"as if done by art"*: Ibid.

30 *"the egg was perfectly fresh"*: Ibid.

31 *(5–40 meters) above the surface*: Poole
1989
30 to 90 percent of the time: Ibid.
half as successful as adults: Ibid.
sluggish fish in deeper water: Poole,
Bierregaard, and Martell 2002
time-consuming feeding strategy: Ibid.

32 *weigh more than five pounds*: Audubon
1840
this species is 0.3 to 0.7 pounds: Poole
1989
400 grams is about the upper limit: Ibid.
birds can release fish underwater: Ruppell
1981 in Poole 1989

KITES

Hook-billed Kite

33 *hierakos, for "a falcon"*: Choate 1973

34 *brown morph like the female*: Friedmann in
Brown and Amadon 1968
gray morphs and more females brown:
Ferguson-Lees and Christie 2001
pale bands and shows a whitish tip: Brown
and Amadon 1968; Howell and Webb 1995
Measurements: Clark and Wheeler 1987
Three subspecies are generally recognized:
del Hoyo, Elliott, and Sargatal 1994
Paraguay and northern Argentina: Ibid.

35 *Grenada and the Lesser Antilles*: Ibid.
resident in eastern Cuba: Ibid.
"resembling an American oriole": Brown and
Amadon 1968
call it very "unhawk-like": Snyder and
Snyder 1991
"a clucking or rattling chatter": Sibley 2000
Texas in Hidalgo and Starr Counties: Lockwood and Freeman 2004 in Heller 2005
two or three pairs nesting regularly: Heller
2005
*in Santa Ana National Wildlife Refuge in
1964*: Fleetwood and Hamilton in Heller
2005
nesting effort there in 1976: Delnicki 1978 in
Heller 2005
"apparently on migration" have been noted:
Ferguson-Lees and Christie 2001
fall migration, 3 in spring: Bildstein et al.
2008
partial to dry tropical forest: Brown and
Amadon 1968

36 *acacia thorn scrub woodlands*: del Hoyo,
Elliott, and Sargatal 1994
occurs mostly in May and June: Kaufman
1996
In places it nests in "loose colonies": Snyder
and Snyder 1991
stick nest is built by both sexes: Kaufman
1996
The clutch contains one or two eggs: del
Hoyo, Elliott, and Sargatal 1994
*buffy white and marked with dark reddish
brown*: Howell and Webb 1995
"very much like that of a dove": Snyder and
Snyder 1991
brings most of the food to the nest: del Hoyo,
Elliott, and Sargatal 1994
"skulking within the canopy": Ferguson-Lees
and Christie 2001
"in groups of two or three": Brown and
Amadon 1968

circling low over open ground: Ferguson-Lees and Christie 2001

transfers the prey to its left foot: Kaufman 1996

characteristically holed shell to the pile below: Ferguson-Lees and Christie 2001

hang upside down to reach prey: Ibid.

to hop about among branches: del Hoyo, Elliott, and Sargatal 1994

on foot on the forest floor: Kevin Karlson, personal communication with author, 2016

37 *tear of fracturing snail shells:* Snyder and Snyder 1991

a wider spectrum of snails: Ferguson-Lees and Christie 2001

snails of different sizes are available: Snyder and Snyder 1991

smaller-billed individuals interbreed freely: Ibid.

frogs, salamanders, insects, and caterpillars: Brown and Amadon 1968

38 *uncommon to rare and often "declining":* Ferguson-Lees and Christie 2001

races in the West Indies are endangered: Kaufman 1996

Swallow-tailed Kite

forficatus, is Latin for "deeply forked": Choate 1973

Measurements: Clark and Wheeler 1987

the northern two-thirds of South America: Meyer 1995

utters shrill piping and ringing whistles: Howell and Webb 1995

most of South America, south to northern Argentina: Brown and Amadon 1968

southern Mississippi, central Louisiana, and eastern Texas: Meyer 1995

breeding range extending north to North Carolina: Bent 1937–38

southwestern Ohio and west to the prairies: Meyer 1995

"in Iowa, Minnesota and Kansas where they breed": Krider 1879

only half of its year in North America: Snyder and Snyder 1991

in late July and early August exceeding 1,200: Meyer 1993 in Meyer 1995

40 *population withdraws by mid-September:* Meyer 1995

to begin the 10,000-mile odyssey: Avian Research and Conservation Institute (ARCI), http://arcinst.org/

along the Gulf Coast of the United States: Avian Research and Conservation Institute blog, Jan. 22, 2015; arci-avianconservation .blogspot.com

41 *radio-tagged adults succumbing in one study:* Meyer in Bildstein et al. 2008

in proximity to prairie and marsh: Goss 1855 in Meyer 1995

cypress swamp forest, and mangrove: Cely 1979; Collopy 1990 in Meyer 1995

may be formed upon or shortly after arrival: Meyer 1995

Courtship and territorial behavior is immediate: Ibid.

"its motions are then more beautiful than ever": Audubon 1840

"on the margin of a stream or pond": Ibid.

42 *"many nests over 100 feet from the ground":* Snyder and Snyder 1991

"over 200 feet in a cottonwood": Sprunt 1955

Both sexes aid in construction of the nest: Meyer and Collopy 1990 in Meyer 1995

"coarse grass and a few feathers": Audubon 1840

used for more than one season: del Hoya, Elliott, and Sargatal 1994

located near the previous year's nest: Ely and Sorrow 1990 in Meyer 1995

dark brown to reddish brown markings: Robertson 1988 in Meyer 1995

These hatch in about 28 days: Snyder 1974 in Meyer 1995

Fledging occurs 35 to 42 days later: Sutton 1955 in Meyer 1995

remain in natal ranges for two or three months: Meyer 1995

share in all aspects of rearing young: del Hoyo, Elliott, and Sargatal 1994

pairs are monogamous: Meyer 1995

43 *to capture insects located behind and below:* Ibid.

return to nests bearing whole wasp nests: Meyer and Collopy 1990 in Meyer 1995

reportedly common in the tropics: Buskirk and Lechner 1978 in Meyer 1995

this species entered into a dramatic range reduction: Kaufman 1996

habitat alteration to favor agriculture: del Hoyo, Elliott, and Sargatal 1994

clutches going for $80 to $120: Skutch in Meyer 1995

a cause of population decline: Meyer 1995

a federally endangered species: Meyer and Collopy in Meyer 1995

"this kite stands at the top of the list": Sprunt 1955

at those hawkwatch sites: Bildstein et al. 2008

White-tailed Kite

44 leucurus *is Greek for "white-tailed"*: Choate 1973

the eastern portion of its North American range: Bent 1937–38

"Only in California": Ibid.

45 *was a lethal combination*: Ibid.

"therefore exceptionally easy to shoot": Ray quoted in Bent 1937–38

"quite the handsomest of the raptors": Dawson 1923

"feathers marked with a substantial ashy bar": Coues 1874 in Dawson 1923

wash on the breast that fades within weeks: Sibley 2000

Measurements: Clark and Wheeler 1987

46 *the smaller* E. l. leucurus *in South America*: Dunk 1995

Juveniles make an Osprey-like whistle: Sibley 2000

the far western counties of Oregon: Dunk 1995

reestablishing itself in south Florida (beginning in the 1960s): Ibid.

the gift of Dr. Ravenel of Charleston: Bent 1937–38

to Chile and central Argentina: Brown and Amadon 1968

reported "common" in northern Argentina: Ibid.

in response to prey availability: Dunk 1995

47 *subject to prolonged winter freezes*: Ibid.

selects in favor of ungrazed grasslands: Bammann 1975 in Dunk 1995

most particularly December through August: Dunk 1995

"near nesting areas after courtship begins": Ibid.

in trees (willows in particular): Dawson 1923

twelve to sixteen feet high: Harrison 1978

Both sexes contribute to nest construction: Watson 1940 in Dunk 1995

"loose but well built": Harrison 1978

"that is high tribute of praise": Dawson 1923

zoologists to restrain their "cupidity": Ibid.

with incubation by the female: Walker 1940 in Dunk 1995

lasting 30 to 32 days: Hawbecker 1942 in Dunk 1995

to capture prey a month later: Waian 1973 in Dunk 1995

48 *a second brood after a successful first nesting*: Stendell 1972 in Dunk 1995

"unsuspicious . . . confiding": Dawson 1923

individuals counted at key communal roosts: Dunk 1995

"more or less gregarious": Dawson 1923

may be only 600 feet apart: del Hoyo, Elliott, and Sargatal 1994

"antagonistic toward most large raptors": Hawbecker 1940 in Dunk 1995

perched atop trees or shrubs, often in pairs: Dunk 1995

kite's principal prey: Fisher 1907 in Dunk 1995

49 *one that targets mice and voles*: del Hoyo, Elliott, and Sargatal 1994

Snail Kite

"gregarious," for its nesting in loose colonies: Choate 1973

50 *only slightly larger than the male*: Friedmann 1950 in Sykes, Rogers, and Bennetts 1995

Measurements: Clark and Wheeler 1987

forest margins of rain forests: del Hoyo, Elliott, and Sargatal 1994

eastern and southern Mexico, as well as Belize: Sykes, Rogers, and Bennetts 1995

This race is smaller than other races: Brown and Amadon 1968

both sexes make a "harsh cackling" ka-ka-ka-ka-ka: Sibley 2000

this raptor species is local but common: Brown and Amadon 1968

outnumbers all other birds of prey: Ibid.

"aquatic vegetation growth": Sykes, Rodgers, and Bennetts 1995

51 *"annual, seasonal, or short-term"*: Bennetts et al. 1994 in Sykes, Rogers, and Bennetts 1995

farther south on the peninsula: Sykes 1979 in Sykes, Rogers, and Bennetts 1995

lakes where apple snails abound: Sykes, Rogers, and Bennetts 1995

"a healthy snail population": Sykes 1978 in Sykes, Rogers, and Bennetts 1995

Roosting sites are "almost always over water": Sykes, Rogers, and Bennetts 1995

may span 10 to 11 months: Snyder and Snyder 1991

may be part of this strategy: Beissinger 1988 and Snyder et al. 1989 in Sykes, Rogers, and Bennetts 1995

52 *apple snail abundance*: Ibid.

15 feet above the water: Brown and Amadon 1968

stand of reeds ("sawgrass clumps"): Nicholson 1926 in Bent 1937–38 *primary cause of death for nestlings:* Snyder and Snyder 1969 in Sykes, Rogers, and Bennetts 1995

"sticks somewhat carelessly arranged": Bent 1937–38

prone to collapse, particularly during severe drought: Palmer 1988

eggs and young overboard: Chandler and Anderson 1984 and Sykes and Chandler 1984 in Palmer 1988

nest failure due to toppling: Kern 1978 in Newton 1979

53 *six eggs were typical before 1940:* Meyer 1995

24 to 30 days: Sykes 1987 in Sykes, Rogers, and Bennetts 1995

23 to 28 days: Chandler and Anderson 1974 in Johnsgard 2004

"can scarcely distinguish them from adults": Menge quoted in Bendire 1892 in Bent 1937–38

"progress was unlikely if not impossible": Snyder and Snyder 1991

"grabbing snails from the water surface": Ibid.

assorted herons, ibis, and vultures: Sykes, Rogers, and Bennetts 1995

daylight hours perched: Ibid.

do not plunge or dive, as some accounts allow: Brown and Amadon 1968

55 *"seizes the prey in its talons":* Sprunt 1955

stretch to 20 minutes or longer: Snyder and Snyder 1991

56 *"eaten whole or torn to pieces":* Sykes and Kale 1974 in Johnsgard 1990

perhaps fewer than 40 birds remained: Sykes 1983 in Palmer 1988

great variation year to year: Sykes, Rogers, and Bennetts 1995

Snail Kite populations in Florida: Stieglitz 1965 in Sykes, Rogers, and Bennetts 1995

Mississippi Kite

"a few miles below Natchez": Wilson 1814

"iris of the eye dark red, pupil black": Ibid.

58 *"tail has 3 incomplete light bands":* Clark and Wheeler 1987

Measurements: Clark and Wheeler 1987

the two are sometimes regarded as a super-species: Parker 1999

"similar to Broad-winged but descending": Sibley 2000

59 *central Kansas, and eastern Colorado, according to J. W. Parker:* Parker 1999

Andes—possibly Manaus, Brazil: Stolz et al. 1992 in Parker 1999

spans late August to mid-September: Bildstein et al. 2008

United States between late April and mid-May: Bildstein et al. 2008

60 *riparian woodlands, and golf courses:* Parker 1999

shelter belts, and even isolated trees: Ibid.

nest trees are usually well foliated: Ibid.

colonies might include 20 pairs: Ferguson-Lees and Christie 2001

may account for the relatively late nesting period: Snyder and Snyder 1991

"The cup is shallow and where found lined with Spanish moss": Parker 1999

usually two bluish white eggs: Harrison 1978

continue to feed for 15 to 20 days: Rolfs 1973 in Parker 1999

"independent of the earth much of the time": Sprunt 1955

few humans have actually been struck by territorial birds: Parker 1999

61 *flocks of up to 100 individuals:* Skinner 1962 in Parker 1999

hawks insects from exposed perches: Bent 1937–38

cicadas are its most important insect prey: Parker 1999

during migration in South America: Davis 1989 in Parker 1999

including frogs, reptiles, birds, bats, and small mammals: Parker 1999

August through November are about 210,000: Bildstein et al. 2008

in 2014, 362,514 were counted: 1997–2015 data, Corpus Christi Hawkwatch (John Economidy, compiler), unpublished

a "positive rate" of change at all sites during the period: Bildstein et al. 2008

SEA EAGLES
Bald Eagle

62 *the white plumage of the head of adult birds:* Choate 1973

"as some assert, one hundred years": Wilson 1814

known to have lived 28 years: Buehler 2000

63 *"but catching live fish, mammals and birds":* Brown and Amadon 1968

"a different stage of color": Wilson 1814

64 *"and is entitled to particular notice":* Ibid.

"'the Eagle pursues him, and takes it from him'": Audubon quoting Benjamin Franklin in Audubon 1840

highly variable as compared to older immatures: Buehler 2000 all-white head and tail by five and a half years: McCollough 1989 in Buehler 2000

65   Measurements: Clark and Wheeler 1987

Nantucket lightship on November 14, 1914: Bent 1937–38

may, in fact, constitute a superspecies: del Hoyo, Elliott, and Sargatal 1994

Bald Eagle (H. l. leucocephalus), first described by Catesby: Buehler 2000

Bald Eagles have a weak, chirping twitter: Sibley 2000

south to Florida and Baja California: Brown and Amadon 1968

66   beginning September to early October: Broley 1947 in Buehler 2000

from late February to mid-April: McIntyre in Buehler 2000

nest building occur from December to January: Hunt et al. 1997 in Buehler 2000

nearly 10 feet across and 20 feet deep: Broley 1947 in Buehler 2000

estimated to weigh two metric tons: Herrick 1932 in Buehler 2000

63 to 70 days later: Harrison 1978

as they gain flying and foraging skills: Buehler 2000

8 to 14 weeks postfledging: Bortolotti 1986 in Buehler 2000

67   they also cruise and soar over food-bearing habitat: Buehler 2000

attempt to secure most prey on the wing: Ibid.

68   Old Abe is exhibited in the atrium: www .army.mil/article/91178

69   Eagles sometimes hunt cooperatively: Ibid.

Eagles eat primarily larger fish: Stalmaster 1987 in Buehler 2000

raccoons reported to be the most common: Mersmann 1989 in Buehler 2000

Early explorers reported it as "abundant": Buehler 2000

owing largely to the impacts of DDT: Ibid.

numbers are assessed to be stable: Bildstein et al. 2008

British Columbia 20,000 to 30,000: del Hoyo, Elliott, and Sargatal 1994

HARRIERS
Northern Harrier

70   a reference to the adult male's blue back: Choate 1973

"to harass by hostile attacks": Clark and Wheeler 1987

appear to have an Old World origin: MacWhirter and Bildstein 1996

71   Measurements: Clark and Wheeler 1987

72   They also winter in the Caribbean: MacWhirter and Bildstein 1996

74   but up to 12 have been reported: Brown and Amadon 1968

some are spattered with pale brown or buff spots: Bent 1937–38

28 to 36 days: Breckenridge 1935 in MacWhirter and Bildstein 1996

five weeks old for their first flight: Ibid.

76   behind the subordinate intruder: Temples 1986 in MacWhirter and Bildstein 1996

77   have also been reported to figure in the diet: MacWhirter and Bildstein 1996

a trend that is reflected globally: del Hoyo, Elliott, and Sargatal 1994

ACCIPITERS
Sharp-shinned Hawk

78   "streaked," referring to the streaks on the undersides: Choate 1973

"active and daring little hunter": Wilson 1814

"the grasp of this little tyrant": Audubon 1840

"bloodthirsty little pirate": Eaton 1914

80   Measurements: Clark and Wheeler 1987

subspecies restricted to the Greater Antilles: Bildstein and Meyer 2000

81   possibly on the coastal mainland: Ibid.

82   the Lower 48 and extreme southeastern Canada: Ibid.

(Mexico, Cuba) are probably resident: Ibid.

birds occasionally winter on Bermuda: Amos 1991 in Bildstein and Meyer 2000

utilizing updrafts off of high-rises: Bob Grant, personal communication with author

preferring forest tracts exceeding 200 acres: Laurie Goodrich, personal communication with author

five days to rest and feed fairly typical: Ibid.

"from sea level to near alpine": Bildstein and Meyer 2000

84   Nest building begins soon after arrival of the pair: Ibid.

the female does most or all of the construction: Ibid.

The nest interior may be lined with bark flakes: Bent 1937–38

variously marked eggs: Bent 1937–38; Harrison 1978

21 to 27 days later: del Hoyo, Elliott, and Sargatal 1994

86   recent declines at most locations since 1980 and 1998, respectively: Bildstein et al. 2008

Cooper's Hawk

New York ornithologist William C. Cooper: Choate 1973

"with short, powerful, rounded wings": Rosenfield and Bielefeldt 1993

88 *known by the name "Great Pigeon Hawk"*: Audubon 1840

89 *Measurements*: Clark and Wheeler 1987

conspecific with A. gundlachi *of Cuba*: Rosenfield and Bielefeldt 1993

(A. c. cooperii *and* A. c. mexicanus): Friedmann 1950 in Rosenfield and Bielefeldt 1993

mewing whistle reminiscent of a sapsucker: Sibley 2000

90 *smaller woodlots and occasionally in isolated trees*: Brown and Amadon 1968

91 *in forested areas and parts of the Midwest*: Rosenfield and Bielefeldt 1993

"thin fringe of trees along streams": Brown and Amadon 1968

large woodland tracts for roosting: Laurie Goodrich, personal communication with author

breed in late March to mid-July: Rosenfield and Bielefeldt 1993

very much influenced by prey availability: Titus and Mosher 1981 in Squires and Reynolds 1997

solitary pines in suburban and urban environments: Laurie Goodrich, personal communication with author

typically situated below the canopy: Johnsgard 2004

(25 to 30 inches in diameter): Palmer 1988

flatter than those situated in deciduous trees: Squires and Reynolds 1997

Cups are typically lined with bark flakes: Meng 1951 in Rosenfield and Bielefeldt 1993

between 35 and 45 feet: Bent 1937–38

The typical clutch is three to five: Rosenfield and Bielefeldt 1993

white to pale blue eggs: Harrison 1978

Incubation is 34 to 36 days: Meng and Rosenfield 1988 in Rosenfield and Bielefeldt 1993

Fledging occurs 30 to 34 days later: Ibid.

for an additional seven weeks: Meng 1959 in Rosenfield and Bielefeldt 1993

92 *"from nowhere and returning thereto as swiftly"*: Sprunt 1955

"wounded bird until it reached some thicket": Krider 1879

93 *"preeminently a 'chicken hawk'"*: Hausman 1938

"causes fear and confusion in their ranks": Audubon 1840

robins, quail, meadowlarks, and jays: Sprunt 1955

94 *considered a "common nesting raptor"*: Palmer 1988, summarizing the opinions of various authors

"young prairie chickens and meadow larks": Krider 1879

"More in evidence in winter": Dawson 1923

but since 1998 declines are noted: Bildstein et al. 2008

Northern Goshawk

95 *birds on which the hawk might prey*: Choate 1973

Gentilis *is Latin for "noble"*: Choate 1973

heaviest-bodied accipiter: Squires and Reynolds 1997

96 *"The hawk followed right up to the skirt but was killed"*: Forbush 1929

capable of killing prey 2.2 times their mass: Squires and Reynolds 1997

solitary, silent, and secretive: Kenward et al. 1981 in Squires and Reynolds 1997

evidently had her nest in the woods nearby: Auk vol. XXIV in Forbush 1929

98 *Measurements*: Clark and Wheeler 1987

As many as ten subspecies are recognized: Stresemann and Amadon 1979 in Squires and Reynolds 1997

British Columbia and coastal Alaska: Webster 1988 in Squires and Reynolds 1997

larger footed than A. g. atricapillus: Brown and Amadon 1968

may, in fact, be a different species: Ibid.

European and North American Goshawk were the "same" bird: Audubon 1840

north of the Brooks Range in Alaska: Swem and Adams 1992 in Squires and Reynolds 1997; also personal observations on the Colville River, Alaska

99 *offering a greater abundance of prey*: Berthold 1993 in Squires and Reynolds 1997

late February to early April—but poorly understood: Squires and Reynolds 1997

New England to Minneapolis and Manitoba: Forbush 1929

Maurice Broun notes "invasions" in 1934, 1935, and 1936: Broun 1948

"incursions" in 1859, 1870, 1905, 1926, 1935, 1954, 1962, and 1982–83: Palmer 1988

significant irruptions in 1982, 1983, and 1991–93: Squires and Reynolds 1997

primarily boreal and temperate forest: Ibid.

it is partial to clearings and edge: del Hoyo, Elliott, and Sargatal 1994

middle-age-growth woodlands: Squires and Reynolds 1997

old-growth forests composed primarily of large trees: Reynolds et al. 1982 in Squires and Reynolds 1997

Some pairs remain near nests year-round: Doyle and Smith 1991 in Squires and Reynolds 1997

in places as early as February: Lee 1981 in Squires and Reynolds 1997

typically the largest tree in the stand: Reynolds et al. 1982 in Squires and Reynolds 1997

100 *18 to 75 feet above the ground:* Bent 1937–38

they may construct and use up to eight nests: Squires and Reynolds 1997

Construction of new nests takes approximately one week: Palmer 1988

35 inches in height: Bent 1937–38

"large hawk nest that I have ever seen": Farley in Bent 1937–38

five unmarked bluish white eggs: Abbott 1941 in Squires and Reynolds 1997

incubation period is 28 to 30 days: Bebee in Squires and Reynolds 1997

for several weeks or until they acquire hunting skills: Squires and Reynolds 1997

"at tremendous speed, over short distance": Palmer 1988

"to flush or kill prey": Cram 1899 in Bent 1937–38

102 *"a freshly killed rabbit which they had eaten":* Ibid.

"he immediately gives chase, soon overtakes them": Audubon 1840

a greatly favored target of Goshawk: Turner 1886 in Bent 1937–38

American Robin and Steller's Jay are favored prey: Palmer 1988

Varied Thrush are especially targeted species: Bebee 1974 in Johnsgard 1990

59 percent of the diet, birds 18 to 69 percent: Storer in Johnsgard 1990

"a scattering of small mammals": Snyder and Snyder 1991

103 *"death grapple":* Forbush 1929

the greatest challenge facing the Goshawk: Palmer 1988

Northern Goshawk appears stable: del Hoyo, Elliott, and Sargatal 1994

A. g. atricapillus "is not considered at risk": Squires and Reynolds 1997

and recent declines in Washington: Bildstein et al. 2008

BUTEOS AND ALLIES
Common Black-Hawk

104 *anthracinus for "coal black":* Clark and Wheeler 1987

106 *their plumage is overall "sooty" black:* Brown and Amadon 1968

Measurements: Clark and Wheeler 1987

107 *but dimorphism is not clearly evident:* Snyder in Schnell 1994

Buteogallus anthracinus occurs in the American Southwest:: AOU Checklist, Seventh Edition Supplement 2015

Cuba and the Isle of Pines: Brown and Amadon 1968

"rendered with great power": Mearns in Bent 1937

southwestern United States to Argentina: Brown and Amadon 1968

rivers draining the Mogollon Rim: Snyder and Snyder 1991

with birds returning in April: Ibid.

Arizona have been from Sinaloa, Mexico: Schnell 1994

streams cutting through arid habitat: Ibid.

mature cottonwoods, sycamores, and walnut: Snyder 1991

small fish, amphibians, and reptiles: Schnell 1994

"of any North American buteonine raptor": Bibles 1999 in Schnell 1994

to touch above and below the body: Schnell 1994

construction, which involves both sexes: Ibid.

Nests are sometimes used for several years: Brown and Amadon 1968

with a clutch size of one or two eggs: Snyder and Snyder 1991

spotted sparingly with dull or light brown: Brown and Amadon 1968

32 to 34 days: Schnell 1994

109 *feeding of the young is usually done by the female:* Ibid.

Young fledge in about 42 days: Ibid.

areas adjacent to active breeding territories: Ibid.

that ranges from a "swooping glide": Millsap in Schnell 1994

to a "pounce": Snyder and Snyder 1991

to attract or herd prey into the shallows: Schnell 1994

The Black-Hawk's flight is "swift and powerful": Mearns 1886 in Bent 1937–38

"the far-famed Frigate or man-o-war Bird": Sprunt 1955

targeting prey that is most abundant and available: Schnell 1994

including grasshoppers and caterpillars: Brown and Amadon 1968

110 most of which are found in Arizona: Schnell 1994

The population is believed to be self-sustaining: Ibid.

in New Mexico and threatened in Texas: Ibid.

Harris's Hawk

a reference to the broad band around the tail: Choate 1973

Measurements: Clark and Wheeler 1987

47 percent heavier than males: Bednarz and Hayden 1991 in Bednarz 1995

112 eastern Mexico and much of Central America: Van Rossem 1942 in Bednarz 1995

P. u. unicinctus inhabits South America: Brown and Amadon 1968

in southwestern Arizona and western Mexico: Ibid.

it was formerly in California, but is now extirpated: Bednarz 1995

described as a raucous, harsh raaak: Sibley 2000

given in a series of five to ten notes: Bednarz 1995

into Venezuela and the interior of Brazil: Brown and Amadon 1968

113 New Mexico, and western and southern Texas: Bednarz 1995

sparse woodland or semiopen desert: Brown and Amadon 1968

frequents palo verde and mixed-cactus habitats: Mader 1978 in Bednarz 1995

mesquite-oak shrublands and thorn scrub vegetation: Bednarz 1995

and nest support are an important component: Bednarz and Ligon 1988 in Bednarz 1995

a possible component of prime habitat: Bednarz 1988 in Bednarz 1995

commonly used as hunting perches: Snyder and Snyder 1991

March in Arizona; slightly later elsewhere: Bednarz et al. 1988 in Bednarz 1995

repaired January through August: Whaley 1986 in Bednarz 1995

in years when prey numbers are low: Bednarz 1995

both members of the alpha pair die: Ibid.

"relatively tall, sturdy structure": Whaley 1986 in Bednarz 1995

may build or repair up to four nests: Mader 1988 in Bednarz 1995

less than 30 feet above the ground: Brown and Amadon 1968

often exposed to direct sunlight: Bednarz et al. 1988 in Bednarz 1995

may be used or an alternate structure chosen: Whaley 1986 in Bednarz 1995

five eggs, with three or four typical: Bednarz et al. 1988 in Bednarz 1995

hunting and nest protection: Bednarz 1987 and Dawson and Mannan 1991 in Bednarz 1995

natal territory for up to three years: Bednarz 1987 in Bednarz 1995

"hunts with other members of the group": Bednarz 1988 in Bednarz 1995

114 during the nonbreeding season, September to March: Bednarz 1995

success increases with hunting party size: Bednarz 1988 in Bednarz 1995

perch together, sometimes on the same branch: Ibid.

115 two birds converge nearly simultaneously: Dawson 1988 in Bednarz 1995

Cactus Wren, and Northern Mockingbird: Bednarz 1995

sometimes on foot in pursuit of prey: Ibid.

116 mammalian prey populations are low: Snyder and Snyder 1991

"Backstanding" may last for up to several minutes: Ibid.

the Colorado River in Arizona and California: Bednarz 1995

Its distribution in Texas is patchy: Brown and Amadon 1968 in Bednarz 1995

"distributed throughout its range in Texas": Oberholster 1974 in Bednarz 1995

Red-shouldered Hawk

117 "occupying entirely separate ranges": Bent 1937–38

118 "be so scarce along our flyway?": Broun 1948

119 Measurements: Clark and Wheeler 1987

B. l. elegans of California and southwestern Oregon: Brown and Amadon 1968

"without hearing its discordant shrill notes": Audubon 1840

colloquial name is "Singing Hawk": Hausman 1938

120 and southern Canada are migratory: Crocoll 1994

whatever forest types are available: Titus 1984 in Crocoll 1994

Western birds favor riparian stands of oak: Crocoll 1994

pair formation begins in February: Bloom in Crocoll 1994

121 *"indulged in every year, even by mated pairs"*: Bent 1937–38

Nests are often located near water: Crocoll 1994

"especially during nesting period": Ibid.

refurbishment may take four or five weeks: Ibid.

dark brown–marked eggs, sometimes four: Harrison 1978

Incubation is about 33 days: Palmer 1988 in Crocoll 1994

typically takes 35 to 45 days: Penak 1982 in Crocoll 1994

continue to roost at or near the nest: Wiley in Palmer 1988

Crayfish are particularly targeted in some areas: Crocoll 1994

"grasshoppers during outbreaks": Brown and Amadon 1968

wounded ducks as favored prey: Audubon 1940

123 *but the population may be "stable overall"*: Bildstein et al. 2008

Broad-winged Hawk

124 pteron *for "wing"*: Choate 1973

"he had never before seen such a Hawk": Wilson 1814

125 *"appeared truly sorrowful"*: Audubon 1940

"the mildest and least suspicious": Hausman 1938

Bent calls the bird "gentle, retiring, quiet": Bent 1937–38

it is "relatively sluggish and tame": Brown and Amadon 1968

126 *Measurements*: Clark and Wheeler 1987

The balance are West Indies endemics: Goodrich, Crocoll, and Senner 1996

Common Buzzard, a Eurasian species: Schmutz et al. 1993 in Goodrich, Crocoll, and Senner 1996

from southern Mexico to Peru and Brazil: Brown and Amadon 1968

They also winter in the West Indies: Goodrich, Crocoll, and Senner 1996

defined as "humid broad-leafed forest": Bailey 1989 in Goodrich, Crocoll, and Senner 1996

(largely forest) habitat types: Goodrich, Crocoll, and Senner 1996

in a variety of rainforest habitats: Bailey 1989 in Goodrich, Crocoll, and Senner 1996

127 *in a two-week period*: Bednarz et al. 1990 in Goodrich, Crocoll, and Senner 1996

tabulated at Veracruz, Mexico: Bildstein et al. 2008

single-day count of over 700,000 birds: Kevin Karlson, personal communication with author

130 *and have exceeded 150,000*: Bildstein et al. 2008

occasionally paired with an adult: Palmer 1988

In Kansas, birds arrive between April 19 and 25: Goodrich, Crocoll, and Senner 1996

established within a week of arrival: Ibid.

131 *same woodland tract for successive seasons*: Bent 1937–38

Primary construction material is dead sticks and twigs: Ibid.

sprig of evergreen to line the nest bowl: Laurie Goodrich, personal communication with author

Construction takes two to four weeks: Mosher in Goodrich, Crocoll, and Senner 1996

A typical clutch is two or three eggs: Brown and Amadon 1968

variously spattered with brown: Mosher in Palmer 1988

28 to 31 days: Matray 1974 in Goodrich, Crocoll, and Senner 1996

an additional four to eight weeks: Ibid.

A sentinel forager: Toland 1986 in Goodrich, Crocoll, and Senner 1996

has been described as "catlike": Brown and Amadon 1968

reptiles, small mammals, and birds: Goodrich, Crocoll, and Senner 1996

particularly favored summer prey item: Hausman 1938

are the most frequent prey: Fitch 1974 in Goodrich, Crocoll, and Senner 1996

nestling birds figure in the hawk's diet: Brown and Amadon 1968

on southern nonbreeding grounds: del Hoyo, Elliott, and Sargatal 1994

North American hawks: Johnsgard 1990

for wintering and migrating birds: Goodrich, Crocoll, and Senner 1996

stable or increasing in North America: Bildstein et al. 2008

threatened by deforestation: del Hoyo, Elliott, and Sargatal 1994

listing as endangered: Ibid.

"stable or possibly declining but unclear": Bildstein et al. 2008

Gray Hawk

132 *Red-shouldered, and Broad-winged Hawk*: Johnson and Peters 1963 in Bibles, Glinski, and Johnson 2002

"narrower tarsi than typical buteos": Bibles, Glinski, and Johnson 2002

133 *mottled with white and buff:* Brown and Amadon 1968

Measurements: Clark and Wheeler 1967

larger than the male: Bibles, Glinski, and Johnson 2002

Gray Hawk's taxonomy is problematic: Ibid.

135 *and Ridgway's Hawk (*B. ridgwayi*):* Snyder and Snyder 1991

a *"descending long, plaintive whistle":* Sibley 2000

commonly heard before the bird is seen: Ibid.

along the Rio Grande Watershed: Bibles, Glinski, and Johnson 2002

in late February through March: Ibid.

(middle to late March in Arizona): Snyder and Snyder 1991

winter records for extreme south Texas: Oberholster 1974 in Bibles, Glinski, and Johnson 2002

bosques that are open at ground level: Glinski in Snyder and Snyder 1991

found in heavier humid forests: Brown and Amadon 1968

same prey as Roadside Hawk: del Hoyo, Elliott, and Sargatal 1994

mesquite-hackberry bosques for hunting: Snyder and Snyder 1991

in mid-March to early April: Davis and Russell 1990 in Bibles, Glinski, and Johnson 2002

especially evident in April: Bendire 1892 in Bibles, Glinski, and Johnson 2002

often concealed by foliage: Brown and Amadon 1968

female shaping the nest: Glinski 1988 in Bibles, Glinski, and Johnson 2002

deposited early to late May: Bendire 1892 in Bibles, Glinski, and Johnson 2002

at about 42 days of age: Glinski 1988 in Bibles, Glinski, and Johnson 2002

136 *it glides to intercept:* Brown and Amadon 1968

flight is "swift and Accipiter-like": Snyder and Snyder 1991

typically hunts below the canopy: Ibid.

80 percent of the Gray Hawk's diet: Glinski in Snyder and Snyder 1991

up to the size of Gambel's Quail: Bibles, Glinski, and Johnson 2002

an "uncommon component in Gray Hawk's diet": Snyder and Snyder 1991

along the San Pedro's watercourse: Ibid.

Short-tailed Hawk

139 *Measurements:* Clark and Wheeler 1987

B. b. brachyurus *occurs in South America:* Brown and Amadon 1968

"drawn-out, sometimes quavering": Sibley 2000

central Mexico south through Brazil: Brown and Amadon 1968

140 *the Florida Panhandle:* Robertson and Wolfenden 1992 in Miller and Meyer 2002

Florida and the eastern panhandle: Ogden 1991 in Miller and Meyer 2002

Everglades to the northern Keys: Miller and Meyer 2002

through May and August through June: Miller and Meyer 2002

counted during fall migration: Bildstein et al. 2008

"extensive forest tracts for nesting": Ogden 1988 in Miller and Meyer 2002

cypress and bay swamps: Millsap 1989 in Miller and Meyer 2002

a variety of open woodlands: Ibid.

humid tropical and deciduous: del Hoyo, Elliott, and Sargatal 1994

(such as prairies, marshes, and pastures): Ogden 1974 in Miller and Meyer 2002

hunt over suburban areas: Millsap et al. 1996 in Miller and Meyer 2002

from early February to late March: Howell 1932 in Miller and Meyer 2002

"sky dancing and tumbling": del Hoyo, Elliott, and Sargatal 1994

Nests in Florida are bulky: Brandt 1924 and Ogden 1988 in Miller and Meyer 2002

The male provides most of the sticks: Brandt 1924 in Miller and Meyer 2002

(especially cypress twigs): Penncock 1890 in BNA

"very dense cypress swamp": Bent 1937–38

use the same nesting area year after year: Millsap 1989 in Miller and Meyer 2002

more than two consecutive years: Ogden 1988 in Miller and Meyer 2002

"usually with brown spots and blotches": Brown and Amadon 1968

Incubation lasts 34 days: del Hoyo, Elliott, and Sargatal 1994

with pairs rearing one brood per season: Miller and Meyer 2002

"rather sluggish, tame buteo": Brown and Amadon 1968

141 *seen diving upon birds in flight:* Robinson 1994 in Miller and Meyer 2002

sometimes found in small groups: Hundly and James 1960 in Miller and Meyer 2002

rodents, lizards, and insects: del Hoyo, Elliott, and Sargatal 1994

up to the size of Sharp-shinned Hawk: Bent 1937–38

this species is never common: Miller and Meyer 2002

"disappeared from that state": Bent 1937–38

Short-tailed Hawks in Florida: Avian Research and Conservation Institute 2004

142 suggest an increase in numbers: Casey Lott, personal communication with Kevin Karlson

but "not globally threatened": del Hoyo, Elliott, and Sargatal 1994

Swainson's Hawk

named it after Swainson: Choate 1973

"rather sluggish, tame buteo": Brown and Amadon 1968

"seen from above, is whitish": Ibid.

144 Measurements: Clark and Wheeler 1987

constitute a superspecies group: Mayr and Short 1970 in England, Bechard, and Houston 1997

145 gives a series of whistled notes: Sibley 2000

west Texas, into northern Mexico: Brown and Amadon 1968

the Northwest Territories "needs clarification": England, Bechard, and Houston 1997

"(individuals unable to make the long migration)": Brown and Amadon 1968

wintered in south Florida: Robertson and Woolfenden 1992 in England, Bechard, and Houston 1997

may exceed 12,000 miles: England, Bechard, and Houston 1997

from February to mid-April: Ibid.

146 "they gradually drift southward": Bent 1937–38

large numbers of grasshoppers before heading south: Snyder and Snyder 1991

"energy source during the long southward flight": Olendorff 1975

intercepting randomly encountered thermals: Kerlinger 1989

near the core of the thermal: Kerlinger 1989

may occur in "patches, zones, or waves": Smith in England, Bechard, and Houston 1997

without resorting to energetic flight: Ibid.

averaging over 118 miles a day: England, Bechard, and Houston 1997

147 may number from 5,000 to 10,000 individuals: Ibid.

counts at Veracruz average 34,537: Bildstein et al. 2008

"since the demise of the Passenger Pigeon": Brown and Amadon 1968

late October to early November: Smith 1985 in England, Bechard, and Houston 1997

Birds reach Argentina in January: Woodbridge et al. 1995 in England, Bechard, and Houston 1997

before birds leave the United States: Laurie Goodrich, personal communication with author

late February to mid-March: England, Bechard, and Houston 1997

in late April and early May: Houston in BNA

traveling to or from Argentina: Snyder and Snyder 1991

148 extensive grasslands, as well as deserts: del Hoyo, Elliott, and Sargatal 1994

as native prairie grasses: Bechard 1992 in England, Bechard, and Houston 1997

sunflowers and corn are abundant: Woodbridge et al. 1995 in England, Bechard, and Houston 1997

grassland habitats with scattered trees: Johnsgard 1990

7 to 15 days after arrival: England, Bechard, and Houston 1997

June, and early July in Alaska: Brown and Amadon 1968

as having found 41 nests: Bent 1937

and now, agricultural landscapes: England, Bechard, and Houston 1997

other species (most notably magpie) are used: Ibid.

"finished off with twigs, leaves and grasses": Bent 1937–38

Most nests are in "commanding situations": Ibid.

Great Horned Owl and Red-tailed Hawk: Newton 1979

"only obscurely and palely marked with brown": Brown and Amadon 1968

34 or 35 days: Olendorff 1973 and Fitzner 1980 in England, Bechard, and Houston 1997

dependent upon adults for food: Fitzner 1980, in England, Bechard, and Houston 1997

fledging takes about 73 days: England, Bechard, and Houston 1997

seven or eight months in Saskatchewan: Houston in England, Bechard, and Houston 1997

they prefer a knoll if one is available: Brown and Amadon 1968

149 shrub steppe, and agricultural land: England, Bechard, and Houston 1997

in alfalfa fields and cropland: White et al. 1989 in England, Bechard, and Houston 1997

"transformed into an alert and skillful hunter": May 1935

on the mound and extracts the gopher: Bechard 1992 in England, Bechard, and Houston 1997

it also follows tractors: Snyder and Snyder 1991

"they hobble about, like half grown turkeys": Brown and Amadon 1968

150 *ground squirrels, pocket gophers, and voles:* England, Bechard, and Houston 1997

"ordinarily nothing larger than gophers": Coues 1874

"their craws stuffed with grasshoppers": Merriam 1888

"the diet of breeding birds": Smith and Murphy 1973 in England, Bechard, and Houston 1997

diet is dominated by insects: Snyder and Wiley 1976 in England, Bechard, and Houston 1997

known as the "locust hawk": Brown and Amadon 1968

with a high count of 943,346 in 2009: 1997–2015 data, Corpus Christi Hawkwatch (John Economidy, compiler), unpublished

151 *increasing across much of North America:* Bildstein et al. 2008

by ingesting poisoned grasshoppers: England, Bechard, and Houston 1997

White-tailed Hawk

caudat'us for "tailed": Choate 1973

found in semiarid open country: del Hoyo, Elliott, and Sargatal 1994

152 *Measurements:* Clark and Wheeler 1987

Three subspecies are currently recognized: Farquhar 1992

northern Columbia and western Venezuela: Brown and Amadon 1968

dark morph ascribed to this subspecies: Ibid.

Brazil to northern and central Argentina: del Hoyo, Elliott, and Sargatal 1994

153 *(B. polyosoma) of the High Andes:* Farquhar 1992

a goat or cry of Laughing Gull: Brown and Amadon 1968

It formerly bred in Arizona: Farquhar 1992

In Texas, the bird is fairly common but local: Clark and Wheeler 1987

adults in the Coastal Bend region: Rappole and Bucklock 1985 in Farquhar 1992

154 *exclusively shrub-steppe in northern Argentina:* del Hoyo, Elliott, and Sargatal 1994

Cultivated and fallow fields are shunned: Farquhar 1992

155 *this species shuns artificial structures:* Stevenson and Meitzen 1946 in Farquhar 1992

5 to 15 feet from the ground or even lower: Brown and Amadon 1968

a commanding view preferred: Ibid.

Nests may be reused but not necessarily every year: Ibid.

with peak laying March 11 to 20: Morrison 1978 in Farquhar 1992

Clutch size ranges from one to three: Brown and Amadon 1998

with two eggs typical: Bent 1937–38

"blotched with brown or unmarked": Brown and Amadon 1968

29 to 32 days: Farquhar 1988 in Farquhar 1992

between 49 and 52 days: del Hoyo, Elliott, and Sargatal 1994

up to 21 months is noted: Mader 1981 in Farquhar 1992

a good deal of its time soaring and gliding: Brown and Amadon 1998

156 *small groups of up to 60 individuals:* Palmer 1988 in Farquhar 1992

they may elect to perch-hunt: Farquhar 1986 in Farquhar 1992

trees, telephone poles, and the ground: Brown and Amadon 1968

The diet is variable: Benners 1987 in Farquhar 1992

targets small to medium-sized birds: Ibid.

Eastern Meadowlark, and Prairie Chicken: Ibid.

"a rather common resident . . . plentifully distributed": Bent 1937–38

"less in evidence now than only a few years ago": Sprunt 1955

200 breeding pairs in Texas: Farquhar 1992

endemic to the coastal prairies: Snyder and Snyder 1991

Zone-tailed hawk

157 *notatus for "marked":* Choate 1973

158 *"its flight is lazy and sluggish":* Bent 1937–38

need some strategic edge to secure prey: Snyder and Snyder 1991

when Zone-taileds were thus escorted: Ibid.

159 *juvenile plumage that is held for one year:* Bent 1937–38

Measurements: Clark and Wheeler 1987

taxonomic position within Buteo is uncertain: Brown and Amadon 1968 in Johnson, Glinski, and Matteson 2000

Red-tailed Hawk, B. jamaicensis harlani: Johnson, Glinski, and Matteson 2000

a "feeble screaming": Brown and Amadon 1968

"clearer and lower than Red-tailed": Sibley 2001

"widespread but rare or local": Brown and Amadon 1968

apparently shuns the rainforest ecosystem: del Hoyo, Elliott, and Sargatal 1994

160 *some overwintering is reported*: Ferguson-Lees and Christie 2001

returns February to March: Johnson, Glinski, and Matteson 2000

foraging over adjacent open country: AOU Checklist, Seventh Edition 1983

Both sexes engage in nest building: Johnson, Glinski, and Matteson 2000

in pines in more mountainous regions: Snyder and Snyder 1991

approximately 200 feet high: Johnson, Glinski, and Matteson 2000

a "rather bulky affair of sticks": Bent 1937–38

late March to mid-May: Johnson, Glinski, and Matteson 2000

"coarsely built and rather bulky": Brown and Amadon 1968

Two egg sets are the rule: Bent 1937–38

"getting to high and open ground": Snyder and Snyder 1991

161 *28 to 34 days*: Johnson, Glinski, and Matteson 2000

35 to 42 days: Snyder and Glinski 1988 in Johnson, Glinski, and Matteson 2000

for another four to eight weeks: Kennedy et al. 1995 and Hiraldo et al. 1989 in Johnson, Glinski, and Matteson 2000

"surpassing even the falcons": Smith in Brown and Amadon 1968

approach "in a shallow stoop": Snyder and Snyder 1991

(chipmunks especially) and lizards: Ferguson-Lees and Christie 2001

specifically collared and spiny lizards: Johnson, Glinski, and Matteson 2000

162 *specialists like the Peregrine*: Snyder and Snyder 1991

"the beds of the streams where it lives": Bent 1937–38

locations north of Mexico: Snyder and Snyder 1991

Red-tailed Hawk

164 *might simply be a matter of age*: Wilson 1814

165 *Measurements*: Clark and Wheeler 1987

14 subspecies are generally recognized: del Hoyo, Elliott, and Sargatal 1994

16 are recognized by various authorities: Preston and Beane 1993

166 *greatest range in size between males and females*: Ferguson-Lees and Christie 2001

almost reach the tail when it is perched: Clark and Wheeler 1987

a tail that is nearly white: Brown and Amadon 1968

167 *"I could not get near them"*: Krider 1878

the Coast Range and interior Alaska: Brown and Amadon 1968

southeastern Alaska to the Queen Charlotte Islands: Ibid.

Arkansas, central Oklahoma, and Missouri: Root 1988 in Bechard and Swem 2002

feathers have dark bars near the shaft: Brown and Amadon 1968

from Alberta to Nova Scotia: Dickerman and Parkes 1987 in Preston and Beane 1993

168 *more Red-tailed may now be wintering farther north*: Laurie Goodrich, personal communication with author

"the widest ecological tolerance of any buteo": Brown and Amadon 1968

170 *a taller tree with a commanding view*: Preston and Beane 1993

a mere four to seven days: Peterson 1979 in Preston and Beane 1993

structure may denote occupancy: Bent 1937–38

171 *dark brown, reddish brown, or purple markings*: Harrison 1978

requiring 34 days to hatch: Hegner 1906 in Palmer 1988

an additional 42 to 46 days: Preston and Beane 1993

another 18 to 70 days: Johnson 1973 in Preston and Beane 1993

for at least another week: Petersen 1979 in Preston and Beane 1993

may be lateral, northerly: Luttich et al. 1971 in Preston and Beane 1993

exclusively upon meadow mice (Microtus): Brown and Amadon 1968

172 *but perhaps stable overall*: Bildstein et al. 2008

Ferruginous Hawk

173 *"royal," in reference to the bird's size*: Clark and Wheeler 1987

"raptors' behavior and voice are much alike": Bent 1937–38

almost reach the tail tip when it is perched: Clark and Wheeler 1987 *a long gape, and large yellow feet:* Sibley 2000

174 *grayish tail shows a dusky subterminal band:* Clark and Wheeler 1987

separated by the Rocky Mountains: Bechard and Schmutz 1995

Upland Buzzard (B. hemilasius*) of central Asia:* Brown and Amadon 1968

dating back to the Bering land bridge: Olendorff 1993 in Bechard and Schmutz 1995

"Juvenile gives high scream": Sibley 2000

overall than that of any other buteo in North America: Snyder and Snyder 1991

176 *northwestern Texas, and western Oklahoma:* Brown and Amadon 1968

short distances or may be sedentary: Bechard and Schmutz 1995

return in late March or early February: Ibid.

south and following grasslands: Schmutz and Fyfe 1987 in Bechard and Schmutz 1995

a bird of grasslands and shrub-steppe: Bechard and Schmutz 1995

"Badlands," says Sprunt: Sprunt 1955

also commonly nests on the ground: Snyder and Snyder 1991

cultivated fields that house pocket gophers: Bechard and Schmutz 1995

nesting territories in early March: Olendorff 1973 in Bechard and Schmutz 1995

February to early March: Smith and Murphy 1973 in Bechard and Schmutz 1995

same nest in consecutive years: Bechard and Schmutz 1995

177 *"I would call extraordinary or acrobatic":* Olendorff 1975

"visited and repaired each year": Ibid.

cow dung to line the bowl: Bechard and Schmutz 1995

primary component of Ferruginous nests: Snyder and Snyder 1991

typically uses the highest available: Brown and Amadon 1968

178 *ground nesting remains common:* Snyder and Snyder 1991

both "massive and high": Harrison 1978

12 to 15 feet high: Brown and Amadon 1968

buffish brown, or light purple: Harrison 1978

depending upon prey availability: Smith and Murphy 1978 in Bechard and Schmutz 1995

32 or 33 days: Palmer 1988

"rarely left unattended": Bechard and Schmutz 1995

38 to 50 days: Powers 1981 in Bechard and Schmutz 1995

several weeks after feeding: Blair and Schitoskey 1982 in Bechard and Schmutz 1995

densities of prey species: Olendorff 1975

half that found in prey-rich years: Smith and Murphy 1979 in Bechard and Schmutz 1995

typically solitary or found in pairs: Bechard and Schmutz 1995

enjoying a high rate of success: Ibid.

when trees or posts are unavailable: Brown and Amadon 1968

abundant but where cover is scant: Wakely in Snyder and Snyder 1991

small and medium-sized mammals: Brown and Amadon 1968

"most frequently captured prey": Olendorff 1993 in Bechard and Schmutz 1995

jackrabbits constitute the favored prey: Smith and Murphy 1978 in Bechard and Schmutz 1995

proliferation of aspen in prairie habitat: Houston and Bechard 1984 in BNA

estimated at 3,000 to 5,600 pairs: del Hoyo, Elliott, and Sargatal 1994

Rough-legged Hawk

179 *probably in reference to the bird's feathered shanks:* Choate 1973

"conspicuous in most other hawks": Audubon 1840

"one of the largest and finest of our hawks": Bent 1937–38

180 *Measurements:* Clark and Wheeler 1987

central-eastern Asia: Johnsgard 1990; Ellis et al. 1999 in Bechard and Swem 2002

181 *and lacks a breast band:* Brown and Amadon 1968

possibly in the Aleutian Islands: Ibid.

It winters in east-central Asia: del Hoyo, Elliott, and Sargatal 1994

more variable than the other races: Brown and Amadon 1968

Melville Island in Nunavut, Canada: Ibid.

tree line and southern Hudson Bay: Bechard and Swem 2002

182 *It strays rarely to the Gulf Coast:* Ibid.

from early March through early May: Ibid.

an average of 487 birds per fall: Bildstein et al. 2008

situated on sides of outcroppings: Bechard and Swem 2002

rarely nests on the ground: Ibid.

correlates well with low ground cover: Ibid.

conifers, cottonwoods, and other deciduous trees: Ibid.

from late April to early May: Kessel 1989 in Bechard and Swem 2002 snowmelt on nest ledges: Ibid.

laying dates are mid-May to mid-July: Bent 1937–38

birds are paired on migration: Brown and Amadon 1968

Both adults participate in nest building: Bechard and Swem 2002

the female constructs the nest: Palmer 1988 in Bechard and Swem 2002

tops of cliffs and outcrops: White and Cade 1971 in Bechard and Swem 2002

183 "cemented together by excrement": Bent 1937–38

suggesting alternate nest use: Brown and Amadon in Bechard and Swem 2002

"the three eggs were lying": Chapman 1885 in Bent 1937–38

five to seven in good years: Brown and Amadon 1968

ledges become snow-free: Kessel in Bechard and Swem 2002

the second week of May: Ibid.

28 to 31 days: del Hoyo, Elliott, and Sargatal 1994

"in the nest for 40 days": Parmelee et al. 1967 in Bechard and Swem 2002

the next two to four weeks: Kessel 1989 in Bechard and Swem 2002

in the vicinity of the nest until migration: Bechard and Swem 2002

may extend into migration: Palmer 1988 in Bechard and Swem 2002

"as soon as they leave the nest": Bent 1937–38

184 like a high-altitude harrier: Ibid.

Most prey is captured on the ground: Bent 1937–38

including ground squirrels and rabbits: Schnell 1967 in Bechard and Swem 2002

"most abundant species of raptor in the world": Palmer 1988

a total of 4,791 Rough-legged Hawks were counted: figure courtesy of Geoff LeBaron, CBC Director, National Audubon Society

185 "below the City of Philadelphia": Krider 1897

species going from "most abundant": Ibid.

Rough-legged Hawk are "evidently declining": Bildstein et al. 2008

Golden Eagle

186 Greek in the third century A.D: Choate 1973

187 "He clasps the crag": Tennyson 1851

188 over four or five years: del Hoyo, Elliott, and Sargatal 1994

some measure of white in the tail: Kochert, Steenhof, McIntyre, and Craig 2002

Measurements: Clark and Wheeler 1987

although some sources cite five or six: Kochert, Steenhof, McIntyre, and Craig 2002

The nominate subspecies, A. c. chrysaetos: Linnaeus 1758

189 "A. c. chrysaetos and A. c. japonica of Korea and Japan": Brown and Amadon 1968

"cheeps and high-pitched chitters": Jollie 1943 in Kochert, Steenhof, McIntyre, and Craig 2002

population extends south to central Mexico: Kochert et al. 2002

across the central and eastern United States: Ibid.

western Texas, and south into central Mexico: Ibid.

begin migrating before the end of September: Kessel 1989 in Kochert et al. 2002

190 "habitats in eastern Great Plains": Menkens and Anderson 1987 in Kochert et al. 2002

birds breeding in northeastern Canada: Michael Lanzone, personal communication with author

"may be seen at almost any month": Brown and Amadon 1968

similar to those of many buteo species: Bent 1937–38

nest construction occur December to January: Hunt 1997 in Kochert et al. 2002

late February to mid-April: Kochert et al. 2002

on manmade structures and on the ground: Ibid.

"deposited on the naked rock": Audubon 1840

little more than scrapes with branches around them: Brown and Amadon 1968

sometimes one, occasionally three: Ibid.

191 "chestnut red and pale gray": Harrison 1978

resulting in asynchronous hatching: Kochert et al. 2002

lasts 43 to 45 days: Brown and Amadon 1968

elder siblings attack and kill younger nest mates: Ibid.

may be tended to by the female: Ibid.

grappling with large animals: Watson 1997

particularly important food source in winter: Kochert et al. 2002

"to get away from a pursuing eagle": Forbush 1927

192 well adapted to the capture of ptarmigan: Watson 1997

used to subdue large prey: Ibid.

"probably have little foundation in fact": Forbush 1927

akin to a messenger of the Great Spirit: Ernie C. Salgado Jr., Soboba Tribal Elder, Jan. 17, 2014; www.theindianreporter.com

"flapped his wings to create the wind": www.warpaths2peacepipes.com/native-american-symbols/

"doctor's rattles and medicine pipes": Ernie Salgado, www.theindianreporter.com/

193 mammals comprise 80 to 90 percent of their diet: Kochert et al. 2002

fish during nesting season: Olendorff 1976 in Kochert et al. 2002

"Whooping Crane, and Great Blue Heron": Phillips et al. 1991 in Kochert et al. 2002

domestic sheep during lambing: Ibid.

194 vertical dive would be "about 180 miles per hour": Brown 1976

"also places the talon points in a position to pierce . . . ": Ibid.

"the most numerous large eagle in the world": Ibid.

estimated to be 70,000 birds in North America: Palmer 1988

estimated at 50,000 to 70,000: Watson 1997

declining numbers have been noted since 1998: Bildstein et al. 2008

there has been an overall increase in sightings: Ibid.

70 percent of Golden Eagle deaths: Franson et al. 1995 in Kochert 2002

FALCONIDAE
Crested Caracara

195 "derived from its call, a low rattle": Jacquin in Choate 1973

196 Measurements: Clark and Wheeler 1987

grouped with three other caracara species: del Hoyo et al. 1994

within the subfamily Falconinae: Griffiths 1999

The number of subspecies has varied: Morrison and Dwyer 2012

distinct from forms found in South America: Morrison 1996

a series of "rattles, cackles and chattering": Ibid.

197 "until my visit to Florida in the winter of 1831": Audubon 1840

river edges, and especially ranch land: Morrison 1996

"creeks and arroyos narrowly skirted by trees": Simmons 1925 in Bent 1937–38

"raptors to begin nesting in Florida": Nicholson 1929 in Bent 1937–38

the onset of the dry season: Morrison 1996

with most Florida birds laying in late January: Ibid.

eggs are laid January through March: Rivera-Rodriguez-Estrella 1993 in Morrison 1996

in Arizona, they are laid April through June: Levy 1988 in Morrison 1996

caracaras overwhelmingly favor cabbage palm: Morrison 1996

they are invariably in the crotch of a large saguaro: Ellis et al. in Morrison 1996

They are also reported to nest on cliffs: Bent 1937–38

"often very bulky and show successive layers": Brandt in Bent 1937–38

"bulky yet woven, well-constructed": Morrison 1996

198 may be delayed up to two months: Ibid.

scrawls, splashes, and spots of darker browns: Bent 1937–38

Incubation lasts from 30 to 33 days: Morrison 1996

young fledge in seven or eight weeks: Dickinson 1996, Layne 1996, JLM in Morrison 1996

typically there is only one brood per season: Bent 1937–38

fed by the parents for several months after fledging: Morrison 1996

199 even include birds in adult plumage: Ibid.

early in the morning and late in the afternoon: Dickinson 1990 in Morrison 1996

they actively search roadsides for roadkill: Morrison 1996

"any animal matter, alive or dead, that it can catch or find": Ibid.

flips over debris or cow pies with one foot: Ibid.

"lands and approaches prey on foot": Ibid.

"in spite of its sharp turns and bounds": Merrill 1878 in Bent 1937–38

"once saw one chase, tire out and kill a white ibis": Bent 1937–38

200 content to grab small scraps: Wallace and Temple 1987 in Morrison 1996

201 an ambush whose objective was a young lamb: Bent 1937–38

202 "perches on fence posts, trees or utility poles": Morrison 1996

victims include Northern Mockingbird and Loggerhead Shrike: Ibid.

nesting Brown Pelicans returning with prey: Bent 1937–38

another fleet-footed hunter, the Secretarybird of Africa: Snyder and Snyder 1991

"generally declined from 1950 to 1980": Oberholser 1974 in Morrison 1996

increase in both population and range: Ortega in Morrison 1996

"as extensive now as it was formerly": Ellis et al. 1988 in Morrison 1996

fairly common to locally abundant: del Hoyo, Elliott, and Sargatal 1994

American Kestrel

falco *from* falx *for "sickle":* Choate 1973

sparverious, *"pertaining to a sparrow":* Ibid.

13 kestrel species found across the globe: del Hoyo, Elliott, and Sargatal 1994

to 14,000 feet in South America: Ibid.

204 *"the prettiest and jauntiest of our Hawks, yet no prig":* Coues 1874

"most light-hearted and frolicsome": Brewster in Bent 1937–38

"Everyone knows the Sparrow-Hawk": Audubon 1840

205 *Measurements:* Clark and Wheeler 1987

F. s. paulus *is found from South Carolina to Florida:* del Hoyo, Elliott, and Sargatal 1994

absent in heavily forested areas, including in Amazonia: Brown and Amadon 1968

through Mexico to at least Panama: Smallwood and Bird 2002

Males winter farther north than females: Ibid.

wooded or heavily vegetated habitat: Roest 1957 in Cade 1982

Kestrels breed March to June: Smallwood and Bird 2002

207 *birds engage in a "prolonged period of pre-laying activities":* Cade 1982

eggs are generally paler than those of most other falcons: Harrison 1978

With clutches of up to seven eggs: Cade 1982

Birds may double-brood: del Hoyo, Elliott, and Sargatal 1994

about 30 days postfledging: Brown and Amadon 1968

1,200,000 breeding pairs in North America: del Hoyo, Elliott, and Sargatal 1994

208 *apparent across much of North America:* Bildstein et al. 2008

annual declines of –2.3 percent between 1983 and 2005: Ibid.

Merlin

210 columbarius *for "a pigeon keeper":* Choate 1973

the Old French name for this species: Sodhi, Oliphant, James, and Warkentin 1993

"possesses great spirit and rapidity of flight": Wilson 1814

description found in Birds of North America: Sodhi, Oliphant, James, and Warkentin 1993

Tom Cade calls it a "doughty little hunter": Cade 1982

212 *Measurements:* Clark and Wheeler 1987

Nine Merlin subspecies are generally recognized: del Hoyo, Elliott, and Sargatal 1994

winter range that extends to northern California: Brown and Amadon 1968

215 *may return to nest sites in late winter:* Cade 1982

found near rivers, lakes, and bogs: Sodhi, Oliphant, James, and Warkentin 1993

on islands in large lakes and burned-over areas: Cade 1982

may commonly nest on the ground: Sodhi, Oliphant, James, and Warkentin 1993

small flocking land birds are found: Cade 1982

females join them several days to weeks later: Ibid.

mid-April to May in Alaska: Laing 1985 in Sodhi, Oliphant, James, and Warkentin 1993

but not necessarily the same site: Cade 1982

concealment and easy access: Sodhi, Oliphant, James, and Warkentin 1993

They deposit at two-day intervals: Cade 1982

Incubation lasts 30 days: Palmer 1988

potential prey and other raptors: Sodhi, Oliphant, James, and Warkentin 1993

216 *prey as large as Golden-Plover, pigeons, and small ducks:* Cade 1982

Most of the falcon's prey (80 percent) weighs less than 1.5 ounces: Ibid.

217 *avian prey species in the area:* Sodhi, Oliphant, James, and Warkentin 1993

prey item in northern urban areas: Oliphant in Cade 1982

800 to 900 birds per year: Cade 1982

shooting, poison, and cat predation: Sodhi, Oliphant, James, and Warkentin 1993

Aplomado Falcon

218 *bright orange feathers on the upper legs:* Choate 1973

long-legged falcon had been extirpated: Brandt 1951

219 *Measurements:* Clark and Wheeler 1987

"kacking of the usual falcon type": Brown and Amadon 1968

"faster and higher than Prairie or Peregrine": Sibley 2000

"coordinate collaborative activities": Keddy-Hector 1986 in Keddy-Hector 2000

closer alliance with Peregrine Falcon (Falco peregrinus): Griffiths 1994 in Keddy-Hector 2000

differentiated subspecies are recognized: Keddy-Hector 2000

United States south locally through Mexico: Brown and Amadon 1968

occurs in South America at low altitudes: Ibid.

220 "darker in color and larger" than northern subspecies: Brown and Amadon 1968

higher elevations during austral winter: Keddy-Hector 2000

a winter resident or vagrant in western Mexico: Ibid.

was in New Mexico in 1952: AOU Checklist, Seventh Edition 1983

above 13,000 feet in the Andes Mountains: U.S. Fish and Wildlife Service 2007

"East to Texas (Ft. Stockton, Pecos, and Brownsville)": Bent 1937–38

historic breeding sites near South Padre Island: Kevin Karlson, personal communication with author

initiated in New Mexico: U.S. Fish and Wildlife Service 2007

high altitudes during the southern winter: Keddy-Hector 2000

favors lightly forested or open country: Brown and Amadon 1968

desert grasslands with scattered yuccas and mesquite: Keddy-Hector 2000

221 breeding habits are very poorly known: del Hoyo, Elliott, and Sargatal 1994

pairs deposit eggs mid-February to late March: Keddy-Hector 2000

and occasionally use bromeliads: Cade 1982

blotches of light brown or chestnut red: Harrison 1978

Fledging occurs four to five weeks posthatching: Keddy-Hector 2000

posts, and telephone poles, often in shadows: Ibid.

comparatively little time hunting: Brown and Amadon 1968

"though more listless than Merlin or Peregrine": Ibid.

222 both in the air and on the ground: Ibid.

"picks its prey to pieces": Brooks 1933 in Bent 1937–38

"it would launch an attack": Grayson in Cade 1982

including small mammals and reptiles: Brown and Amadon 1968

"catching and eating insects on the wing": Howell and Webb 1995

the mate, waiting overhead, engages: Keddy-Hector 2000

twice as successful as solo efforts: Keddy-Hector 1986 in Keddy-Hector 2000

they capture some on the ground: Cade 1982

for the decline of this species: Snyder and Snyder 1991

223 "because of inadequate or corrupted data": Keddy-Hector 2000

in the vicinity of Fort Huachuca, Arizona: Bent 1937–38

"which is another desert mystery": Brandt 1951

doing well, with 700 adults released: Tweit 2008

244 young fledged since 1995: U.S. Fish and Wildlife Service 2007

Gyrfalcon

224 "circle," and geier, for "greedy": Choate 1973

a reference to the bird's remote breeding habitat: Ibid.

"most majestic of the long-winged hawks": Cade 1982

extending to 82 degrees north latitude: Ibid.

"over even the Peregrine in strength, speed, courage": Ibid.

225 over the ocean between Greenland and Iceland: Burnham and Newton 2011

few individuals wander south of 55 degrees north latitude: Cade 1982

broad tail, and a heavy body: Forsman 1999

"handling of large mammals": Cade 1982

226 "grayish brown with slightly paler tail": Forsman 1999

Measurements: Clark and Wheeler 1987

"mostly white . . . dark or intermediate": Clum and Cade 1994

birds are 50 percent white and 50 percent dark: Ibid.

the most widespread color morph: Sibley 2000

now known to winter on the pack ice: Ellis et al. 1992 in Clum and Cade 1994

"more trumpeting quality than Peregrine": Sibley 2000

to 55 degrees north: Cade 1982 in Clum and Cade 1994

Ontario, and occasionally farther south: Clum and Cade 1994

tend to be female and juvenile: Ibid.

breeding below 70 degrees north: Norment 1985 in Clum and Cade 1994

winter territory is typically in October and November: Clum and Cade 1994

as early as March and April: Ibid.

ptarmigan numbers remain supportive: Cade 1982; Nielson and Cade 1990 in Clum and Cade 1994

"often along rivers and seacoasts": Clum and Cade 1994

maritime, riverine, and montane: Cade 1982

227 sea level to at least 4,500 feet: del Hoyo, Elliott, and Sargatal 1994

nest site and the abundance of prey: Cade 1982

similar to that of Rock Ptarmigan: Cade 1960 in Clum and Cade 1994

"precipitous cliff faces": Ibid.

usurps the nest of another species: Potapov and Sale 2005

more common in the Palearctic: Ibid.

broadly March through July: Clum and Cade 1994

from mid-February to early March: Cade 1982

a high degree of fidelity to territories: Ibid.

offering a shielding overhang: Potapov and Sale 2005

228 between 2,360 and 2,740 years ago: Burnham et al. 2009

(with a range of 6 to 200 feet): Potapov and Sale 2005

bare substrate or accumulated debris: Clum and Cade 1994

when Gyrfalcon begins nesting: Potapov and Sale 2005

in years marked by food extremes: del Hoyo, Elliott, and Sargatal 1994

lasts 35 or 36 days: Clum and Cade 1994

most prey overall: Poole and Brag 1988 in Clum and Cade 1994

mid-July to early August: Cade 1982

adults for at least a month: Ibid.

affected by ptarmigan numbers: Brown and Amadon 1968

during lemming irruptive years: Cade 1982

employing a flap and glide: Ibid.

similar to that of Golden Eagle: Clum and Cade 1994

may be used in combination and in succession: Potapov and Sale 2005

229 over long distances, exhausting it: Cade 1982

ground than to snatch it in the air: Ibid.

rather than the ringing-up manner of a Peregrine: Clum and Cade 1994

"Ridge hopping" is a common hunting tactic: Potapov and Sale 2005

prey on or near the ground: Clum and Cade 1994

Gyrfalcons eat chiefly birds: Brown and Amadon 1968

230 (such as longspurs) to ducks and geese: Ibid.

Pairs at higher altitude take more mammals: Cade 1982

Gyrfalcons approximates 11,106 pairs: Potapov 2005

estimates and calculated 7,000 to 9,000 pairs: Cade 1982

(with most birds occurring in Canada): Shank and Poole 1994 and Swem 1994 in Potapov and Sale 2005

Peregrine Falcon

"caught in their passage from the breeding place": Choate 1973

"is of astonishing rapidity": Audubon 1840

"probably, of our reputation": Wilson 1814

232 "Kings in the seventeenth century": Peterson in Cade 1982

"adult bird different from that of young": Krider 1897

233 wingtips fall short of the tip of the tail: Sibley 2000

Measurements: Clark and Wheeler 1987

234 except for the Pacific Northwest: White, Clum, Cade, and Hunt 2002

from Alaska to Greenland: Ibid.

as well as many oceanic islands: Cade 1982

"have not been able myself to find its nest": Krider 1879

into an "enormous" winter range: White, Clum, Cade, and Hunt 2002

central Argentina and southern Chile: del Hoyo, Elliott, and Sargatal 1994

Peregrines have been counted in a single season: Bildstein et al. 2008

the previous single-day count record by over 800 birds: Florida Keys Hawkwatch Data, Raphael Galvez

peak migration April through May: White, Clum, Cade, and Hunt 2002

236 It favors cliff ledges and crags: Cade 1982

in patches of heath surrounded by bog: Ibid.

two months prior to egg laying: Nelson 1970 in White, Clum, Cade, and Hunt 2002

Courtship continues until egg laying: White, Clum, Cade, and Hunt 2002

in favor of preferred nest sites: Ted Swem, personal communication with author

occasionally five or six: White, Clum, Cade, and Hunt 2002

"shades of pink, fawn, buff and cream":
Ratcliffe 1980

hatch in 33 to 35 days: Haggard in Bent
1937–38

fledge in five to six weeks: Ratcliffe 1980

seldom visiting the nest ledge: Ibid.

young for about five or six weeks: White,
Clum, Cade, and Hunt 2002

(40 to 55 miles per hour): Cade 1982

may exceed 100 miles per hour: White,
Clum, Cade, and Hunt 2002

small mammals, and nestlings on foot: Ibid.

would come to the "report": Audubon 1840

237 *vertical to a tempered 20 degrees*: White,
Clum, Cade, and Hunt 2002

diving falcon was 223 miles per hour: Cade
1982

"not admit to so violent concussion": Wilson
1814

238 *"the hawk employs only its talons"*: Ibid.

"toes are splayed at impact": White, Clum,
Cade, and Hunt 2002

240 *even consuming egg shells*: Ratcliffe 1980

*British scientists Norman Moore and Derek
Ratcliffe*: Ibid.

241 *"rarely reptiles and small mammals"*: White,
Clum, Cade, and Hunt 2002

ranging in size from passerines to geese: Ibid.

and herons: Cade 1982

preferred wherever they occur: Ibid.

200 species would "not be out of order": Ibid.

bats, but also small rodents: White, Clum,
Cade, and Hunt 2002

territories in North America: Faulk and
Moller 1988 in White, Clum, Cade, and
Hunt 2002

approached complete recovery: White,
Clum, Cade, and Hunt 2002

Prairie Falcon

242 *An "irascible, excitable bird"*: Brown and
Amadon 1968

"courageous and 'noble' as Peregrine": May
1935

"altogether capable and determined hunter":
Cade 1982

243 *Measurements*: Clark and Wheeler 1967

Gyrfalcon, Lanner, and Saker: Brown and
Amadon 1968

closer kinship to Peregrine": Helbig et al.
1994 in Steenhof 1998

report several color phases: Anderson and
Squires 1997

Gyrfalcon's array, but more subdued: Wreng
and Cade 1977 in Steenhof 1998

similar to Peregrine but higher: Sibley 2000

"scream in a high-pitched voice": Anderson
and Squires 1997

of the North American falcons;: Cade 1982

and western and northern Texas: Anderson
and Squires 1997

Utah, Montana, and California: Ibid.

"quite unevenly spread within this range":
Cade 1982

244 *do not use the same site in consecutive years*:
Steenhof 1998

sites show a high rate of occupancy: Runde
in Anderson and Squires 1997

Canadian birds vacate their natal areas:
Steenhof 1998

Great Plains and the Great Basin: Ibid.

Prairie Falcons are tallied every autumn:
Bildstein et al. 2008

in Utah October to March: White and Rose-
neau 1970 in Steenhof 1998

descend from the mountains: Brown and
Amadon 1968

"steppes of interior North America": Ibid.

concentrations of larks: Ibid.

"irrigated croplands, cattle feedlots": Steenhof 1998

late February through March: Ibid.

the clutch is nearly complete: Enderson in
Steenhof 1998

becoming active aboveground: Cade 1982

on cliff faces but also in trees: MacLaren et
al. 1984 in Steenhof 1998

and on power line structures: Roppe et al.
1989 in Steenhof 1998

the upper half of cliff faces: Steenhof 1998

usually on south-facing cliffs: Enderson 1964
in Steenhof 1998

246 *"sometimes more heavily marked"*: Harrison
1978

lasts 29 to 31 days: Enderson 1964 in Steenhof 1998

47 days posthatching: Steenhof 1998

areas where food is abundant: Brown and
Amadon 1968

"long, low-angle stoop at prey": White in
Steenhof 1998

247 *in a low, slow harrier-like manner*: Anderson and Squires 1997

"marking each unsuccessful effort": May
1935

found in Prairie Falcon eggs: Fyfe in Anderson and Squires 1997

"5,000 to 6,000 breeding pairs": del Hoyo,
Elliott, and Sargatal 1994

in 19 states for falconry: Steenhof 1998

NEW WORLD VULTURES
Black Vulture

249 *"clothed in black" as for mourning:* Choate 1973

(the defining characteristic of the raptare*):* Kemp in Newton 1990

Measurements: Clark and Wheeler 1987

from northern Ecuador to northern Bolivia: Wetmore 1962 in Buckley 1999

250 *southeastern New York and southern Maine:* AOU Checklist, Seventh Edition 1998

fall migration through Panama: Skutch 1969 in Buckley 1999

251 *apparently mating for life:* Rabenold 1986 in Buckley 1999

near prospective nest sites: Buckley 1999

never lay more than two eggs: Audubon 1840

252 *concentrated at the larger end:* Harrison 1978

lasts 38 or 39 days: Thomas in Buckley 1999

fledging takes 10 or 11 weeks: Harrison 1978

they leave the roost the following day: Buckley 1999

"slaughterhouses, which are their favorite resort": Audubon 1840

"indolent, loitering for hours in one place": Wilson 1814

grist for the bird's mill: Ibid.

253 *"fixing their claws on each other's head":* Ibid.

"But these instances are rare": Ibid.

dismembering the hapless piglet: Nick Germanio, personal communication with author

254 *in the Western Hemisphere:* Buckley 1999

the bird's close association with humans: Ibid.

central Tennessee, and southwest Alabama: Price et al. 1995 in Buckley 1999

Turkey Vulture

aura *is the South American name for the bird:* Choate 1973

this aerial scavenger rarely: Kirk and Mossman 1998

". . . are protected by a law": Wilson 1814

"effortless conquest of the air currents": Broun 1948

slightly larger on average: Kirk and Mossman 1998

255 *Measurements:* Clark and Wheeler 1987

not in the Americas, but in France: Newton 1990

256 *originated in the mid-Pleistocene:* Miller 1942 in Kirk and Mossman 1998

somewhat larger than today's birds: Hertel in Kirk and Mossman 1998

Central and South America: Kirk and Mossman 1998

six subspecies are recognized: Stressmann and Amadon 1979 in Kirk and Mossman 1998

breeders may be resident: Kirk and Mossman 1998

It winters from Mexico to Panama: Ibid.

Uruguay and northern Argentina: Brown and Amadon 1968

Patagonia and the Falkland Islands: Ibid.

make a low-pitched nasal whine: Pemberton 1925 in Kirk and Mossman 1998

257 *and even the Falkland Islands:* Brown and Amadon 1968

"in portions of the Great Plains": Kirk and Mossman 1998

258 *than western populations:* Ibid.

Florida in early October: Ibid.

"A very few remain": Audubon 1840

early March to early April: Kirk and Mossman 1998

259 *11,404 vultures are tallied:* Bildstein et al. 2008

setting a record with 4,000: Stevenson in Kirk and Mossman 1998

mid-March to early April: Jackson 1983 in Kirk and Mossman 1998

boulders and shallow caves: Coles 1944 in Kirk and Mossman 1998

on the ground beside stumps: Mossman and Hartman 1992 in Kirk and Mossman 1998

chaparral, and shrubs: Bendire 1892 in Kirk and Mossman 1998

an important component of chosen sites: Kirk and Mossman 1998

reddish brown to lilac splotches: Harrison 1978

39 to 41 days: Ibid.

takes 10 or 11 weeks: Ibid.

261 *the anus, genitals, mouth, or nostrils:* Kirk and Mossman 1998

small stranded live fish: Bendire 1892 in Kirk and Mossman 1998

"widespread and abundant": del Hoyo, Elliott, and Sargatal 1994

gut piles they feed upon: Carpenter 2003

California Condor

262 *the bird's unfeathered head:* Clark and Wheeler 1987

263 *"so gentle a ghoul":* Dawson 1923

more extensive North American range: Snyder and Schmitt 2002

Measurements: Clark and Wheeler 1987

"we are not prepared to say": Dawson 1923

264 *This is a monotypic species:* AOU Checklist, Seventh Edition 1983

*King Vulture (*Sarcoramus papa*):* Snyder and Schmitt 2002

may have represented a subspecies: Ibid.

placed in protective custody: AOU Checklist, Seventh Edition Supplement 1998

They forage for the most part: Snyder and Schmitt 2002

support extensive soaring: Ibid.

augment a running start: Pennycuick 1996 in Snyder and Schmitt 2002

pairs remain together for multiple years: Snyder and Schmitt 2002

bare soil, gravel, or a rocky floor: Bent 1937–38

265 *a giant sequoia in 1984:* Snyder and Snyder 1991

occurs 163 to 178 days later: Ibid.

perhaps another half-year: Koford 1953 in Snyder and Schmitt 2002

rapid running and hopping: Snyder and Schmitt 2002

"which is anything but graceful": Audubon 1840

"preen themselves by the hour": Dawson 1923

at their roost site: Brown and Amadon 1968

primarily carrion: California Condor 2013 Annual Report, U.S. Fish and Wildlife Service, Northwest Region

108 miles from nest sites: Snyder and Snyder 2000 in Snyder and Schmitt 2002

266 *"weeks without ingesting food":* Snyder and Schmitt 2002

"singly or in irregular groupings": Ibid.

"by its power of vision": Audubon 1840

Golden Eagles, and ravens: Snyder and Schmitt 2002

"Condor appears in the area": Brown and Amadon 1968

subservient to Golden Eagles: Snyder and Schmitt 2002

ingesting little hide: Ibid.

in the wild and in captivity: California Condor Recovery 2014 Annual Program Population Report–U.S. Fish and Wildlife Service

"more than two or three at a time": Audubon 1840

"while the getting was good": Dawson 1923

267 *miring in oil:* Koford 1953 in Snyder and Schmitt 2002

"an unsustainable decline": Snyder and Snyder 1991

268 *vicinity of the Grand Canyon:* California Condor Annual Report: www.fws.gov/ CNO/es/CalCondor/Condor.cfm

keep birds lead-free: Snyder and Schmitt 2002

It did not survive: The Peregrine Fund, http://peregrinefund.org/

wild birds and those held in captivity: Ibid.

"to eventually thrive": Ibid.

linked to lead poisoning: Ibid.

274 *an organophosphate compound:* Goldstein et al. 1999

275 *39 birds (mostly raptors) in this way since 2011:* Bell 2015

Bibliography

American Ornithologists' Union (AOU). 1983. *Checklist of North American Birds,* seventh edition. Washington, DC: American Ornithologists' Union. Supplements 1998, 2015.

Anderson, Stanley H., and John R. Squires. 1997. *The Prairie Falcon.* Austin: University of Texas Press.

Audubon, John James. 1840. *Birds of America.* Vol. 1. Philadelphia: J. B. Chevalier.

Avian Research and Conservation Institute. 1995. *Swallow-tailed Kite Migration, a Ten Thousand Mile Odyssey.* http://www.swallow-tailedkites.org/feeds/posts/default.

Bechard, M. J., and Josef K. Schmutz. 1995. "Ferruginous Hawk." In *The Birds of North America,* no. 172. Edited by A. Poole and F. Gill. Philadelphia, PA: Academy of Natural Sciences, and Washington, DC: American Ornithologists' Union.

Bechard, M. J., and T. R. Swem. 2002. "Rough-legged Hawk." In *The Birds of North America,* no. 641. Edited by A. Poole and F. Gill. Philadelphia, PA: The Birds of North America, Inc.

Bednarz, J. A. 1995. "Harris' Hawk." In *The Birds of North America,* no. 146. Edited by A. Poole and F. Gill. Philadelphia, PA: Academy of Natural Sciences, and Washington, DC: American Ornithologists' Union.

Bell, Cathy. 2015. "Raptors and Rat Poison." *Living Bird,* Summer.

Bent, Arthur Cleveland. 1937–38. *Life Histories of North American Birds of Prey,* Vols. 1 and 2. Washington, DC: Smithsonian Institution.

Bibles, B. D., R. L. Glinski, and R. R. Johnson. 2002. "Gray Hawk." In *The Birds of North America,* no. 652. Edited by A. Poole and F. Gill. Philadelphia, PA: The Birds of North America, Inc.

Bildstein, K. L., and K. Meyer. 2000. "Sharp-shinned Hawk." In *The Birds of North America,* no. 482. Edited by A. Poole and G. Gill. Philadelphia, PA: The Birds of North America, Inc.

Bildstein, Keith L., Jeff P. Smith, Ernesto Ruelas Inzunza, and Richard R. Veit. 2008. *State of North America's Birds of Prey.* Cambridge, MA: Nuttall Ornithological Club, and Washington, DC: American Ornithologists' Union.

Brandt, Herbert. 1951. *Arizona and Its Bird Life.* Cleveland, OH; The Bird Research Foundation.

Broun, Maurice. 1948. *Hawks Aloft.* New York: Dodd Mead Company.

Brown, Leslie. 1976. *Eagles of the World.* New York: Universe Books.

Brown, Leslie, and Dean Amadon. 1968. *Eagles, Hawks and Falcons of the World,* Vols. 1 and 2. Feltham, Middlesex: Country Life Books.

Buckley, Neil. J. 1999. "Black Vulture." In *The Birds of North America,* no. 441. Edited by A. Poole and F. Gill. Philadelphia, PA: The Birds of North America, Inc.

Buehler, D. A. 2000. "Bald Eagle." In *The Birds of North America,* no. 506. Edited by A. Poole and F. Gill. Philadelphia, PA: The Birds of North America, Inc.

Burnham, K. K., William A. Burnham, and Ian Newton. 2009. "Gyrfalcon, *Falco rusticolus,* Post-Glacial and Extreme Long-term Use of Nest Sites in Greenland." *Ibis* 151: 519–522.

Burnham, K. K., and I. Newton. 2011. "Seasonal Movements of Gyrfalcons *Falco rusticolus* Include Extensive Periods at Sea." *Ibis* 15 (3): 468–484.

Cade, Tom J. 1982. *The Falcons of the World.* Ithaca, NY: Cornell University Press.

Carpenter, James W., Oliver Pattee, Steven Fritts, Barnett Rattner, Stanley Wiemeyer, J. Andrew Royle, and Milton Smith. 2003. "Experimental Lead Poisoning in Turkey Vultures (*Cathartes aura*)." *Journal of Wildlife Diseases* 39 (1): 96–104.

Cely, J. E. (1979) in Myer, Kenneth D. 1995. "Swallow-tailed Kite." In *The Birds of North America,* no. 128. Edited by A. Poole and F. Gill. Philadelphia, PA: Academy of Natural Sciences, and Washington, DC: American Ornithologists' Union.

Choate, Ernest A. 1973. *The Dictionary of American Bird Names.* Boston: Gambit.

Clark, William S., and Wheeler, Brian K. 1987. *A Field Guide to Hawks of North America.* Boston: Houghton Mifflin.

Clum, N. J., and Tom. J. Cade. 1994. "Gyrfalcon." In *The Birds of North America,* no. 114. Edited by A. Poole and F. Gill. Philadelphia, PA: Academy of Natural Sciences, and Washington, DC: American Ornithologists' Union.

Coues (1874) in Dawson, William Leon. 1923. *The Birds of California,* Vol. 4. San Diego: South Moulton Co.

Crocoll, S. T. 1994. "Red-shouldered Hawk." In *The Birds of North America,* no. 107. Edited by A. Poole and F. Gill. Philadelphia, PA: Academy of Natural Sciences, and Washington, DC: American Ornithologists' Union.

Dawson, William Leon. 1923. *The Birds of California*, Vol. 4. San Diego: South Moulton Co.

del Hoyo, J., A. Elliott, and J. Sargatal, eds. 1994. *Handbook of the Birds of the World*, Vol. 2: *New World Vultures to Guineafowl*. Barcelona: Lynx Editions.

Dunk, J. R. 1995. "White-tailed Kite." In *The Birds of North America*, no. 178. Edited by A. Poole and F. Gill. Philadelphia, PA: Academy of Natural Sciences, and Washington, DC: American Ornithologists' Union.

Eaton, Elon Howard. 1914. *Birds of New York*. Albany: University of the State of New York.

England, A. S., M. J. Bechard, and C. S. Houston. 1997. "Swainson's Hawk." In *The Birds of North America*, no. 265. Edited by A. Poole and F. Gill. Philadelphia, PA: Academy of Natural Sciences, and Washington, DC: American Ornithologists' Union.

Farquhar, C. C. 1992. "White-tailed Hawk." In *The Birds of North America*, no. 30. Edited by A. Poole and F. Gill. Philadelphia, PA: Academy of Natural Sciences, and Washington, DC: American Ornithologists' Union.

Ferguson-Lees, James, and David A. Christie. 2001. *Raptors of the World*. Boston: Houghton Mifflin.

Fish, Allen. 2013. "Rodenticides and Raptors: A Deadly Relationship." Pacific Raptor Report Number 35.

Forbush, Edward Howe. 1925–1929. *Birds of Massachusetts and Other New England States*. Commonwealth of Massachusetts. Norwood, MA: Berwick and Smith Co.

Forsman, Dick. 1999. *The Raptors of Europe and the Middle East*. London: T & AD Poyser.

Gill, Frank B. 1990. *Ornithology*, Second Edition. W. H. Freeman.

Goldstein, M. I., T. E. Lacher, B. Woodbridge, M. J. Bechard, S. B. Canavelli, M. E. Zaccagnini, G. P. Cobb, E. J. Scollon, R. Tribolet, and M. J. Hooper. 1999. "Monocrotophos-Induced Mass Mortality of Swainson's Hawks in Argentina, 1995–96." *Ecotoxicology* 8(3): 201–204.

Goodrich, L. J., S. T. Crocoll, and S. E. Senner. 1996. "Broad-winged Hawk." In *The Birds of North America*, no. 218. Edited by A. Poole and F. Gill. Philadelphia, PA: Academy of Natural Sciences, and Washington, DC: American Ornithologists' Union.

Hamerstrom, Frances. 1986. *Harrier Hawk of the Marsh*. Washington, DC: Smithsonian Institution Press.

Harrison, Colin. 1978. *A Field Guide to the Nests, Eggs, and Nestlings of North American Birds*. Glasgow: William Collins Sons & Co., Ltd.

Hausman, Leon Augustus. 1938. *The Hawks of New Jersey*. New Brunswick: New Jersey Agricultural Experiment Station.

Hausman, Leon Augustus. 1948. *Birds of Prey of Eastern North America*. New Brunswick: Rutgers University Press.

Heller, Dick D. 2005. "Hook-billed Kite." *Texas Breeding Bird Atlas*. College Station and Corpus Christi, TX: Texas A&M University System. http://txtbba.tamu.edu (accessed 2005).

Houston, C. Stuart. 1997. In England, A. Sidney, Marc J. Bechard, and C. Stuart Houston. "Swainson's Hawk." In *The Birds of North America*, no. 265. Edited by A. Poole and F. Gill. Philadelphia, PA: Academy of Natural Sciences, and Washington, DC: American Ornithologists' Union.

Houston, C. Stuart, and Marc J. Bechard. 1984. In England, A. Sidney, Marc J. Bechard, and C. Stuart Houston. "Swainson's Hawk." In *The Birds of North America*, no. 265. Edited by A. Poole and F. Gill. Philadelphia, PA: Academy of Natural Sciences, and Washington, DC: American Ornithologists' Union.

Howell, Steve N. G., and Sophie Webb. 1995. *A Guide to the Birds of Mexico and Northern Central America*. Oxford: Oxford University Press.

Johnsgard, Paul A. 1990. *Hawks, Eagles, and Falcons of North America*. Washington, DC: Smithsonian Institution Press.

———. 2004. *Hawks, Eagles, and Falcons of North America*. Washington, DC: Smithsonian Institution Press.

Johnson, R. R. L., L. Glinski, and S. W. Matteson. 2000. "Zone-tailed Hawk." In *The Birds of North America*, no. 529. Edited by A. Poole and F. Gill. Philadelphia, PA: The Birds of North America, Inc.

Kaufman, Kenn. 1996. *Lives of North American Birds*. Boston: Houghton Mifflin.

Keddy-Hector, Dean P. 2000. "Aplomado Falcon." In *The Birds of North America*, no. 549. Edited by A. Poole and F. Gill. Philadelphia, PA: The Birds of North America, Inc.

Kerlinger, Paul. 1989. *Flight Strategies of Migrating Hawks*. Chicago: University of Chicago Press.

Kirk, D. A., and M. J. Mossman. 1989. "Turkey Vulture." In *The Birds of North America*, no. 339. Edited by A. Poole and F. Gill. Philadelphia, PA: The Birds of North America, Inc.

Kochert, M. N., K. Steenhof, C. L. McIntyre, and E. H. Craig. 2002. "Golden Eagle." In *The Birds of North America,* no. 684. Edited by A. Poole and F. Gill. Philadelphia, PA: The Birds of North America, Inc.

Krider, John. 1879. *Forty Years Notes of a Field Ornithologist.* Philadelphia: Press of Joseph H. Weston.

Lockwood, Mark, and Brush Freeman. 2004. *Texas Breeding Bird Atlas.* College Station and Corpus Christi, TX: Texas A&M University System.

MacWhirter, R. B., and K. L. Bildstein. 1996. "Northern Harrier." In *The Birds of North America,* no. 210. Edited by A. Poole and F. Gill. Philadelphia, PA: Academy of Natural Sciences, and Washington, DC: American Ornithologists' Union.

May, John Richard. 1935. *The Hawks of North America.* New York: The National Association of Audubon Societies.

Merriam (1888) in May, John Richard. 1935. *The Hawks of North America.* New York: The National Association of Audubon Societies.

Meyer, Kenneth D. 1995. "Swallow-tailed Kite." In *The Birds of North America,* no. 138. Edited by A. Poole and F. Gill. Philadelphia, PA: Academy of Natural Sciences, and Washington, DC : American Ornithologist's Union.

Miller, K. E., and K. D. Meyer. 2002. "Short-tailed Hawk." In *The Birds of North America,* no. 674. Edited by A. Poole and F. Gill. Philadelphia, PA: Academy of Natural Sciences.

Morrison, Joan L. 1996. "Crested Caracara." In *The Birds of North America,* no. 249. Edited by A. Poole and F. Gill. Philadelphia, PA: Academy of Natural Sciences, and Washington, DC: American Ornithologists' Union.

Morrison, Joan L., and James F. Swyer. 2012. "Crested Caracara." In *The Birds of North America Online.* Edited by A. Poole. Ithaca, NY: Cornell Lab of Ornithology. Retrieved from Birds of North America Online: http://birds.cornell.edu.bnaproxy.birds cornell.edu/sna/species/249.

Mullarney, Killian, Lars Svensson, Dan Zetterstrom, and Peter Grant. 1999. *Birds of Europe.* Princeton: Princeton University Press.

Newton, Ian. 1979. *Population Ecology of Raptors.* Vermillion, SD: Buteo Books.

———. 1990. *Birds of Prey.* New York: Facts on File, Inc.

Olendorff, Richard R. 1975. *Golden Eagle Country.* New York: Alfred A. Knopf, Inc.

Oliphant (1974) in Sodhi, L. W., S. L. W. Oliphant, P. C. James, and L. G. Warkentin. 1973.

"Merlin." In *The Birds of North America,* no. 44. Edited by A. Poole and F. Gill. Philadelphia, PA: Academy of Natural Sciences, and Washington, DC: American Ornithologists' Union.

Palmer, Ralph S. 1988. *Handbook of North American Birds,* Vols. 4 and 5. New Haven: Yale University.

Parker, J. W. 1999. "Mississippi Kite." In *The Birds of North America,* no. 402. Edited by A. Poole and F. Gill. Philadelphia, PA: The Birds of North America, Inc.

Penncock (1890) in Miller, K. E., and K. D. Myers. 2002. "Short-tailed Hawk." In *The Birds of North America,* no. 674. Edited by A. Poole and F. Gill. Philadelphia, PA: Academy of Natural Sciences, and Washington, DC: American Ornithologists' Union.

Poole, Alan F. 1989. *Ospreys: A Natural and Unnatural History.* Cambridge: Cambridge University Press.

Poole, A. F., R. O. Bierregaard, and M. S. Martell. 2002. "Osprey." In *The Birds of North America,* no. 683. Edited by A. Poole and F. Gill. Philadelphia, PA: The Birds of North America, Inc.

Potapov, Eugene, and Richard Sale. 2005. *The Gyrfalcon.* United Kingdom: T & AD Poyser.

Preston, C. R., and R. D. Beane. 1993. "Red-tailed Hawk." In *The Birds of North America,* no. 52. Edited by A. Poole and F. Gill. Philadelphia, PA: Academy of Natural Sciences, and Washington, DC: American Ornithologists' Union.

Ratcliffe, Derek. 1980. *The Peregrine Falcon.* Vermillion, SD: Buteo Books.

Rosenfield, R. N., and J. Bielefeldt. 1993. "Cooper's Hawk." In *The Birds of North America,* no. 75. Edited by A. Poole and F. Gill. Philadelphia, PA: Academy of Natural Sciences, and Washington, DC: American Ornithologists' Union.

Salgado, Ernie. 2014. "Government to Allow Wind Energy Industry to Kill Eagles." *The Indian Reporter,* January 17. www.theindian-reporter.com/ernie_salgado/killing_eagles/.

Schnell, J. H. 1994. "Common Black-Hawk." In *The Birds of North America,* no. 122. Edited by A. Poole and F. Gill. Philadelphia, PA: Academy of Natural Sciences, and Washington, DC: American Ornithologists' Union.

Sibley, David Allen. 2000. *The Sibley Guide to Birds.* New York: Alfred A. Knopf.

Simmons, Robert E. 2000. *Harriers of the World.* Oxford: Oxford University Press.

Smallwood, John A., and David M. Bird. 2002. "American Kestrel." In *The Birds of North America,* no. 602. Edited by A. Poole and F. Gill. Philadelphia, PA: Academy of Natural Sciences, and Washington, DC: American Ornithologists' Union.

Snyder, N. F. R., and N. J. Schmitt. 2002. "California Condor." In *The Birds of North America,* no. 610. Edited by A. Poole and F. Gill. Philadelphia, PA: Academy of Natural Sciences, and Washington, DC: American Ornithologists' Union.

Snyder, Noel, and Helen Snyder. 1991. *Birds of Prey: Natural History and Conservation of North American Raptors.* Stillwater, MN: Voyageur Press.

Sodhi, L. W., S. L. W. Oliphant, P. C. James, and I. G. Warkentin. 1993. "Merlin." In *The Birds of North America,* no. 44. Edited by A. Poole and F. Gill. Philadelphia, PA: Academy of Natural Sciences, and Washington, DC: American Ornithologists' Union.

Sprunt, Alexander, Jr. 1955. *North American Birds of Prey.* New York: Harper & Brothers.

Squires, J. R., and R. T. Reynolds. 1997. "Northern Goshawk." In *The Birds of North America,* no. 298. Edited by A. Poole and F. Gill. Philadelphia, PA: Academy of Natural Sciences, and Washington, DC: American Ornithologists' Union.

Steenhof, Karen. 1998. "Prairie Falcon." In *The Birds of North America,* no. 346. Edited by A. Poole and F. Gill. Philadelphia, PA: The Birds of North America, Inc.

Sykes, P. W., J. A. Rogers, and R. E. Bennetts. 1995. "Snail Kite." In *The Birds of North America,* no. 171. Edited by A. Poole and F. Gill. Philadelphia: Academy of Natural Sciences, and Washington, DC: American Ornithologists' Union.

Tweit, Robert C. 2008. "Aplomado Falcon." *The Texas Breeding Bird Atlas.* College Station and Corpus Christi, TX: Texas A&M University. http://txtbba.tamu.edu/species-accounts/aplomado falcon/.

U.S. Fish and Wildlife Service. 2007. "Aplomado Falcon Fact Sheet." www.fws.gov/endangered/esa-library/pdf/aplomado_falcon_fact_sheet.pdf.

U.S. Fish and Wildlife Service, Pacific Southwest Region. "California Condor Count Information." www.fws.gov/CNO/es/CalCondor/Condor.cfm (April 28, 2015).

Watson, Donald. 1977. *The Hen Harrier.* Hertfordshire, England: T & AD Poyser Ltd.

Watson, Jeff. 1997. *The Golden Eagle.* London: T & AD Poyser Ltd.

White, C. M., N. J. Clum, T. J. Cade, and W. G. Hunt. 2002. "Peregrine Falcon." In *The Birds of North America,* no. 660. Edited by A. Poole and F. Gill. Philadelphia, PA: The Birds of North America, Inc.

Wilson, Alexander, and Charles Lucien Bonaparte. 1814. *American Ornithology,* Vol. 1. Philadelphia, PA: Porter & Coates.

Index

Page numbers in italics refer to species accounts.

insecticides, 274
intrusion on birds of prey, 274, 275

Kestrel, American, 4, *202–10*
Kite
    Black-shouldered, 46
    Everglades, 50
    Hook-billed, *33–38*
    Mississippi, *56–61*
    Plumbeous, 58
    Slender-billed, 50
    Snail, *49–56*
    Swallow-tailed, *38–43*
    White-tailed, 15, *44–49*

lead poisoning, 273–74

Merlin, 4, *210–17*
    Black, 212, 213
    Prairie, 212, 214–15
    Taiga, 1, 211, 212, 213, 215, 216

Osprey, 4, 12, *22–32*

Pandion
    haliaetus, 4, 12, *22–32*
    haliaetus carolinensis, 24
    haliaetus cristatus, 24
    haliaetus haliaetus, 24, 26
    haliaetus ridgwayi, 24
Pandionidae overview, 13
Parabuteo unicinctus, 4, 9, 105, *110–16*
    harrisi, 111–12
    superior, 112
    unicinctus, 112
photographers and birds of prey, 275, 276

poisoning
    lead poisoning, 273–74
    secondary poisoning, 274–75

reverse dimorphism, 11
Rostrhamus
    hamatus, 50
    sociabilis, *49–56*
    sociabilis levis, 50
    sociabilis major, 50
    sociabilis plumbeus, 50
    sociabilis sociabilis, 50

Sarcoramus papa, 263
secondary poisoning, 274–75
shooting birds of prey, 271, 272

taxonomy of diurnal birds of prey
    families overview, 11, 13–19
    overview, 3–5
threats to birds of prey (overview), 271–75
    See also conservation of birds of prey
        (overview)
traits of birds of prey (overview), 1–11

visual acuity (summary), 8, 10
Vultur gryphus, 263
Vulture
    Black, *248–54*
    King, 263
    Lesser Yellow-headed, 256
    Turkey, 8, *254–61*, 272

wind turbine collisions, 271
windows and birds of prey, 273, 276
wire collisions, 271